Letters to the Editor

CONFESSIONS OF A FRUSTRATED CONSERVATIVE

Jon Michael Hubbard

iUniverse, Inc.
New York   Bloomington

Letters to the Editor
Confessions of a Frustrated Conservative

Copyright © 2009 Jon M. Hubbard

iUniverse books may be ordered through booksellers or by contacting:

iUniverse
1663 Liberty Drive
Bloomington, IN 47403
www.iuniverse.com
1-800-Authors (1-800-288-4677)

ISBN: 978-0-595-52981-0 (pbk)
ISBN: 978-0-595-63630-3 (cloth)
ISBN: 978-0-595-63034-9 (ebk)

Printed in the United States of America

iUniverse rev. date: 3/10/2009

WARNING

This is a book of opinions. Although they are my own opinions formed over time through observations of certain actions taken by a growing collection people who have placed the future of this nation at great risk, I am convinced that these very same opinions are shared by thousands, and even millions of real Americans throughout this country. The survival of America is at stake, and we are quickly running out of time in which to retake our nation!

As the author of this book, I feel it only fair to advise you that I am not a professional writer and have never before attempted to have a book published. I am simply a very concerned American who fears for our future if certain events continue to happen. This book will not likely be confused with any best-selling novel, but it is my fervent wish that those concerned Americans reading it just might begin to see themselves in the role of its author, and realize the urgency to act.

My purpose in writing this book is to encourage others to voice their own feelings and fears about what has been happening in this country. This unique America cannot and will not survive the liberal conspiracy now underway to transform the economic system of this country from capitalism to liberal socialism. What is every bit as dangerous as this conspiracy itself is the ideological brainwashing by liberal educators who have been indoctrinating generations of our young people that socialism is the way of the future. Real Americans have been abandoned by those in whose hands we had mistakenly placed our trust, and we must examine the voting and performance records of those legislators, and recall any and all who are not performing up to the standards and expectations of their constituents.

The time for true Americans to act is now, and this just might be our final opportunity to change the destructive course of this nation!

Contents

DEDICATION

Down through our history, whenever the call went out for Americans to come to the defense of our country, that call was answered by patriots who saw it as their duty, and never hesitated to act. It is those patriots who are the real heroes of America, and to whom we all owe an undying debt of gratitude!

This book is dedicated to those brave and courageous men and women of our military who have unselfishly chosen to lay their lives on the line, and more specifically to those who have made the ultimate sacrifice to protect freedom, democracy, and our American way of life. Many times these young men and women have made their choice to serve their country in our military, having overcome the evaporation of the standards and values advanced by a liberal-dominated educational system, and many times while delaying their pursuit of more lucrative occupations outside of the military.

Like those patriots of past wars, our men and women in uniform today represent what is the very best within this nation, and they would be the source of much pride to our founding fathers. They are carrying on the rich tradition of those American patriots who have come before them and who did not hesitate to serve their country when called upon to do so.

May God bless this nation, and may God bless these wonderful men and women who realized and understood their responsibility to serve their nation, and have dedicated themselves to fulfilling that responsibility.

INTRODUCTION

WHY I WROTE THIS BOOK

If any success is attained as a result of writing this book, it will come when those reading it will see their own thoughts and feelings jumping off these pages right at them. To understand the purpose of this book, one must first understand and realize that this nation we call America is like no other nation ever devised by mankind. The true American is unlike any person found in any other country, but unfortunately, not everyone who calls America home is capable of being a true American. It has nothing to do with one's race, color of skin, nation of origin, or the economic status into which they were born. But, it has everything to do with their love of their God, their family, and their love for this country. They simply will not allow their sense of the values and long-held traditions of this nation to be compromised. They acknowledge the remarkable history of this nation, they understand that this country owes them nothing, but they also realize that they have an obligation to come to this nation's defense if called upon to do so. Writing this book has helped me to understand some things about myself I never realized before. I knew that I loved my lord and savior Jesus Christ, and my family, and writing this book has greatly reinforced those feelings within me. But perhaps the most important thing I learned about myself was just how much I truly love my country.

I am a Christian, first and foremost! I am also an American, a conservative, and I am very frustrated at what I see going on within this country. I am very concerned about what will happen to this country if certain things are not changed. I could no more continue to contain my feelings than I could run a four-minute mile, and I couldn't come close to running a four-minute mile on the very best day of my life. In writing this book I am actually shouting my feelings and concerns from the rooftop. Before this book, I have never

1

published anything, except for a group of letters to the editor printed in my local newspaper. If this book achieves anything at all; my hope is that it will inspire other everyday Americans like me to do the very same thing. If you don't like what you see happening in this country, express yourself, either in print or by telling it to anyone who will listen. Remember, for most of us, this is our home, and the only country we have or will ever have. This is where we were born, where we live, where we love, where we raise our families, where we fought, and where we will die. If we allow this country to go down the tubes, we will have absolutely nothing left. If you love this country—if you really love this country—tell someone. Tell everyone. Tell them why you love this country. Tell them what it is about this country that you like. Tell them what makes you proud to be an American. Tell them what it is that you just cannot sit back any longer and allow to happen. Do this, and you'll never regret that you did!

Before we move to the subject matter of this book, I must first apologize for my obvious lack of journalistic expertise. I don't know if I can blame it on having a few senior moments or not, but you will likely notice some repetition of thought in various areas of this book, and for this I must also humbly apologize. Please understand that I am like many of you who might be reading this book, a very concerned American citizen who fears for the direction in which our nation is headed. This book was written straight from the heart, and I may tend to ramble as well as being repetitive at times, so please bear with me in my efforts to express my sincere frustrations as a very concerned and conservative American. Please also keep in mind that my letters were written at various stages during the 2008 political season, and some of the topics of these letters were resolved before this book went into print, but at the time they were written, they were still undecided and very relevant to the outcome of the election.

What might cause an average U.S. citizen to write a book about his country? If we are truly satisfied with what we see happening in this country, there would be no reason to write a book such as this one. If we look at what has been going on in this country, however, and if what we see indeed causes great concern, then maybe even an average U.S. citizen like me or you just might have cause to write a book such as this.

There definitely are reasons for great concern, some of which are due to the fact that the sanctuaries we should be able to turn to for help have actually become a major part of the problem. We find ourselves in the hands of an incompetent government headed by the most inexperienced and radical liberal who has ever sat in the White House; a Congress that is totally out of control and presided over by two clowns in the person of Nancy Pelosi and Harry Reid, and with a cast of characters that go by the names of Barney

Frank, Chuck Schumer, Christopher Dodd, and a bunch of liberal, socialist Democrats and a weak band of Republicans who have lost their backbone to challenge liberals.

One very obvious problem that has an enormous impact on many of the other problems is that we have allowed our own Christian principles to become devalued under the pretense of not allowing them to offend other religious groups. Anti-American organizations such as the ACLU have been given carte blanche in their efforts to destroy the very traditions and values this nation was founded upon. When the American people suffered through the indignity of just sitting back and allowing themselves to be herded like cattle to the slaughter as the ACLU went about their attack on America, a huge part of the great American spirit seemed to die in the process, and the rest of it just evaporated as a result of our feeble attempts to protect it. After becoming indoctrinated into a more politically correct liberal theology, in the interest of not offending anyone, Christians were told to become more tolerant of and submissive to other religions, even to the point of forgoing our own traditions and beliefs. In this game of politically correctness, even the Ten Commandments have become expendable.

The right to life of the yet-unborn has become secondary to the right of a woman to choose, and liberals have identified and even justified abortion as just another form of birth control. I do not disagree with a woman's right to choose, but I see that choice as being whether or not to use a safe method of birth control before or during the act instead choosing to kill a yet-unborn child afterward. There are circumstances where a reasonable argument for abortion can be made, but this should be limited to when rape or incest has occurred, and most assuredly when the life of the mother is at stake. Abortion of a yet-unborn child should never be allowed to become just another method of birth control.

The liberal ideology has been working to destroy the American family unit for decades, and with the help of Hollywood and the ACLU, this has proven to be an easy task. They have introduced the assumption that the gay lifestyle is normal and that same-sex marriage is just another form of liberty. Hollywood joined in this charade by continuously expanding the definition and boundaries of what is decent and appropriate for viewing by the general public. Of course, family values became the victim of this attack, and the motto: "If it feels good, do it," has become the law of the land.

We find ourselves today deep in the clutches of an invasion of illegal immigrants, the dangers of which the liberal, socialist Democrats refuse to acknowledge, as they simply see these invaders as another bloc of potential voters. To further entice additional border jumpers, liberals have chosen to dangle the carrot of entitlement programs to lure them in. To the liberal politician, anything is possible where a vote is concerned.

Thanks to a mass infestation of liberal educators in our public schools, our educational system is in shambles and shows little chance of recovery. This nation once enjoyed an educational system that was second to none, where progress and achievement were the prizes available to anyone willing to take advantage of everything available to them. This once-great system of learning has become a place where excellence has been sacrificed in the interest of making sure no one will ever experience failure. The once dedicated and highly qualified teacher has been relegated to being a glorified babysitter, one who many times has to fear for his or her very safety in an atmosphere where the inmates are running the asylum. Far too much attention and expense has been devoted to political correctness instead of educating students.

Race relations within this country has long been a major issue, and it has become so greatly influenced by the constant liberal bombardment reinforcing the farce that today's white community is solely responsible for the institution of slavery. How ridiculous! This makes no more sense than insisting that this world owes us a living simply as a result of our being born. Racial problems in this country are not solely the responsibility of the white race, and the sooner the black community realizes and understands this fact, the more likely we are to see real improvement in this area. This country has made great strides through the years to include the black community in the American way of life, but this process can only be successful when each side takes every advantage of the abundance of opportunities America has to offer. Race relations within this country are indeed a two-way street, and they will not be improved upon until both sides accept their own responsibility to improve this relationship. Entitlements should not become a way of life. Education is the only way to pull one up by the bootstraps.

The United States of America is indeed the best place on the face of this Earth. If we are wise enough to appreciate the fact of having been born here, and smart enough to take advantage of the opportunities available to us here, then the only limitations we cannot overcome are those we place upon ourselves.

The time has come for all of us to overcome our frustrations by correcting those things that are within our own ability to control, and not to worry about those things that are beyond our own ability to control.

God bless this nation and our troops!

WHAT ARE LETTERS TO THE EDITOR?

Reading a letter to the editor will not be confused with reading a novel or the biography of a famous person. A letter to the editor represents something that comes from our thoughts and concerns. They do not necessarily have any certain flow, but they are descriptions of feelings ignited by certain events that cause fear or anger. People often find themselves and their letters going up against an editor of one of the mainstream, liberal media outlets who sees their role as to edit out any views that are different than their own. To give the false illusion that they are being fair, they allow a few selected letters to be printed, but they have no intention of allowing their readers to be educated about something that is in direct conflict with their liberal agenda.

Letters to the editor are not frivolous or contrived nonsense articles written by a bunch of crybabies. They are the honest, heartfelt, and fearful feelings submitted by concerned American citizens. These are citizens who see this country taking a path that will surely lead to the destruction of the nation that our founding fathers put their lives on the line to create. Many writers of these letters see this as the only way to express their feelings and concerns to the public.

Letters to the editor are sometimes flashes of thought that just appear in one's mind. They can be brought on by something we see in a newscast or some knee-jerk statement of political one-upmanship uttered by one of our grossly underachieving legislators. They are very likely something that each one of us has given thought to or wanted to say, but for some reason, we didn't. These are your thoughts and mine. They are your feelings and fears. They are the things that make us so mad when we see or hear them, but for one reason or another, have managed to escape from our consciousness by the time we could write them down. They are possibly something that we wanted to say but could not grab the words that would allow us to best describe our feelings, at the time when those feelings were very fresh upon our memories.

Do people actually read letters to the editor? Sure they do. People have told me that one of the first things they look for in their newspaper each morning is the editorial section and the letters to the editor. I am amazed at the number of times I have received phone calls about one of my letters from people I have never met but who have read my letters and called to say thank you for saying something they have felt or wanted to say for a long time. I remember a lady who once told me that my letters were sometimes discussed in her Sunday school class. I am by no means a professional writer, but I have become compelled to express and share my feelings about things I see happening in this country every day.

Again, if there is one thing I hope to accomplish by writing this book, it is to encourage everyone to be more eager and comfortable in expressing his or her thoughts. Expressing my thoughts has proven to be somewhat therapeutic and has given me the courage to continue to express my feelings, and even to have a better understanding of what my feelings truly are.

PROBLEMS WE FACE

Take a look at some of the major problems facing our nation today. We will examine some of them and see what can be done to correct them. People with vision have come to understand that our survival as a nation can only be achieved when government is not allowed to interfere with ambition, initiative, and desire, those wonderful and vital ingredients of American progress of times past. Webster defines "Americanism" this way: "Devotion to the United States and its institutions; a custom, trait, or thing peculiar to the US; a word especially characteristic of English spoken in the United States." This definition seems to have become lost somewhere between the visions of our founding fathers and the degrading and corrupt policies of liberal politicians. It is our responsibility to understand and deal with these issues.

National Security

This is by far the most important priority, bar none! If we do not do whatever is necessary to protect this nation against all enemies, both foreign and domestic, everything else has no significance whatsoever! We all recognize that it is important to protect our interests around the world, but it is just as important to protect our interest within our own borders. To do this, we must stop sending our National Guard overseas, and we must recognize that their value is better utilized in protecting our interests within our home borders.

Energy

Energy consumes much of our concerns today and rightly so. We are dealing with a liberal Congress that has used childish political games to vent its hatred toward a president it has refused for eight years to cooperate with. As a result, high energy prices have been passed along to the public. The time has come for citizens to ban together and force legislators to either do what we are directing them to do or be recalled from office. Energy costs are a major factor in the wholesale and retail price of all goods we use today, and we have allowed our energy policies to be dictated primarily by a corrupt congress, a narrow-minded oil industry, and our out-of-step auto industry. Although it is true that oil companies are in the business of finding and refining petroleum, they have been allowed to stifle any progress in the area of alternative energy sources. Just as many typewriter and adding-machine companies adapted themselves to move into the computer age, many did not adapt and are no longer in business. Petroleum is a product with a limited life span, and unless the major oil companies diversify and move toward developing other energy sources, they too will become ancient history at some point, just like those adding machine companies. Many of today's oil company executives are in the golden years of their careers, and their emphasis is only on the short-term profits to sweeten their own financial status, and long-term concerns are not a priority.

Oil industry executives must be convinced that they can play a vital role in ensuring that our future energy needs are met without interruption. A portion of today's oil profits can be used in the R&D of the primary energy sources of tomorrow. A mutually beneficial working relationship between government and today's oil industry will ensure that we are dependent only upon American ingenuity for our future energy needs. This not only will ensure the security of our future energy needs but will also lead to the growth of many new industries for future employment needs.

Education

Although education is not in the number-one spot on our list of priorities, it could easily be considered to be the most important element in the successful implementation of all other choices. Without a great educational system to teach us those things we need to know, the accomplishment of all other aspects of a successful nation become unattainable. Our successful educational system has also fallen victim to liberalism, and only the elimination of liberal concepts and principles can resuscitate it. Our schools have been allowed to become glorified day-care centers where working parents drop off their children to be entertained while they devote their energies to advancing their careers or just putting food on the table. Political correctness has developed an atmosphere where gaining an education and absorbing knowledge has taken a back seat to surviving the day in a world of gangs and malcontents. Personal achievement has been replaced with policies that do not allow for the experience of failure in any form. Without experiencing failure, success cannot be appreciated; therefore, we have turned out generations of average and below-average students who are not allowed to experience what it means to fail, while at the same time de-emphasizing the possibility of an educational experience that can only be realized by overcoming failure.

American Industry

The auto industry, for one, is in grave trouble today, but many of the problems are of its own making. That being said let us not forget our own government's role in the financial woes of the auto industry. Our government has consistently listened to the pleas of environmentalists and has required automakers to build cars with an emphasis upon pollution control, with the initial costs of these modifications to be borne by the automakers. Auto companies have also flooded the market by overproducing vehicles year after year, and year after year they have relied upon the general public to bail them out by constantly trading in fairly new cars for brand-new cars. It is hard to believe that our parents and grandparents kept their vehicles for five, ten, or more years before trading them in. I can remember when my dad would trade in our family car, and all of the men on our block would come over to check out the new car. This created another reason for neighbors to get together.

Aside from the fact that the labor unions have raped the American industries for decades, automakers have also been in bed with the American oil companies and have produced vehicles built more with style in mind than economy or ecology. They are now acting like the current energy crisis happened overnight and was totally unexpected, and are now taking on the same victim label that has been used successfully for years by minorities, laying the blame for their own faults everywhere except where it rightly belongs.

Race Relations

I don't think anyone can honestly deny that there is still much more that can be done to improve race relations in this country, but there is much debate as to where this improvement should be coming from. Both sides of this issue are guilty of not doing enough to make satisfactory improvements in this area, but the assumption that the blame for the lack of satisfactory progress belongs exclusively to the white race is in itself a big part of this problem. During the most recent fifty to seventy-five years, many of those who have passed themselves off as leaders of the civil rights movement have become very wealthy at the expense of their black brothers and sisters. If race relations did indeed make significant improvement, many of those so-called leaders who have become wealthy as a result of their roles in the civil rights movement would see their gravy train pull out of the station without them. Comfort in wearing the victim tag is one of the major reasons many blacks will not move forward and work to improve race relations in this country. This is not a one-sided issue, and until both sides accept their own responsibility, this issue will never be solved.

Military

To ensure that the strength of our military remains at a level that can successfully meet and overcome any threat to our national security, the time has come to reinstate the military draft. Those who are not willing to give two years out of their lives to serve this nation do not deserve the right to take advantages of all of those things for which they have refused to protect and defend. The draft could be expanded to include service in areas such as a version of the Peace Corps or community service agencies within our borders. Service to our country seems to be one of the primary areas liberalism has tried to make disappear, along with family values, sound and solid educational policies, and our religious beliefs and traditions. The draft would not only help introduce discipline and responsibility to many of the young people of today, but it would also help keep tabs on their activities, thereby allowing much less opportunity for getting into trouble.

Immigration

The immigration issue, both legal and illegal, will one day mean enormous hunger and poverty for all of us, if not addressed. The overpopulation problem will affect food supplies, housing availability, employment, crime, and health care. The developed nations will at some point see the necessity of placing birth-rate restrictions on their people to compensate for the population explosions within the Third World countries. Overpopulation will lead to planned wars or extermination to relieve this problem, and although this now seems to be barbaric and uncivilized, it will at some point become as necessary as eating and breathing. The lack of education within the underdeveloped countries will prove to be as dangerous in the future as threats from an unprincipled rogue dictatorship are today.

Subversive Elements (Liberals, ACLU, etc.)

The primary goal of liberal Democrats is to transform America into a socialist state. It is their contention that bigger government is better, and that this bigger government should control every aspect of our lives from the cradle to the grave. Liberals have never been capable of understanding what it means to be an American, a true American, that is, and they cannot understand why this country has become so successful without a suffocating government to control everything.

Liberals have the perfect answer to the question, "What do we do for those who do not want to work; who do not want to make any positive contributions to this nation; or for those who keep having children out of wedlock; or even for those undocumented potential voters who constantly sneak across our borders from other countries?" Their answer is very simple: "Make every entitlement program possible available to them, and keep them dependent upon the Democrat Party for their every need." The plan of the presidential candidate of the Democrat Party offers nothing to improve this country, except to tax and spend, and to speed America toward socialism. Democrats are not concerned when their candidate's glaring weaknesses are exposed, and this extends to a total lack of concern when their candidate will not even attempt to answer simple and legitimate questions. The blind followers of liberal Democrats simply cannot, or will not, see what is happening to them. They have been brainwashed into the idea that big government is better government, and as long as there is someone to take care of them, why change it?

When legal issues come up, or if liberals simply want to discredit or even eliminate the Christian values and traditions that have guided this nation throughout its amazing history into a superpower, they turn to their satanic legal team, that defender of un-American ideals, the *ACLU*. When these two champions of un-American activities join hands, the virtues of *truth, justice, and the American way* find themselves under attack from everyone and everything that is wrong with this country.

Going up against the likes of the Hitler's and the Soviet Union's, or any other outside opponent was much easier to deal with because we knew what we were up against. But, fighting enemies who pretend to be Americans is a totally different story. If America can survive the constant assaults from these two evil and subversive organizations, then anything else thrown at us will seem like a walk in the park.

Traditions, Values, and Principles

Family values, the Ten Commandments displayed in public buildings, opening doors for ladies, putting one's hand over the heart during the playing of the national anthem, pulling over to the side of the road while a funeral procession passes, showing respect for authority, church socials, picnics on the grounds, standing at attention when the American flag passes, a man's word is his bond, just doing the right thing—these are just a few traditions, values, and principles that were once important but which seem to have lost a measure of importance in today's world. Perhaps one of the most important values is to know and acknowledge the fact that, in spite of all of our faults, America is good, America is unique, and there is no better place on the face of this Earth!

I know this might seem trivial, but I think one of the best examples to show how our values have changed for the worse during the past several decades is the way our young people dress. Remember when going to the movies or taking a date out to dinner meant dressing up? What we see today is far different, and it says a lot about the pride of today's young people. The more sloppy one looks today, the better they like it. What do you think?

Some other problems that need attention are as follows:
- Religious values
- Abortion
- Border control
- Same-sex marriage
- Taxes
- U.S. participation in the United Nations
- The role of government in our lives
- Socialism vs. capitalism
- The job descriptions of our legislators
- Term limits on legislators
- Government entitlements
- "NAFTA superhighway"
- Family values

We must first ask ourselves if this nation is really worth fighting for. Are we truly willing to do our part to protect the sovereignty of this nation? If we had the choice, would we rather live in the United States or in another country? How we answer these questions could very well determine whether or not this nation will survive into the future.

CONSERVATIVES

What I Believe

Like many people who voted the same straight Democrat ticket as our ancestors had done up through the time of JFK, I began to question which party really shared and supported my true beliefs and values. With the emergence of Ronald Reagan, I discovered that my values had not changed, but the political party that shared and supported those values indeed had changed, and I found that my values were now more closely aligned with the Republican Party than with the Democrat Party. I do not consider myself to be a radical by any means. I do, however, hold dear the same values and traditions that our founding fathers and my own ancestors incorporated into this American fabric during the formative years of this great nation.

First and foremost, I believe that there is a supreme being and that this nation was founded upon Christian principles, traditions, and beliefs, many of which have been allowed to become diluted over time by groups of liberals who have lost their commitment to their own convictions. They somehow see religious commitment and the belief in a supreme being as a human weakness, one that must be replaced with the assumption that only government can take care of its people. Liberals see their role in life as being caretakers of the black race, a race they see as weak and incompetent. What liberals fail to tell us is that as long as they can convince the black race (for whom they pretend to have assumed a certain responsibility) that they are incapable of taking care of themselves, then blacks will accept this fallacy as reality, and their own self-worth and ambition will disappear from their souls. Unfortunately, there are members of the black race who see it as their self-anointed role to make sure this dependency mind-set continues.

I believe that the purpose of government is not to control each and every aspect of the lives of its citizens. Government should be there only to help provide those necessities that its people do not have the ability to perform for themselves, such as during a disaster, or defending this nation against those who hope to see it destroyed. I believe that the role and size of our government should be limited to that which is necessary to provide those necessities—no less, but certainly no more! The basic size and function of government should only be that which is necessary to perform those duties that single or small groups of its citizens cannot perform for themselves. It should not be the role of government to promise to fulfill each and every need of its people from the cradle to the grave, thereby increasing the size and expense of government to operate the programs required to oversee those needs, and in turn requiring a tax burden to be placed upon the shoulders of its people to support and sustain those government programs. This history of entitlement programs has almost single-handedly destroyed the ambition of entire generations and reduced this nation from one of pride and self-determination to one that is almost totally dependent upon its government.

We have allowed feelings of guilt for something that happened to a race of people many decades ago to replace common sense. Instead of making available to that proud race of people the tools necessary to control their own destiny, we have allowed ourselves to become caretakers of generations who have been convinced that they either cannot or should not take care of themselves.

THE WAY AMERICA SHOULD BE

Obviously, the conservative idea of how America should look is vastly different from that of liberals. We have been subjected to what America will look like under the liberal agenda, and this is nothing like the vision our founding fathers had when they put their plan for this unique nation into motion.

First, the real history of this nation would be an excellent place to start in order to find the true and factual way America was to evolve. The true intentions of our founding fathers should be studied in depth as to their vision for this unique nation. Although there was no government-endorsed religion, our laws and customs were patterned after those of God-fearing and hardworking people who were dedicated to peace, prosperity, and harmony. Whether someone became actively associated with a religion or not, if their lives were patterned after those who did, America would be a much better place in which to live and raise a family. And, as far as the legislative branch of our government is concerned, a term limit should be enacted to prevent any grand illusions of a birthright as that envisioned by our career politicians of today. A free enterprise system would be strongly encouraged, and those who understand how to create and grow wealth by creating jobs would be allowed to grow and prosper without suffocating government intervention.

Maybe the best way to envision how America would look in a conservative world would be to look at our real history books, at *Currier & Ives* and *Norman Rockwell* paintings, and see the America as it was in years past. The downtown area contained the business centers of most cities and towns, and the stores and restaurants were often busy with shoppers. For those of us fortunate enough to remember living in what has been called *small town America*, the memories of our parents taking us to a nearby city or town to go Christmas shopping was something very special. We would navigate the crowded sidewalks and be drawn to the animated Christmas displays in the storefront windows which would lure us into the magic world that would be found inside. Once inside, the aroma of fresh popcorn and candy filled the air. Small children were mesmerized by the network of the overhead chutes and cables that transported credit slips and buyer orders for merchandise to the upstairs business offices, where they would be entered into the customer's store charge account records. Somewhere toward the middle of the store we would find the lineup of children who had been waiting all year to sit on Santa's lap and tell him what they wanted for Christmas.

Our lifestyles were a little slower and less hectic back then. Families seemed to spend more time together, and our schools and churches were the centers of community activities. It is sometimes hard to recall now, but the idea of going to a downtown movie theater which had only one screen could be so exciting. Going back even further in time, I can remember my parents telling about band concerts held at the bandstand in city square on Sunday afternoons. These wonderful gatherings are considered corny and uncool by today's standards, but they are all a major part of life in America during a time that being an American was something special.

Schools concentrated on educating students in the basics of reading, writing, and arithmetic that would allow them to function in their everyday lives instead of offering a curriculum that many of them would never have a need for. They also taught our nation's history as it actually happened instead of the more politically correct version that is now being forced upon us by liberal college professors. Dedicated teachers and administrators knew how to deal with those few unruly punks who seemed more interested in disrupting the learning process than they were in taking part in it. Smaller rural schools were the focal point of their towns and communities, and when we gave up these centers of pride by consolidating them into larger school districts in distant towns, we seem to have lost a lot more than we gained in the process, not to mention the death of many of these same small towns and communities.

Now, one reason this slower and more peaceful lifestyle was possible is because crime was kept under control much better then than it is today. We could take our families shopping, go to a movie or out to dinner in the downtown area without fearing for our very lives in going from place to place, or to and from our cars. One thing that played a much larger role than most people realize in controlling crime in America was the military draft. Not only did the draft keep our armed forces supplied with the numbers necessary to protect and defend our nation, but it also served as an employer who instilled a certain amount of discipline into many of the undisciplined type that are now spending their time in our jails and prisons after committing crimes on our streets and in our neighborhoods.

Immigration has become a major problem in today's America, and it is just another example of what liberals will allow to happen to our country in return for a few extra votes. People from other countries coming here must do so legally, or not at all! Repeat offenders of our immigration laws should be incarcerated in prisons at hard labor, and I don't mean prisons that even remotely offer conditions like the country-club environments enjoyed by those detainees at Club Getmo on a daily basis. Anyone who chooses not to take advantage of the vast educational opportunities found in this country would be given a choice between induction into the military or enrolled into a trade school where they would learn a skill. Those who showed no interest in working would not be compensated with welfare entitlements, unless they were legitimately disabled, or were physically or mentally unable to hold down a job. If laziness was the only disability someone might have, they would be encouraged to move to another country that accepted and supported their deadbeat lifestyles as a matter of policy.

I guess it could be said that my version of how America should look is old-fashioned, and where the idea of progress may have even been forgotten. But, from what we have seen happen to the American way of life in the name of progress, we just might want to ask ourselves if that kind of progress is worth it.

THE CONSERVATIVE PARTY

It has long been said that if two parties reach the point where they share the same goals and ideas, one of them is totally unnecessary. The two-party system in this country has worked well for the political balance of this nation; that is, up until the time it became difficult to distinguish the differences between the two parties. True conservatives have long been the heart and soul of the Republican Party, but that party has now turned its back on them. The old saying, "If it looks like a duck, walks like a duck, and quacks like a duck, it probably is a duck," applies to today's Republican legislators. Now that these

RINOs (Republicans in Name Only) have chosen to abandon their principles and join forces with the liberal Democrats in Congress, they have proven themselves to be no longer useful or necessary to our two-party system. I am not advocating a third-party movement just at this time; instead I propose simply replacing one dysfunctional party with one that is not afraid to stand up and fight for its true principles.

The time has come for the conservative arm of the GOP to reassert itself and put a halt to the plans of the liberal Democrats and their RINO cohorts to convert this nation into a socialist state—to come forth as a true conservative party, one supported by those who really love this country but who have been abandoned by the present-day GOP! The need for a return to a party of Reagan-style conservative values was never more evident than it is today. We cannot continue to cling to the memory of the old GOP, because that political party no longer exists. The very survival of America depends upon entrusting the leadership of this nation, not into the hands of those who are consumed by guilt over something that happened over 150 years ago, but instead to those who understand that the real success of this unique nation was predicated upon adherence to the strong principles, traditions, values, and beliefs of our founding fathers and must not be compromised.

Everyone knows that the mainstream media has long favored and promoted liberal Democrats, using lies and deception to discredit what once was a proud and conservative Republican Party. Conservatives should have realized something was up when the mainstream liberal media began to throw its phony support behind John McCain as the Republican Party nominee. They perceived (and correctly so) McCain to be easier for their newly invented and inexperienced darling candidate Barack Hussein Obama to defeat, so they did whatever was necessary to see that McCain became the nominee instead of more conservative GOP candidates who would have presented a stark contrast to any liberal, socialist candidate the Democrats offered up. With the success of this charade well in place, the media, as expected, has now turned its attack upon McCain, and now true conservatives discovered that there was no candidate for them to identify with or to rally around.

We must remember that the function of this nation is as a democracy, and not a perpetual yard sale for liberals to offer at bargain prices!

REINTRODUCING TODAY'S CONSERVATIVE REPUBLICAN PARTY

Hello, I have someone I would like for you to meet. Say hello to today's Republican Party—the conservative Republican Party.

The Republican Party has long been one of the most well-kept secrets we have ever witnessed. What is a Republican? A Republican is one who appreciates, and in his or her heart agrees with, the basic principles and values that have made this nation the greatest nation mankind has ever seen. What does the average American think of when hearing the word "Republican"? They will likely say rich, wealthy, big-business tycoons and almost anything with a negative connotation that liberals have been using to brainwash the general public for years. We may not be willing to admit it, but what the average citizen doesn't realize is that while their values and beliefs have not changed, the name of the party that fights for these values and beliefs definitely has changed. Today's conservative Republican Party is not the party of the same name from a century or even a half century ago; it is the party that has positive plans to propel this nation and its people successfully into the future. The conservative Republican Party is definitely not the party that believes in *something for nothing*. Today's conservative Republican Party is the party with a conscience.

Ted Kennedy, Hillary Clinton, Harry Reid, Nancy Pelosi, and the rest of the liberal Democrats have done everything within their power to destroy the very heart and soul of this great nation and are rapidly moving to transform our country into a second-rate socialist nation! The general public has for years voted for and supported the Democrat Party, mainly because they have been brainwashed into believing that the word "Democrat" stands for the same values today that it did decades ago. The most surprising thing here is why the Republican Party has not used this more to its advantage. People think they are still supporting the same party that their parents, grandparents, and great-grandparents supported for over a century, when today's Democrat Party has nothing in common with the Democrat Party of decades ago except for the name itself.

A majority of American voters share the same conservative values that Republicans have championed for years, yet this glaring fact is rarely considered when the lever is pulled at the voting booth. Republicans have long supported strong family values; a belief in God; the idea that marriage is the union between one man and one woman; the idea that abortion cannot be used as just another method of birth control, and that except in cases of rape, incest, or danger to the life of the mother, abortion is *wrong*; the idea that English is *the* language of this nation, and if people want to *legally* immigrate here, it is their responsibility to *learn* and *use* English as their *primary* language, and not the responsibility of Americans to convert to the language of their former country. It has not been the Democrats who have fought for these issues, but why is it so difficult for intelligent people to see through this?

How do we educate the general voting public? Today's conservative Republican Party must go out and meet the people *face-to-face,* shake their hands, and ask them to share with us their values and beliefs that have been handed down to them by their parents. We must share with them that the values and beliefs that have made this country strong are the very same values and beliefs that the conservative Republican Party goes to battle for daily. We can no longer afford to offer candidates that we hope will go out into the neighborhoods with the purpose to work hard and win over the voters, only to find out after the elections that these voters never knew what our candidates actually stood for. The voters of this nation have been the real losers when this happens, and as a viable political party, we cannot afford to allow this travesty to continue!

What have the Democrats done for America during the past several decades?

1. They have allowed the *ACLU* to become their legal mouthpiece.
2. Democrats have convinced many of today's minorities and low-income earners that this nation owes them a living, and that a good education is not necessary, or that they don't need health insurance, because the Democrats will take care of them if they don't do these things. They do this to keep these very same people from becoming educated and self-sufficient, hoping that they will remain dependent upon the Democrats, who will receive their votes in return.
3. Democrats promote the idea that any reference to God is at best unfair, and at worst illegal, and that the posting of our Ten Commandments might offend someone; thus, Democrats are working to see that this document is removed.
4. Democrats support the assumption that *illegal* immigrants should have the same (or sometimes even better) rights as those of the legitimate citizens of this nation, and that we should adapt our customs and laws to accommodate all immigrants, instead of the other way around.
5. During their times of occupying the White House, Democrats have depleted our military resources to the extent that even today we remain in danger of becoming vulnerable to any rogue regime that wants to take over the world.
6. Democrats offer no legitimate plans for the longevity and prosperity of this great nation, but they routinely denounce any Republican plans for achieving such results, whether they agree with them or not, as evidenced by their plan to roll back President Bush's tax cuts.

In short, the loyal voters of this nation have been brainwashed into thinking that the Democrat Party of today is the same party of their ancestors decades ago. With role models like Hillary Clinton, Ted Kennedy, Harry Reid, and Nancy Pelosi, you know something is dreadfully wrong! Each one of these career politicians is constantly looking for ways to keep giving away this country to anyone who thinks the world owes them a living. With luck and a very determined effort to educate the public, we will prevail in returning this nation to the grassroots beliefs and values of our founding fathers. These selfless pioneers guided our country into becoming the beacon of liberty and democracy, and they did not intend for this land to be entrusted to those who would take whatever they could take, but would give nothing back in return. The philosophy of a political party cannot be one that believes that this great land is for sale to anyone who might have a vote.

Rebuilding the GOP

Conservative Republicans find themselves in a dilemma. We all know that John McCain and Barack Hussein Obama are the candidates of their respective parties in the 2008 general election. We also know that John McCain has not shown himself to be a champion of conservative values, which have long been the heart and soul of the GOP platform. We also know that Barack Hussein Obama is the most liberal of a very liberal Democrat Party, which is really saying something.

Now we come to the dilemma. What can conservatives do to make sure that the United States of America does not become another socialist state, a carbon copy of a weak group of European nations who are terrified of offending those invaders who have infested their countries? These immigrants have been turning Europe into a place that resembles the one from which they came, and immigrants from those same places are intent upon doing the same to the United States, thereby putting an end to the visions and intentions our founding fathers had when they set up this most wonderful and unique nation over two hundred years ago. Even though conservatives find it hard to get totally behind John McCain, if they fail to do so, this will guarantee that the most liberal candidate to ever seek the office of president of the United States of America will ascend to that lofty office, and this nation will never be the same. The dilemma is not a choice between the lesser of two evils. This is truly a choice between the very survival of this *unique* nation we call America, or becoming just another liberal socialist state. If *socialism* reigns, this unique nation will be no more!

John McCain is strong on national defense, while the liberal Obama says he will quickly withdraw U.S. troops from Iraq. John McCain will likely strengthen our military, while many expect Obama to weaken and draw down our military, making us vulnerable to attack by any one of several rogue nations. John McCain says he will extend the Bush tax cuts, while Obama has pledged to let them expire, and he will move to immediately increase taxes on all Americans, under the pretense of raising taxes only on the wealthy. McCain now says he is in favor of offshore drilling for energy, while Obama professes to use the ever-increasing rise in the price of oil to force Americans to conserve energy by not driving, by living in far less comfortable conditions, and by making sure we keep our tires properly inflated. Although McCain does not seem to interject his personal religious beliefs into his political platform, Obama hints that everything we have learned about the Christian religion is all wrong, that we should forget our own traditions, while allowing the traditions of those who came to this country from other lands to proceed unaltered.

Although conservatives are not completely comfortable with McCain, we are terrified at the thought of an Obama administration. Incentive for businesses to create jobs will quickly disappear, and applying for entitlement programs will become an occupation.

CONSERVATIVE CANDIDATES

Republicans have apparently lost their ability to distinguish themselves between a true conservative and a liberal. It has always been relatively easy to recognize a liberal, but when someone presented themselves as a Republican candidate, we automatically assumed that they could be counted upon to protect true conservative values. Could it be that the Republican Party has finally abandoned the ideals of Reagan conservatism?

Although the definition of a true conservative has not changed during the past eight years, the voice of the true conservative seems to have lost its messenger. John McCain campaigned as a Republican, and conservatives were duped into thinking that this meant that he would fight for true conservative values. If we had examined his legislative history in more detail, we should have understood that he has been more liberal than conservative on many issues. Americans truly appreciate John McCain's military service to our country and deeply regret that he had to go through the hell of being a POW, but his political designs are about as liberal as the Democrat candidates. If this were not true, why would the *New York Times* have supported Hilary Clinton and John McCain as the presidential candidates of their respective parties?

It is a well-known fact that true conservatives favor smaller government, lower taxes, the right to life of the yet-unborn, and a strong military. We oppose same-sex marriage, pork-barrel government spending, illegal immigration, and the death tax. Other than on the right-to-life issue, John McCain is more closely aligned with liberals than he is with true conservatives. If this is how the Republican Party has chosen to redefine itself, then the time has come for true conservatives to divorce themselves from the Republican Party of John McCain and support a true conservative party that will promote real conservative values and principles.

If conservatives are choosing a candidate simply on the issue of electability, then we are losing our reason for being a political party. Winning the hearts and minds of the voters is very important, but when selling our soul for a vote becomes more important than the values we look for in a candidate, then we have lost our focus of what the purpose of a political party should be. One way to say it is: "It's the issues, stupid!" The 2006 election showed us just what can happen when those we send to Washington to represent us totally abandon the reasons we sent them there in the first place.

McCain Throws In the Towel

The actions of John McCain during the 2008 presidential campaign and after the election itself are perfect examples of what true conservatives tried to warn the rest of the Republican Party about all along. John McCain was not a conservative! He was more closely aligned with the Democrat Party than he was with the Republican Party, and to think that he would be one who would conduct a campaign that would defeat the liberal menace just shows how senile the GOP has become since abandoning their heart and soul conservative values.

In 2000 and again in 2004 John McCain convinced us that he really wanted to be president of the United States, and I believe he was sincere at that time. In 2008, however, after a long and hard-fought primary contest, Senator McCain apparently became more interested in running a more honorable and politically correct campaign than in launching a campaign that would defeat anyone the liberals ran as their candidate. To be perfectly honest, John McCain has nothing to prove to anyone concerning his devotion to and love for his country, but his will to be the true leader of this country had disappeared. Perhaps he unknowingly realized that the job of president of the United States was just too demanding a task to take on at this point in his life, just as President George H. W. Bush appeared to realize during the 1992 campaign. After a long and dedicated career of service to his country, Senator McCain understood the strain that the job of president would put on any person, and after witnessing firsthand the shameful daily assaults to which liberals subjected George W. Bush, this battle-scarred warrior decided that his golden years would not be spent in this way.

The 2008 presidential contest, both the Democrat and Republican primaries, were entirely and totally orchestrated and choreographed by the unscrupulous and unethical liberal mainstream media. To those who understand just how this sleazy group operates, how could anyone be surprised at the eventual outcome? McCain finally understood that he had been chosen and set up by this deceitful media to win the GOP primary over younger and more formidable conservative candidates whom the media knew were much more likely to defeat their invented, darling candidate, Barack Hussein Obama. The liberal mainstream media did to this great American patriot in six months what six years in a Vietnamese prisoner-of-war camp could not do. They convinced John McCain to throw in the towel. Anyone who thinks John McCain lost this race because he is not a fighter has no idea what this man is made of. He simply came to realize that taking on one of the most influential and destructive elements in America today, who wants to push this nation into socialism, was just too much for him to take on at his age. John McCain has certainly earned the right to enjoy his golden years, but fighting an evil conspiracy made up of the liberal Democrat Party and their liberal mainstream media propaganda mill were just more than he wanted to take on at this point in his life. In another time, John McCain might have made this liberal den of thieves deeply regret even the thought of trying to trick him and the American people. God bless, John McCain.

THE PERFECT PRESIDENT

Have you ever asked yourself, "If we could design the perfect president, how would that person be described? What would he or she do to make this world a better place in which to live?"

We definitely want someone who would be honest, dependable, incorruptible, and unafraid of making correct but difficult decisions, regardless of whom those decisions might anger. One who understands that being "politically correct" would be far down the list of considerations when making these decisions, and that the primary consideration must be whether it is truly in the best interest of this nation.

Without question, the number-one priority of anyone holding this office must be our national security! If our economy depends upon our ability to obtain certain sources of energy; and if our ability to obtain those sources of energy through mutual agreement is threatened by any nation or region, our president must do whatever is necessary to ensure that our supply of those sources of energy is not compromised. With that thought in mind, our ability to become totally energy-independent must also be a critical priority!

Other issues to which the perfect president should give high priority are reducing the size of government, maintaining a strong military, supporting education, a strong economy, improving race relations, and stopping illegal immigration.

The person who can successfully attack these issues and bring together both political parties to seek out solutions to these issues would indeed be the perfect president.

WHAT HAPPENED TO OUR AMERICA?

I am much like many of you in that I am an everyday citizen, and one who has become very concerned, with each passing day, that this nation is quickly losing its battle to remain that unique nation our founding fathers intended it to be. Those who are intent upon separating the people of this nation from the ideals of our founding fathers have managed to weaken those ideals and values that made this nation the great beacon of democracy. Those same liberties that were granted by our constitution to make this the most wonderful place upon the face of the Earth are now being used to destroy this nation. Those liberties, which have encouraged us to be ambitious and resourceful, are now being redefined and used against us. This was a nation built through the efforts of a very diverse collection of people who only wanted a chance to succeed. Today, this nation is overflowing with people who think the world owes them a living, and who feel no responsibility to do their part to keep this nation strong. They are perfectly content to refuse to contribute anything positive to a nation that has given them everything necessary for success.

The American dream, that wonderful monument to freedom and democracy into which Thomas Jefferson and our other founding fathers breathed that first breath of life, has been watered down to a mere shadow of its former self. We have reluctantly taken a back seat and watched as pseudo-Americans have gained a foothold in our courts and in the U.S. Congress. They have used these positions to distort the precepts and intentions of our unique and wonderful constitution and to frame their own socialist agenda. If we continue to sit back and allow these traitors to run unchallenged, then whatever is left of that most wonderful monument to man's ingenuity will not be worth the dirt used to bury it.

We must take immediate steps to point our road signs back in the right direction and place this nation on a solid path toward rebuilding its strengths. U.S. citizenship can once again be something of which we are extremely proud. We need to realize that it is something very special to be called an American, and we need to shout it from the rooftops. We need to let the rest of the world know that the days of the United States rolling over and playing dead are ancient history. The strongest possible military is vital to the survival of this nation, and those who do not understand and accept their own responsibility to this end should no longer be allowed to benefit from the many blessings of this nation.

The unique history of this nation is vital to the understanding of our young people and lets them know just how special this wonderful country really is. We must never again allow our history to be relegated to the status of an insignificant footnote, as proposed by the liberal educational community to fit their own liberal agenda. Administration of our education system must be transferred from the hands of government bureaucrats and radical liberals, and placed in the capable hands of true and able educators. Anyone not wishing to benefit from a superior educational program should be given the choice of taking part in a skilled trade curriculum or spending two years in the military or a service organization similar to the Peace Corps. The idea or opinion that it is okay for anyone to take advantage of whatever this nation has to give them, while giving nothing back in return, must come to an end! For many Americans, their citizenship credit card limits have been exceeded, and the time has come to pay up.

The disasters of big government have been strangling the very life out this nation, and government must be restructured to providing only basic and necessary services. We must also reinforce the concepts of capitalism and encourage businesses to return their corporate infrastructure to this country. This can be done through tax incentives designed to encourage and reinforce compliance with these strategies.

Organizations such as the ACLU have been allowed far too much leeway in attacking and almost destroying the original spiritual concepts of our founding fathers. If people do not believe in or agree with the teachings of the Christian faith, then they can worship in the traditions that honor their own faith, as long as no one attempts to limit or diminish the rights of the people of other religions to peacefully worship their own god.

Truth vs. Political Correctness

Have you ever heard the old saying, "Everything has its price" or "You get what you pay for?" Well, it is very true! If you sell your soul for a vote, or if you trade your dignity and independence for your vote, then you get what you deserve.

The time has finally come for conservatives to either put up or shut up! In fact, that time is long overdue. We have allowed those once-meaningful words "truth" and "common sense" to be replaced with empty phrases such as "political correctness." If we are lucky, we may still have one final chance to save this nation from ourselves. We can save this nation from joining the likes of our European brothers and sisters, who have become lulled into the false security of accepting anything and anyone with open arms, even to the extent of throwing away their own long-held values and traditions.

How could this happen? We have allowed ourselves to just sit back and watch as the very conscience of this wonderful nation is placed into the hands of a bunch of guilt-ridden liberals. The people in this group, made up primarily of Democrats, but with a few misguided Republicans sprinkled in, are so consumed by an enormous and burdensome guilt complex that they can no longer allow themselves to live in a nation where success was built, not by the handing out of government entitlements (as they would prefer), but by human ingenuity and ambition. Liberals are now promoting the fatal illusion that it is the role of government to take the total wealth and assets from those who actually created and earned them, and divide them between those who chose not to become involved in the positive growth of this nation, except of course by increasing the number of their dependent offspring.

The benefactors of this liberal Democrat *share-the-wealth* windfall scheme (in return for their votes, of course) have apparently become so comfortable being dependent that they see no reason to question the true intent of the liberals' generosity toward them. To ensure that this group remains beholden and loyal, Democrats have for decades perpetuated the illusion that this group has been persecuted since the beginning of time, and that they (liberals) will take care of them. Liberals have continuously brainwashed their subjects into believing that they cannot make it without their help, and unless they continue to blindly support them with their vote, they stand no chance of ever pulling themselves out of their designated plight. The plain and simple truth is that the biggest fear of liberals is that the people in this group might someday come to their senses and realize that they have been duped for generations.

Now, to many, this will seem racial, bigoted, degrading, unfair, and oh, yes, *politically incorrect*. It is nothing less, however, than the plain and simple truth! No group of people can be held down indefinitely unless they lack ambition and are comfortable with being dependent upon others. If any group of people has become so satisfied with the position of being forever dependent, then they deserve their self-imposed plight. The secret to pulling oneself up by the bootstraps is found through education. If people do not have the desire to improve themselves through education, then they are destined to accept whatever is left over for them.

Self-imposed dependency becomes a sickness, and once addicted to it, it becomes almost impossible to break away from. Many within this group have been very disappointed that so many within their very own race will not realize what has been happening to them and take steps to correct their situation. Many did not accept this dependency, but there is far too many who do nothing to challenge their dependency. If someone does not have a feeling of self-worth, then being dependent upon someone else doesn't really bother him.

THE LEGACY OF THE BABY BOOMERS

Well, fellow baby boomers, we have come a long way, haven't we! As we limp into our golden years, we realize that we are now looking at a world which we hardly recognize. We inherited a world from our parents that, for the most part, was somewhat better than the one they inherited from their parents, and from their parents before them. This nation had just emerged from a World War that firmly established the United States of America as the dominant nation on Earth, and we were about to see great innovations that would make life much easier and more interesting for mankind.

As the 1950s and 60s became the 1970s and 80s, it looked like we were in the process of greatly improving upon the legacy our parents had placed into our care, and things had never looked better for the United States of America. We were sending men into space and landing on the Moon with such regularity that it was becoming boring. During our watch the computer forever changed the way we did things; the way we did everything! Advances in science and medicine were extending our life expectancy to ages previously thought impossible. General Motors, AT&T, Sears, and Exxon had long been the unchallenged leaders of the business world, but with the emergence of the mega-corporations such as Wal-Mart and Microsoft, our economy soared to heights never before imagined. As we watched, the Dow climbed from 1,000 to 3,000, then to 5,000, 8,000, and on to 10,000 and beyond, and the only question was, "How high would it go?" And oh yes, with the fall of our old nemesis Russia and the Soviet Union, there seemed to be nothing that would prevent us from being the most dominant nation on Earth. But, as so often happens, while we were reveling in our own success and the unprecedented growth of our economy, we forgot to take care of some of those so-called little things along the way.

The integration of our public schools was a major challenge that was designed to close the gap between blacks and whites in the area of education. After the initial shock of this decision, it was understood that by bringing blacks and whites together into a common school system, it would eventually be a good thing for everyone. One of the stated purposes of school integration was to bring black students up to a level close to that of white students. But, to the great disappointment of everyone, the results of this theory worked exactly in reverse of its intended purpose, and instead of black students rising to the educational levels previously attained by white students, the white students dropped to the level of black students. To make matters worse, the lack of discipline and ambition of black students soon became shared by their white classmates, and our educational system has been in a steady decline ever since. This is not a racist statement, but a valid and realistic evaluation of what has actually happened to our schools. One totally unexpected result of public school integration was that along with the decline in educational achievement in this country came a dramatic rise in crime over that same time period.

Now that the torch has been passed to our generation, and with the wonderful examples of what our ancestors did for us firmly in our thoughts and minds, what kind of world would we leave to our children? The answer has become painfully obvious. Where it was the decision of our parents to sacrifice so we would have a better life than they did, we seem to have done the exact opposite. Instead of continuing in the tradition of making sacrifices for our children, it will now be left up to our children and grandchildren to pay the price for destructive decisions made by the baby boomer generation.

THE KEYS TO SUCCESS

With all of our many faults, make no mistake about it: America is still by far the most wonderful country on the face of the Earth. Do we have our problems? Sure we do, just like any other country, but far fewer than most.

Some people who complain about their own personal situations are justified in doing so; however, many who complain about their inability to achieve success in life are simply not willing to do that which is necessary to improve their lives. We are much more in control of our destiny than many people are willing to admit. This country offers almost anyone the opportunity to succeed in life, but the fruition of these opportunities depends greatly upon whether or not we are willing to do what is necessary to take advantage of them. Although luck often plays a big role in one's success, those who are the beneficiaries of luck have taken certain calculated steps to be at the right place and at the right time to take advantage of this luck.

There are certain qualities that most successful people have in common. Perhaps the most important, even more so than one's birthright, is *ambition*. Without ambition, one is not likely to achieve success to any great degree. Once ambition and motivation have taken over one's thought processes, then comes the realization that education in some degree is vital to success, and this is when success becomes reality. Many people equate ambition and motivation with hard labor, when in reality it simply means working smarter instead of working harder. One's fate in life is determined more by a lack of ambition and education than it is by one's birth situation. Granted, there are exceptions to almost any rule, such as being born a Rockefeller or one of Sam Walton's children; but for the most part, we control our own destiny to a much greater extent than we realize. Those who understand the importance of earning an education will always be better-off than those who see earning an education as a waste of time. If someone is satisfied with just getting by from day to day or week to week, then that will very likely remain their fate. On the other hand, if someone is not satisfied with depending upon government or charity for his or her very existence, then he or she will move heaven and earth to make sure that this does not happen to them.

Too many young people today look at professional athletes who are making obscene salaries, and that is the only definition of success they can comprehend. Once they have refined their definition of success to a more realistic version, maybe, just maybe, they can do their part to bring some logic and common sense back into this equation.

Killing the Golden Goose

One of Aesop's fables tells of a goose that laid golden eggs. In this story a farmer and his wife have a goose that lays one golden egg each and every day. Instead of patiently waiting for their goose to lay the single golden egg each day and allow their wealth to accumulate over time, they decide that this goose must surely be made of gold, and that if they kill it, they can take all of its golden contents at one time. After killing and cutting open their goose, they find that it was just like any other goose. In their haste for riches, they lost their one sure thing: getting the one golden egg this goose had been giving them each day.

This story contains a very real and valuable lesson for the future of this nation, but only if we are wise enough to comprehend what it is telling us. In their farsightedness, our founding fathers envisioned this nation as the "last great hope of mankind." Aliens coming into this country, both legally and illegally, seem to realize something that many of our own citizens have failed to grasp: the very uniqueness of this land. The theory of a unique nation is so impossible for some people to comprehend that they just cannot appreciate how fortunate they are to call America home. As in Aesop's fable, many people are willing to destroy their golden goose for something they expect to be much better. Even those considered to be living in poverty in this country would be seen as being well-off in many other countries. It is a hard truth to accept, but not everyone is intended to be rich, nor is everyone capable of handling wealth, as evidenced by many who won the lottery, only to end up in a much worse financial condition than before winning the lottery.

It seems that these old stories and fables are no longer important tools for liberal educators to introduce to our young people today, but this problem extends farther back than this current generation of young people. Many parents of today were not taught these old stories, and they did not have knowledge of them to pass on to their own children; thus many valuable lessons in life have been allowed to disappear into the black hole of time. Aesop's fable about the goose that laid the golden eggs is certainly one of these stories that taught very valuable lessons but have now been lost in time. Why is it that this country seems to be the chosen destination of so many people from many other countries of this world? Just what do these people see in this country that so many of our own people cannot see? Liberals have tried to convince us for decades that this nation is so bad that we must separate ourselves from the teachings of our founding fathers.

Have you ever wondered why the young people of today do not seem to have the strong patriotic feelings of past generations? You do not need to look very far to find that the teaching of our nation's history has been de-emphasized over past decades. Strangely enough, this erosion in American patriotism coincides with the appearance of the liberal policy of "political correctness," which mandates acknowledgment of the history and religious practices of other people who have immigrated here, but at the expense of our own values and beliefs. What is it that makes people want to come to this country? Plain and simple, they see what liberals cannot or will not acknowledge, and that is the reason this unique nation is so necessary to the future of mankind.

TIME: WHERE DID YOU GO?

Ah, how often have we longed for a return to the good old days? For those of us who are no longer spring chickens and are looking back at our golden years instead of forward to them, we remember thinking that a lifetime was like a string winding its way into the future, and with no end in sight. Some of us were even convinced that we were invincible and that we had the world by the tail. Some of us even were convinced that we would somehow retain our youthful appearance and not show the signs of aging as our parents, grandparents, and others did as they grew older. We felt no need to buy life insurance or to plan for retirement. Little did some of us realize that the innocence of our youth would somehow be substituted with the ignorance of our youth.

Back then, the primary disappointment for many of us might have been that we were not better athletes, or that we hadn't made better grades in school, or that we didn't have that sporty car we always wanted, or that we weren't born rich. But we knew that it was only a matter of time before many of these symbols of success would fall right into our laps. The world was just waiting for our arrival with open arms, and when we were ready to accept our destiny, everything would then be perfect, just as it should be. Some of us even thought that all of this would happen regardless of how well or how poorly we had prepared ourselves for the future, and boy, would we be ready to reap our rewards.

Then, as life has proven time and time again, reality began to set in. For many of us it happened shortly after graduating from high school or college, but it did happen to all of us, none-the-less. We had to get jobs, and many of us soon got married and started our families. Some of us realized that we owed our country time in the military. Most of us didn't think that we would soon be facing the same realities that had faced our fathers and grandfathers before us, or that we would also be fighting to preserve democracy and our way of life. Isn't it funny how history has a way of repeating itself?

Moving into our middle-aged years, some found their success, while others would come to realize that success has different faces, and that personal wealth is not always one of them. It didn't matter whether our fate in life included personal wealth or not; the one fact that each and every one of us soon began to realize was that if we lived long enough, we too would age and grow old, some more gracefully than others. Time was something that became more and more precious as it began to pass us by. Regardless of one's wealth, when our time is up, there is absolutely nothing we can do about it! Once we finally realize this fact, life takes on an entirely different meaning.

As we look around at our changing world today, we see several very disturbing trends that have emerged over the past several years. The decline in family values might seem like an insignificant issue to some, but a strong family is at the very core of a strong nation. An increase in crime, illegal drug use, violence in our schools, children born out of wedlock, and single-parent households are prime examples of what happens when our core values are ignored or forgotten entirely. The importance of receiving a quality education and respect for authority in our schools and government are also elements of a value system that are now portrayed as being old-fashioned and unnecessary. The constant attack upon these core values by liberals in our government and in Hollywood just might be the one obstacle we cannot overcome.

This baby boomer generation remembers the prediction made by Nikita Khrushchev, the Russian premier during the 1950s and 60s. He predicted that the United States would destroy itself from within and that Russia would not need to fire a shot. Perhaps he could see even then that this nation was weakening and primed to be destroyed from within by a progressive liberal movement that was already underway.

So, where did the time go? In many ways, we didn't know how good we had it back then. In other ways, however, life is better now than ever before. If we could find some way to take the best of both eras and combine them, how wonderful life would be.

WHERE HAVE THE REAL AMERICANS GONE?

What happened to the conservative or traditional candidates who once convinced voters that they were going to fight to preserve the values that have made this nation strong for almost 250 years? We sent people to Congress, whether they were Democrats, Republicans, or Independents, who promised the voters that they would fight for these values. Among these precious values were, (1) a strong national security, first and foremost, (2) rights of the unborn, (3) that the only definition of marriage would be the union between one man and one woman, and (4) that the securing of our borders against illegal intrusion in any form was mandatory to protect the sovereignty of this nation. Instead, we have managed to send to Congress a group of spineless and unpatriotic American pretenders who didn't have the courage to stand up for the principles on which they campaigned to get elected in the first place.

There are just a few economic systems that have been implemented by mankind, and the only ones that have lasted for any period of time are capitalism, socialism, and communism. Of these, the only one that has actually encouraged its citizens to become wealthy is capitalism. When we give serious consideration to any candidate who says that he wants to take all of the wealth within this nation and divide it equally among everyone, we are either, blind, stupid, or so gullible that we will believe anything regardless of how unrealistic it is. The ones who had the ambition and skill to become the business and industrial leaders of this nation were able to do so when others either, tried and failed, were afraid to try, or were content to take whatever was given to them. It has been said that we could take all of the wealth of world, divide it equally among everyone, and within ten years this wealth would return to the hands of those who knew how to create it in the first place.

It is a sad truth, but even when someone goes to Congress with good intentions, many of them soon lose sight of what they were sent there to do; and before they know it, they have become just as corrupt as those same *career politicians* who see Congress as their personal kingdom. This group has been moving this once-proud nation in the direction of becoming something that is nothing like the nation our founding fathers envisioned when they risked their lives to set into motion something that had never been seen before. This nation has always been unique, but we are allowing liberals to turn it into something that is very similar to the European countries that have lost their will to be world leaders, or the Third World countries that have never understood what it means to be a nation that the rest of the world respects and looks up to.

Liberals will contend that conservative values are outdated and not suited for today's modern world, but successfully maintaining our conservative values is what has made this nation different from any other nation this world has ever seen. This nation was once a place where pride dwelled deep within the hearts of those who would wear its uniform to defend it from anyone or anything that wanted to destroy it. Our founding fathers also understood the simple fact that acknowledging the existence of a supreme being was a primary reason that this nation would prosper like no other nation ever had before. Just another one of those *conservative values*, I suppose?

Now that we know what real Americans are, it is imperative that they now step up and take charge. America, and the rest of the world, are waiting!

RIGHT THE SHIP

What would your reaction be if this announcement appeared in today's newspaper?

Obituaries

The United States of America, age 232. The cause of death was said to be a decline in the number of citizens wanting to see this nation maintain its role as the prominent nation of the world. No immediate survivors could be located at the time of death, and a public but lightly attended memorial service preceded burial in an unmarked grave. Although the deceased had requested prior to death that donations to the cause of world peace be made in lieu of flowers, few contributions were received, and the requested movement for world peace was later abandoned.

After reading this announcement, would you feel surprised, disappointed, upset, heartbroken, ashamed, or simply relieved? Some reading this book might say that these are just the warped views of another right-wing conservative war hawk. At one point in my life, I would have been in total agreement with that opinion. But after seeing the liberal wing of the Democrat Party doing whatever they could to destroy the very fabric of what our founding fathers tried to incorporate into their vision for this fledging nation over 230 years ago, I fear that the dream that was once "the land of the free and the home of the brave" is being allowed to just die of old age or just a lack of attention. Far too many Americans who could have stepped up to take control and preserve everything that was once sacred and good about this country now seem to have lost interest and have lost their will to fight. If this trend continues, this nation will soon resemble something not very different from the many Third World countries that once depended upon the United States to solve all of their problems.

What must happen to this country before its own people finally wake up to the reality that this nation is being exploited by a strong and vocal liberal element whose goal is to turn the United States into a socialist state where incentive and initiative becomes lost in translation? It appears that a segment of people in this country seem to be burdened with guilt over the success of the hardworking citizens whose fortunes have risen, not from their participation in entitlement programs, but due to their own efforts and from the sweat of their brows.

When did we lose sight of what made this great nation successful, and how did we allow the icons of our values to become so dangerously distorted? Is it too late to *right the ship* and return the United States to its former place as the one and only great hope of mankind? *Of course it is not too late!* Not as long as there are still people who understand the difference between right and wrong, between good and evil, and between prosperity and despair. Once we get our priorities straight and return to the ideals and values that our founding fathers envisioned for us as they were designing and building the roadmap for the future of this nation, we will return this great nation to its proper place, where we will once again be in control of our own destiny!

PUTTING AMERICA BACK ON TRACK

What will it take to put America back on track and return this nation to being the wonderful and safe land it was supposed to be? Our government is totally out of touch with the American people, and many of our cities have become every bit as dangerous as some of those lands where our troops have been deployed to curb violence and international terrorism. It really would not take much to make believers out of those who prey upon the innocent citizens of this country, but it would take an attitude adjustment of enormous proportions by politicians to allow these measures to be placed into action.

One of the vital initial measures will be to make certain adjustments that will guard against those seemingly lifetime appointments of *career politicians* who are totally out of touch with the real world, and who have become so powerful that it is almost impossible to remove them from office. Term limits must be implemented to guard against the stranglehold upon the American taxpayer by these *career politicians*. This will greatly limit corrupt political machines from placing this nation under siege and put our economy back on track by encouraging initiative and ambition to start and grow new businesses. An infusion of concerned everyday American citizens who have firsthand knowledge of what is going on in this country will then have a chance to carry the message of the American people straight to the floor of

Congress. We have been sold down the river by a group of *career politicians* who think it is their birthright to own and occupy a seat in the Senate or the House of Representatives. This group doesn't have the first clue about how it feels to anxiously wait for the next payday so they can pay their bills, or who has lost their job because their factory or place of business has moved to some third-world country, or who must find a second or even third job to feed their family. These *career politicians* have been accepting campaign contributions and payoffs that have assured their continued stay in Congress, in return for their promise to push through legislation that will unfairly benefit those contributors, but at the expense of the American people. A great example of this is the recent mortgage crisis forced upon banks and financial institutions by *career politicians* Barney Frank, Christopher Dodd, and other liberal scalawags, and for which the bill to pay for this outrage is now being scandalously dumped into the lap of the American taxpayer. Not only do these corrupt politicians not deserve to return to their places in Congress, but they should be tried in a court of law, and if found guilty, be sent to prison at hard labor. In another day and time, this group would have been dragged kicking and screaming from these hallowed halls of Congress, and forced to answer for their despicable actions. This is the kind of legislative scandal that has brought capitalism to its knees, and totally validates my reasons for making this suggestion to rid ourselves of the *career politician*.

On the issue of working to bring the crime rate in America under control, once our troops have completed their job abroad and returned home, we can deploy them into high crime areas, and along our southern borders, a duty for which our state militia or National Guard was originally intended. This might appear to some to be police state tactics, but drastic times call for drastic measures. Uniformed and non-uniformed squads could patrol areas looking for gang and illegal drug activity and illegal border jumpers. Once these problem areas become places where people could conduct their activities in complete safety, many patrols could be phased out over time, while keeping these areas under surveillance to discourage a return of the criminal element. Rescuing American cities and towns from criminal activity should take priority over claims of racial profiling, especially if it means that those involved in these criminal activities are taken off of the streets as a result of these actions. This cannot be done unless liberal groups such as the ACLU, NAACP, and other watchdog groups realize that the rights of criminals do not take priority over the rights of the American public, and that these measures are necessary to take back our cities. Those who see crime prevention as racial profiling need a big dose of reality and common sense.

MESSAGE TO OUR LIBERAL FRIENDS

To those liberals who have lost sight of what it means to be an American, a real, true American, this book is intended to help open your eyes. The reason America has been successful for so long is that it is unlike any other country on this Earth, and the only way America can remain successful is for it to continue to be unlike any other country on this Earth. We do not need to pattern ourselves after those weak European nations that have lost their own identity in their futile attempt to be all things to all people. If that is the kind of country you want to call home, I am sure those countries would welcome you with open arms. As long as liberals are satisfied and content with being just like everyone else, they will never understand what it means to a be real American.

Real Americans still hold dear such values as having a strong belief in God; the desire to obtain an education; developing a strong work ethic, the desire to take responsibility for your own actions and future; taking on the responsibility of raising and supporting your own family; coming to the defense of your country if called upon to do so; appreciating the great history of your country; and feeling an overwhelming sense of pride when our flag passes in front of you. If you think that holding such values dear signifies a weakness in someone's makeup, then you have proven beyond a doubt that you are totally incapable of being a true American. If you really feel this way, this clearly answers the question of why you are so unhappy living in this wonderful land, and you would very likely be much happier living in some other country where your beliefs are welcomed. America is definitely not one of those countries!

For those who think socialism is the way to go, then by all means please move to Canada, or France, or one of the other European countries that are now so deep into socialism that they don't realize what hit them. Liberals have just never understood what makes capitalism tick. Just as non-Christians do not understand what it means to be saved by the blood of Jesus Christ, then they would likely be miserable spending an eternity in heaven. Likewise, as liberals just cannot comprehend what it means to be a true American, they are miserable living in a land where opportunities are unlimited to those who are willing to work and to do what is necessary to take advantage of those opportunities. Anyone who thinks that an existence through entitlement programs promotes a productive lifestyle will never understand the satisfaction that comes from ambition, initiative, achievement, and bringing home a well-earned paycheck. Liberals, obviously being unable to understand the beauty of capitalism and the American spirit, will never be happy living in America.

And oh yes, my liberal friends, one more thing …

America—
love it or
leave it!

LIBERALS

The total absence of common sense within our liberal friends never ceases to amaze me. The following is a collection of letters to the editor submitted by me to a local newspaper, along with responses from liberal contributors who will remain anonymous.

Letter from a Liberal Writer
July 19, 2006
Bring Our Troops Home
While I am neither a "liberal" nor a "radical Republican," I can lament the death of any American soldier or any Iraqi killed, whether civilian or those who are resisting the unjustified U.S. invasion.

I am particularly incensed when I see rabid Republicans trying to make saints out of every soldier in Iraq. The U.S. military has already acknowledged that the dead soldiers were from the same platoon (a group of thirty men) that was involved in the vicious rape and murder of a young woman in Iraq. Having raped her, they burned her body. This kind of conduct is the act of thugs, not decent U.S. soldiers. This atrocity was more than enough to silence any criticism of the deaths of the soldiers. Isn't it odd that those wanting criticism of *barbaric acts* against U.S. troops are strangely silent themselves when atrocities are committed here and in Haditha by U.S. troops?

It's always odd to see everything in uniform defended as *saints* by these people who seem to believe that the rape and murder of young Iraqi women and killing ten-year-old girls is a "deserved form of recreation" for U.S. soldiers in Iraq.

Yes, I care about the deaths of U.S. soldiers. I wish I could say that these war supporters actually cared about the crimes being committed by their *saints*. If Bush would bring all of our troops home today, none of us would be lamenting the meaningless death and destruction on both sides in Iraq.

My Response
July 27, 2006
This Right to Comment

I find it very amusing that Mr. ___ continues to send his letters all the way from his home state of ___ to show Arkansans just how much he hates anything George Bush says or does. If he and his liberal cronies should ever get the chance to hold this high office again, maybe he would not feel so frustrated all the time.

In his latest tirade he tries to justify his obvious hatred and disdain for all U.S. troops and military personnel by linking them to the group of alleged,— and this point they are still "alleged"—killers who have been accused of murdering and raping a young woman in Iraq. If these people are truly guilty of committing these horrible crimes, then they deserve to be punished to the full extent of the law. Just wearing the uniform of our (including his) country, however, does not mean that they are all guilty by association.

After reading his numerous submissions to "letters to the editor," he seems to take pleasure in attacking anything and everything done or proposed by the Bush administration, even if it may even be something he actually agrees with. The members of our military, who are once again fighting to allow such people as Mr. ___ the right and opportunity to use this outlet to spew his obvious disdain for authority, have once again become his target. He seems to have lost sight of the fact that if he were a citizen of the government of one of these Middle Eastern countries he now seems to be constantly defending, he would be executed on sight for opening his mouth.

I too would love to see all of our troops brought home. I can see, however, that we will likely be in this tumultuous region of the world for some time to come. I have always had a hard time totally accepting the fact that the United States needs to be the "policeman of the world." I have come to realize, however, that if we don't crush these radical Islamic militants and all groups like them before they aim their weapons (WMDs) at the mainland United States, as they have vowed many times to do, Mr. ___ and all of those like him may finally get their chance to become subjects of a government controlled by these radicals.

Just how long, then, does he think he would get to keep his head if he were to spout his antigovernment feelings, as he so often does here? He should take every opportunity to thank his God that these brave men and women, whom he is constantly berating, are still willing to risk their own lives to give him, and those like him, that right to complain.

Letter from a Liberal Writer
January 3, 2007
Saddam Was Brave

The execution is over, but at least Saddam Hussein showed the United States how a brave man faces death. Saddam's bravery was quite a contrast to the Americans' and Iraqis' hiding behind hoods to carry out the execution.

The shameless method of execution was a striking reminder of George W. Bush's "Iraqi democracy," which lies in the midst of the ashes of the three thousand dead Americans and the twenty thousand wounded and crippled American military. Bush invaded a country based on lies and executes the head of state while hiding behind masks. This is so typical of the Bush-conducted war.

My Response
January 24, 2007
Brave Saddam?

Once again, Mr. ___ has used this newspaper to teach us dumb ol' Arkies a lesson. In his letter to the editor shortly after Saddam's execution, Mr. ___ appears to be expressing his feelings of loyalty to an enemy of the United States. He praises Saddam Hussein for "showing the United States how a brave man faces death." He contrasts this with the Americans and Iraqis hiding behind hoods to carry out this execution.

I must have missed something, because I haven't seen any pictures of Americans "hiding behind hoods" or anything else while carrying out the execution of his "brave Saddam," as Mr. ___ suggests. I wonder how Mr. ___ knew that there were Americans involved in this execution of his buddy Saddam, if the participants indeed wore hoods, as he claimed. I also can't understand how Mr. ___ can continue to allow himself to suffer such an indignity as remaining here in the United States, when he could just pack up his bags and join his heroes, Saddam's followers, whom he seems to hold in such high regard.

I truly believe that time will validate the fears of the many American people today who believe that it is the goal of these militant Muslim fanatics to conquer the world in the name of Islam, and that they plan to eliminate any person, any group, or any nation who tries to get in their way. I also think history will one day thank people like President George W. Bush, who saw this movement as it truly was, and who pursued a very unpopular course to stop this global threat before it was too late. There is no doubt that there have been many mistakes made, but I shudder to imagine the fatal mistake of mankind to allow these radicals to achieve their goal of world domination. Maybe someday Mr. ___ will recognize and understand the difference between good and evil.

My Letter
February 10, 2007
Americans in Name Only

What is there about being an American that seems to make some people feel that our way of life is not worth defending? Fortunately, many brave Americans do understand that the future of our nation depends upon those who are willing to take up arms if necessary to fight against the forces that want to see our way of life come to an end. Unfortunately, not all enemies of America are those envious and misguided Muslim radicals that want to kill anyone who believes differently than they do. It seems that we also have several enemies of this country who call America home.

Our enemies can count among their numbers those who try to call themselves Americans but who just can't seem to allow themselves to grasp and enjoy a lifestyle that is like no other this world has ever seen, one in which even the lower economic levels within this country are better-off than the middle and even upper levels in many countries. America's enemies can count on the likes of Jane Fonda, Cindy Sheehan, Susan Sarandon, and Sean Penn to give their best efforts to try to poison the American spirit. They also have the ACLU, who encourages us to replace common sense with "political correctness." They have the glamorous Hollywood "elite," who devote their time to corrupting the moral fiber of what once was a strong, Christian people.

We also have the liberal media, which just can't bring itself to acknowledge any American successes in a war against a proven enemy of freedom and liberty. We have liberal politicians who try to convince us that "capitalism" is a dirty word, but these same politicians have quietly tucked away large personal investment portfolios supported by stocks of the very same corporations that they try to tell us are evil. These liberal politicians hope to promote a socialist state where the government will take care of all of its citizens, but they fail to advise us that this socialist state will require a suffocating tax base to pay for itself. Hugo Chavez and Fidel Castro would fit right in with this group. Many liberal politicians, like Ted Kennedy, Hillary Clinton, Harry Reid, and Nancy Pelosi, have no idea what it is like to hold down a real job, but they will spend their time telling the real working people of this nation that they really know what is best for us.

Granted, our way of life certainly is not perfect, but it is much closer to perfection than the Sodom-and-Gomorrah lifestyle that these liberals and so-called Hollywood elite would have us embrace. This nation was founded by groups of people who basically believed in God, and who wanted, among other things, religious freedoms. How can something so simple be made to look so difficult? If we allow this nation to turn away from God, which is the direction that the supporters of "political correctness" are trying to point us in, this great nation of ours is doomed!

Response from Liberal Writer
February 20, 2007
Defending America

Mr. Hubbard tries to make believe that only Republicans believe in defending America. Of course, it's a twisted argument created only to defend Bush's war in Iraq. It's foolish to suppose that all of the people who fought and died in the Civil War, World War I, World War II, the Korean War, Vietnam, and both Iraq wars were Republican, and a child can see through Mr. Hubbard's thoughts. Neither are all veterans of these wars "pure Republican."

The war in Iraq has always been about one thing: oil. Bush and his friends pushed for the Iraq war because of their intent to remove Saddam Hussein, install a puppet government, install a large body of American military permanently in that country, and turn the management of the oil resources over to Bush's Republican backers, the barons of the United States. Bush pushes to maintain the military presence in Iraq due to his desperate hope to ultimately gain control of its oil resources. Unfortunately, Bush has found he cannot end the sectarian fighting in Iraq, because the major political factions there also want control of the oil. Obviously, Bush doesn't believe Iraqis should own and control Iraqi oil.

Mr. Hubbard only tries to cloud the issue by pretending that the Iraq war is about "defending the American way of life." The Iraq war has absolutely nothing to do with defending America's way of life. Don't be fooled by people preaching that garbage.

My Reply
March 16, 2007
Defending America 2

It is not surprising to see that Mr. ___ has misunderstood and misquoted my thoughts from a previous letter. In his recent letter to the editor titled "Defending America," he said my views were "twisted, foolish, clouding the issues, and preaching garbage." This is how he sees anyone whose views are different from his own.

I did not say, nor do I feel, that only Republicans believe in defending America. Even Mr. ___ can't believe I said that. Veterans who have bravely served our country have been Democrats, Republicans, and even people with no political affiliation at all. I truly believe they did so to defend their country and their own way of life.

My youngest son is at this very minute in his second deployment in Iraq, fighting to defend the right of people like Mr. ___ to speak their mind. He also said that a child can see through my thoughts. I don't know what group of children Mr. ___ has been using as his advisers, but he might want to consider changing his source.

I would prefer that there never were any wars to need defending. However, as long as there are religious fanatics who have vowed to force their religious beliefs upon the entire world and to kill anyone who believes differently than they do, then yes, there is definitely a very real need to defend America's way of life. This is the point he has been missing all along.

I do agree with Mr. ___'s statement that oil is a major reason we are over there. The problem, as Mr. ___ has failed to comprehend, is that these vital oil supplies are essential to every nation on this Earth, and they are in danger of falling under the control of this group of fanatical Islamic murderers. If the rest of the world does not soon wise up to this reality and protect their own interests in this global emergency, then the entire world will suffer at the hands of these enemies of mankind.

My Letter
November 7, 2007
He Proved the Point

Thanks to Mr. ___ for his valuable help in proving a point! In his response to Mr. Ron Miller's recent letter concerning Nancy Pelosi's veiled attempt to buy Armenian votes by condemning Turkey for something that happened almost a century ago, he had a question of his own for Mr. Miller. In challenging him to reveal the facts to back up his statement in which he said, "The Democrats in Congress are absolutely dedicated to a total defeat in Iraq," he asked Mr. Miller, "What possible reason could a Democrat or anyone else have for wishing for a defeat of the U.S. military?"

By asking that question, he unintentionally joined me and many other Americans who have long been asking this very same question about the Democrats' true intentions concerning the outcome of this Iraq war. He claims that Mr. Miller's statement was "silly and unfounded." However, he seems to have conveniently forgotten an earlier statement made supposedly out of earshot by the Democrats' No. 2 person in the House, James E. Clayburn, when he said something to the effect that if this surge is successful, it will mean big trouble for the Dems politically. How about that?

This statement provides all of the facts and proof that Mr. ____ or anyone else should ever need, assuming of course that they are open-minded enough to comprehend what it actually implied. Mr. ____ then went on to complete his question by adding, "Especially since many of them [Dems] have sons or daughters there [Iraq]." This statement sadly suggests exactly what the Democrats' truly sick objective has been all along, which is that nothing is sacred or exempt, their own sons and daughters included, in their fanatical quest to make this Bush administration look bad. Their real motive has become so transparent over time that it is no longer possible even for the Democrats to totally conceal their true political objectives.

It is very sad to admit, but to the true Democrat power broker in Congress, an American military defeat in Iraq is much more acceptable than any perceived military victory that can be attributed to this Republican administration!

Response from Liberal Writer
November 14, 2007
Shameful Politics

I have often pointed out how many Republicans attempt to twist words to justify their fanatical support of the war in Iraq and the corrupt political practices of this administration over the past six years.

Now comes Mr. Hubbard of Jonesboro suggesting I have "proved" his point that Democrats care so little for their sons and daughters that they would trade their lives for political advantage. I made no such statement, implied or real, and Mr. Hubbard should be ashamed.

I would suggest that Mr. Hubbard go ask the mothers and fathers of these dead and crippled Americans, Democrats and Republicans, if they are happy to have their sons and daughters dead in their graves or crippled for life simply to gain control of Iraqi oil resources. Perhaps he will get back to us with his findings of the number of actual Democrats and Republicans who are "happy" to have their sons and daughters dead.

There is no question that Democrats are no more filled with joy at the deaths of their families than the Republicans. It is foolishness of the highest level for Mr. Hubbard to suggest this. I am a veteran, and I have never at any time found any joy in the death of any U.S. military (or anyone else) and would not trade their deaths for any political purpose.

I deeply resent anyone trying to twist words to suggest Democrats or any American family would do this, regardless of politics. It is a shame Mr. Hubbard would rather twist words than tell the truth about Americans.

My Response
December 1, 2007
Confused Again

A recent contributor to letters to the editor is apparently confused over who "twisted" whose words. In his attempt to distort what I said about how Democrats would do almost anything to get back at George Bush, this person has accused me of saying that the parents of our brave American heroes who have made the ultimate sacrifice in Iraq were "happy" (his sick word, not mine) they were dead. The actual wording of my letter, which this person had right in front of him as he deliberately misquoted me, was that "nothing is sacred nor exempt, their own sons and daughters included, in the Democrats' fanatical quest to make the Bush administration look bad." So who really twisted whose words?

This person has also chosen to conveniently ignore indisputable evidence that Rep. James E. Clyburn, the #2 Democrat in the U.S. House of Representatives was overheard and recorded making his statement, "If this surge is successful, it will mean big trouble politically for us Democrats." This confirms the true Democrat intention, which many people have known all along. Ask yourself now what is more important to Democrats: preserving our American way of life, or selling their souls to buy more votes?

I am a Vietnam-era veteran and the proud father of a brave young man who has just returned from his second deployment to Iraq. I do not look forward to this nation's involvement in any war, and I am far from happy with the way George Bush has handled this war in particular. The important thing now is that every American accept the fact that we are involved in this war, and instead of wishing for a total defeat of our own military in Iraq, as the Democrats have so shamelessly chosen to do, we must now all pull together as one nation and do whatever is necessary to ensure a satisfactory outcome to this war. George Bush has finally brought on board a general who understands how to execute this war, and although this has been given little credibility by liberal media and legislators, General Petraeus has implemented a strategy that is finally turning the tide. For this, all Americans should be extremely proud and very grateful. Total victory, and not throwing in the Democrat's surrender towel, is the best and only way to bring our troops home from this war!

THE GREAT LIBERAL DISGUISE

It appears that many people in the South have continued to call themselves "Democrats" more out of habit than out of shared ideals and beliefs. For many years the South had voted solidly "Democrat" because their beliefs were the same as those shared by the Democrat Party of that day. These values and beliefs are those still shared by a majority of the American people today, but over time the goals and principles of the two major political parties in our country seem to have flip-flopped, and it is now the Republicans who share those old time values and beliefs, and not the Democrats.

Beliefs such as abortion for any reason other than to protect the life and health of the mother is wrong, that marriage means the union between one man and one woman, and that we do not have to accept the immoral lifestyle of gays and lesbians as being normal. Our ancestors also believed that the words *God* and *Jesus* referred to our lord, savior, and creator, whose teachings have guided this great nation throughout its history. Today we are told that these very same words have a totally different meaning, and that they now stand for something that is evil, dangerous, and a faith that does not welcome others. This is how liberals and the American Civil Liberties Union now try to define Christianity.

Today's liberal Democrats would have us believe that we must judge our actions according to whether they are *politically correct* rather than *morally correct*, such as removing the word *God* from anywhere it could be found. By its very definition, being a conservative means "one who opposes fast change," not accepting something new simply because it is different from that which we have long believed and practiced, even if it is totally contrary to what we feel to be right or wrong. Being "politically correct" is how liberals justify their reasons for selling out this great country of ours. Being "politically correct" usually proves itself to be acting against good common sense, or even accepting something *immoral* as being correct. All too often it has become the cowardly way to justify doing something they know is wrong.

The good people of this country need to wake up before it is too late!

WHAT'S IN A NAME?

Americans seem to get caught up by the names we choose to call ourselves. Where politics are concerned, does it really matter whether we call ourselves Democrats or Republicans? Is it the name that is important, or is it what that name really stands for? After all, what is in a name? Shouldn't it really be more about supporting a political philosophy that shares one's true values and beliefs rather than supporting a political philosophy simply because it goes by a name that was supported by our ancestors many years ago? After taking a closer look at this question, it appears that many of us have developed an identity crisis. We have become confused as to what political party actually supports the same views that we believe in.

Consider this. Generations of Americans have a history of calling themselves Democrats and voting for candidates who ran as Democrats simply because they were following what their parents and grandparents had done before them. It is the long-held belief of many people that Adolf Hitler could win an election in America if he ran as a Democrat. We are indeed creatures of habit, but do we not owe it to ourselves to know and understand what the candidates we honor with our vote really stands for? For far too long the motto has been, "Vote for anyone, as long as they are a Democrat."

When we examine the findings of several recent polls, we find that the majority of Americans consider themselves more closely aligned with the Christian faith; oppose abortion except in cases of rape, incest, or to protect the life and health of the mother; agree with the definition of marriage as "a union between one man and one woman"; support strong family values; favor the idea of lower taxes and smaller government; feel that our national security is of the utmost importance; hold to the idea that anyone wanting to immigrate to this country must follow our laws and assimilate our language and customs, and not the other way around; and would like to see less instead of more government intrusion into our private lives. If we are honestly looking for the political party who shares this philosophy with us, we just might find that we are more closely aligned with Republicans than we are with Democrats.

Far too many Americans have allowed themselves to be taken in by a group of career politicians who, in exchange for a vote, would give away this country to anyone who feels that this world owes them a living. This group will never agree with nor attempt to support George W. Bush on any issue, regardless of their personal feelings about the issue. How often have Harry Reid, Nancy Pelosi, Ted Kennedy, or Hillary Clinton searched to find fault with anything and everything this president says or does? Regardless of how you feel about him, he is the president of this nation. They have encouraged the erosion of respect for the very office of president itself, simply because the person now holding that office is a member of what they see as the opposition party. When was the last time we heard any of this group say anything positive about this president, or about our country, for that matter? How often have we heard this group acknowledge the fact that there has not been another terrorist attack upon our shores since 9/11? They shamefully promote the belief that if anything bad ever happens to this nation, we surely must deserve it, because we probably did something bad to have caused it. They hold sacred very little that was once valued by our forefathers and ancestors, including religion, family values, or even the premise that anything worth having is worth working for. They place more importance upon their own political gains than they do upon what is truly in the best interest of this nation. A perfect example of this is the financial calamity caused by Barney Frank, Chris Dodd, and their liberal cohorts who forced financial institutions to loan money to people who couldn't, and in many cases had no intention of paying it back, including undocumented illegal aliens.

This doesn't necessarily mean that our ancestors were wrong in their choice of political affiliations, but it just might mean that the political party that shared and supported their values and beliefs once upon a time has changed. When we wonder why the politicians we have elected to office rarely seem to fulfill the promises they made to get elected in the first place, we just might conclude that we voted for the wrong person after all. In the South especially, the name "Republican" once referred to the party of the rich, big business, and big government. But when we examine the aims and goals of today's political parties in more detail, Republicans have evolved into the party that supports the old-time values and beliefs that have long made this nation strong. When we finally realize this fact, we can then begin to restore the pride, honor, respect, and love of country that once overflowed in the hearts of all true Americans.

WHAT LIBERALS DON'T WANT US TO KNOW

The American people are smarter than we are given credit for being. Career politicians think they can keep spouting their unexplained statements, which the general public will continue to blindly accept as fact simply because some politician said they should. Democrats keep repeating their same old song and dance over and over about not agreeing with President Bush's plans for the "surge," but without explaining any specific reasons why they are against it.

Democrats claim that they really care about our troops; however, they knew that President Bush would veto any bill that included their cowardly "surrender date" as a condition, even if it provided the funds so desperately needed by our troops. They would then point all blame toward the president, reminding the American public that he had just vetoed their bill that would have provided funding for our troops. The real truth is that the Democrats are so deathly afraid that any success by this president will hurt their chances to gain the White House in 2008 that they are willing to sacrifice the pride and respect of this nation, and even the lives of our brave troops, just to prove their point.

The "surge" refers to an immediate and hopefully short-term increase in troop strength. The objective of this "surge" is to guarantee the successful completion of the mission objective, which is to allow enough time for the Iraqi government to take over all aspects of the security and military operations. There are several objectives that must be accomplished for this "surge" to be successful, but they will not happen overnight. Some of these objectives are as follows.

1. Overwhelm the insurgents with a number of troops that will be used to decrease and dismantle their previous strongholds, from which they have launched their terrorist attacks and manufactured their car bombs and IEDs. This will put this enemy on the run and disrupt their entire plan of attack. Once these insurgents are forced to move out of their comfortable strongholds, their leadership and chain of command will become dysfunctional, and their will to succeed will be broken. The sooner this process begins, the sooner our mission can be accomplished and our troops can come home.

2. Provide for the inspection of Iraqi neighborhoods, routing and flushing out embedded bands of insurgents to secure these neighborhoods. This will allow the Iraqi police and military personnel to take over all security operations within these neighborhoods. Local leadership endorsed by the Iraqi government can then begin introducing democratic reforms, providing the Iraqi citizens with confidence in the successful implementation of the same democratic process they once risked their lives by voting for. Once they can feel secure in their own neighborhoods, they will begin to resume a somewhat normal lifestyle, which hasn't been possible under the current conditions. The feeling of security will go a long way toward convincing the Iraqi people that a normal lifestyle is indeed possible. This process will then be repeated in other neighborhoods and will gain strength as more and more neighborhoods become secure and the people begin to accept and participate in their own version of democracy.

3. As this process continues to gain strength and momentum, and the Iraqi people finally take control over their own destiny, our troops can then prepare to come home. This increased number of "boots on the ground" will provide the protection and support necessary for the safe and orderly withdrawal of our brave young men and women from this war-torn region.

LIBERALS VS. CHRISTIANITY

Although Christianity and Judaism do not totally share the same beliefs about religion, both faiths were founded upon biblical teachings and philosophies, which teach that the children of Israel are God's chosen people.

With that thought in mind, it would appear that God will bless those who view Israel as a friend, and will look less than favorable upon those who would wish death to his chosen people. The liberal's policy of placing very little importance upon America's continued support for Israel in their efforts to simply exist in the hostile Middle East region, only gives credibility to the assumption that liberals also place very little importance upon biblical history as well. If America abandons Israel, as many liberal politicians have suggested, then America will lose its one friend in that volatile region of the world.

Israel, a small nation surrounded by its enemies who seek its total annihilation, has managed to stand firm against these enemies with little or no assistance outside of that received from the United States of America. If our liberal-controlled government chooses not to support Israel, then we can expect to see some of those very same enemies of Israel bringing their wrath and ideology of hate attacks to our doorstep.

Liberals and their satanic law firm, the ACLU, have made it very clear that they see little value in the Christian faith, its teachings, or its traditions. Understanding that this policy will likely be implemented, the future of the nation of Israel and the Christian faith itself is in for a long and hard battle. We will better understand what we are up against once we realize who the true enemies of America and Christianity really are, and chart our course accordingly. In that great Christmas movie *It's a Wonderful Life*, Uncle Billy explained to Mr. Potter, "Not all of our enemies are in Germany and Japan." Likewise, real Americans have our hands full trying to defeat those same un-American ideals found right here.

If America turns its back upon Christianity and Israel, we can be assured that God will turn his back upon America!

LIBERALS VS. THE PEOPLE

As the history of the liberal wing of the Democrat Party has demonstrated over the years, their most basic method of operation is to identify their enemy, then *attack, attack, attack!* If current trends in the 2008 presidential race continue, we could very well see a Democrat-controlled House, Senate, and (heaven forbid) White House. If this happens, with no opposition majority in the House, Senate, or White House for liberals to target, who then will they turn upon as their enemy?

It doesn't take long for the real answer to reveal itself. First, we must understand that liberals are just not happy unless they are at war with someone or something, and to even justify their own existence they must specifically identify who their enemy is. If there is any group that fits the liberal definition of *their enemy* (which means anyone who can stop or even challenge the liberal, socialist agenda from moving forward), that group *must be eliminated* at all costs! According to how liberals identify their enemy, there is only one group left who fits the definition, and that would be—you guessed it—*the American people* themselves.

Obama feels a need to apologize for me and the rest of the American people for what he perceives to be our crimes against the rest of the world. Obama wants to spread the wealth of this nation, earned through the ambition and ingenuity of the American people, equally among everyone, including those who haven't lifted a finger to earn it. Obama says he supports the Great American Dream of business ownership; that is, as long as the success of that business does not exceed $150,000. At that point, that successful business becomes the *enemy* of the liberals, and the Great American Dream then becomes the Great American nightmare.

Anything that does not conform to the liberal, socialist agenda quickly becomes their target, and attacking their target is what makes life worth living for liberals. With help from their satanic law firm, the ACLU, liberals have targeted prayer at sporting events, the *Ten Commandments*, and the most basic of Christmas holiday displays that have been exhibited on public grounds for decades. Other examples of their anti-American activities include: attacks upon dedicated educators who attempt to maintain control and discipline within our schools or toward those who encourage strong family values, and traditional lifestyles. But, their most damaging and destructive attack of all has been their relentless, malicious, and deliberate attacks upon the very character of this nation, which was built upon strong Christian values and beliefs that were the cornerstone of this nation's success. They have tried to force us to forsake our own beliefs while becoming tolerant of the beliefs of those who chose to immigrate to this great country, but who also want to turn our country into a mirror image of the countries they left behind.

After all of the brilliant speeches and hypnotic hype aimed at the perceived *guilt* of the American people, it has become very clear that the idea of liberal socialism is truly not in the best interest of this nation. Do we honestly want to follow in the footsteps of France and Canada down that fatalistic road to socialism, or do we choose instead to rely upon the genius and guidance of our forefathers, who led this *unique* nation to the unprecedented success that the rest of this world can only dream about?

OBAMA AND THE MOB

After finding out that the Illinois governor Rob Blagojevich attempted to sell Obama's seat in the U.S. Senate to the highest bidder, it is certainly not too far-fetched to suspect that a Chicago political campaign organization might have ties to the underworld. With that thought in mind, might there be a possibility that the Obama political machine and Al Capone's gangster regime in Chicago during the Roaring Twenties have anything in common? Is it too much of a stretch for anyone to suspect that Obama's close ties to criminals such as Tony Rezko and William Ayers is not too unlike that of Capone and his group of thugs who pulled off the St. Valentines Day massacre in Chicago in 1929. Now we see where a group of Obama supporters, operating as lawyers and sheriffs in Missouri, may have taken a page straight out of Al Capone's underworld playbook when they threatened to arrest anyone who spoke out against their beloved and manufactured candidate? It is very easy to recognize this exactly for what it is; a scare tactic intended to intimidate and frighten off anyone who might consider bringing out questions about Obama's background and character.

There is no doubt that such an order would have come straight from the smoky back rooms of the clandestine wing of the Obama political organization. This is the very same group who has flooded the liberal main stream media with anything negative they could dream up about Sarah Palin or John McCain, whether unfounded or not, and which, of course, would have been immediately denied and even repudiated by their majestic leader, Barack Huessain Obama. Even though this order was withdrawn a short time after being made public, it very likely achieved its desired results to a great extent. They even attempt to give legitimacy to Obama's candidacy by rolling out a choir of young children to sing his praises, children far too young to have established any true political values of their own. They seem to have touched all bases in trying to present Obama as a true man of the people; except for the fact that after almost two years of campaigning for president, we still know very little about this man.

Is this the kind of administration we want occupying our White House; one whose possible resemblance to the Chicago Mob of the 1920s is utterly terrifying? The Obama storm troopers will no doubt attack this suggestion as being wild, crazy, racist, or even unpatriotic. Yet, their own failure to respond to even basic questions about their stealth candidate greatly serves to give credibility to such theories. What do they have to hide? A simple come-clean approach might dispel many fears and mysteries about Obama. The still unanswered question of Obama's Constitutional qualifications to hold the office of president could have been settled long ago if his organization would have simply produced a valid and legitimate birth certificate that would show his record and place of birth. Accusations suggesting that he was born in Kenya, or that he gave up his American citizenship when he was adopted and/or declared by his Indonesian stepfather in order to become enrolled in an Indonesian school, are valid questions that American citizens have a moral and legal right to know. This is a direct slap in the face to the American citizens who want to make sure that their president is constitutionally qualified to hold this high office. To ignore their request to have these questions answered, especially when the truth should be so easy to verify, is an outrage!

Instead of attacking anyone with suspicions about their unknown candidate, why doesn't the Obama political organization try being open and honest for a change, and put these fears to rest by finally telling us the truth? Or, could it just be that the truth would indeed prove these theories to be valid after all?

Obama's National Security Force

The idea of a large civilian militia composed primarily of unemployed Obama supporters with some degree of policing authority is not a very comforting feeling for a majority of Americans. If it is their role to patrol their own neighborhoods to discourage gang violence, then that is one thing. But, early images of who might actually be filling these roles might even suggest that many of them could also be the very ones being sought as criminals. For those who watched Adolf Hitler's growing military machine in Germany expand to include many aspects of what was once routine life, Barack Obama's idea of creating a civilian National Security Force evoked memories that were down right terrifying. Obama said we can no longer rely on our military in order to achieve the national security goals *he* has set. He further described plans for forming a civilian security force that would be just as powerful, just as strong, and just as well funded as our military.

The idea of seeing military groups such as *Hitler's Children*, the *Brown Shirts*, and even the *Gestapo*, which became the much dreaded and feared secret police, takes one's thoughts back to the days of Nazi Germany. Might this also be one of those *changes* Obama has in store for the American people? Get ready, America!

Our Last Christmas

I truly hope that I am wrong in my feelings about this matter, but I fear that Christmas 2008 just might be the final Christmas where the true meaning of the season can be celebrated, both openly and legally. The results of the 2008 presidential election, the circumstances surrounding our nation's economy, and the current political climate in this country suggest that the powerful principles and traditions that once made America strong just may be allowed to become only a faded memory. Our incoming president has already proclaimed during his election campaign that America was no longer to be considered a *Christian nation*. His true intentions in making this statement were not clear, but the fear of what he actually meant has increasingly grown due to many unanswered questions about his hidden past. The constant and deliberate attacks by the ACLU and by liberals in Congress, who have lost their courage and their will to stand up for what is right, have weakened America in a way that just a few years ago would have seemed totally impossible.

It didn't happen overnight. No, this change has been in the making over the past several decades. Commercialism played a big role in transforming the Christmas season, but the naiveness of the American people also played a role in allowing this to happen. We have placed the future of this country into the hands of various groups of people who have never been able to understand or appreciate the real reasons for the success and prosperity of this nation. For example, the true meaning and intent of the First Amendment to the Constitution regarding the separation of church and state has been transformed to mean anything and everything the anti-American liberals and the *ACLU* wanted it to mean. Our framers and founding fathers intended that there be no religion sponsored or endorsed by our government, such as was the case in England where the *Anglican Church* was the *Church of England*. But, the true meaning of this amendment has been revised to allow for the outlawing of almost anything that mentioned *God, Jesus*, or the Christian faith to be displayed in public. Although the traditions and presence of Christianity have been encouraged to disappear, at the same time the customs and traditions of the Islamic religion have been given free reign to incorporate itself into our schools and public facilities, and at some point very likely into our future laws, as we saw happen in Europe.

The governor of the state of Washington turned her head as an atheist group was allowed to display their poster attacking Christianity itself right next to the *Nativity* scene in the rotunda of the state capitol. This governor saw no need to either condemn or question the actions of this satanic group that went against specific regulations for such displays.

If we enjoyed and even looked forward to the Christmas season as a child, we did so perhaps because of the gifts we might receive, but also for that very special feeling that was a big part of the Christmas season. If these politically correct troopers are allowed to advance their liberal agenda, then the Christmas season of 2008 could very well be the last time we can experience that very special feeling again. And, may I say, for what might be the final time, *Merry Christmas.*

THE THREE AMERICAS

We have heard liberal Democrat John Edwards try to make sure that this country remains divided by suggesting that there are two Americas: one for the rich or wealthy (to which he obviously belongs), and one populated by the poor, mistreated, and downtrodden. There is no doubt that this country, like any other country, does indeed contain more than one group, separated by the various degrees of comparison that are found in any country. But, I will go one step further than John Edwards and suggest that America contains not two, but three distinct groups of people, and characterized differently than our liberal politicians would have us believe. These groups of Americans are indeed three separate and very distinct groups of people, but all of them refer to themselves as Americans.

The first group is made up of those Americans who create and build the wealth of this country through ambition, imagination, creativity, and perseverance. Many of these people have been denied success many times before their dreams were finally realized, but through hard work and a never-say-die attitude, they eventually develop something that is necessary to mankind. People in this group eventually become the developers of commerce, the creators of industry, and the movers and shakers within our unique economic system known as capitalism. But, they are viewed simply as *big business* by those who are less fortunate.

The second group is made up of those Americans who work for the wealth builders, and provide the manpower to create and build the wealth of this nation through their hard work. This group is the very backbone of this nation, and without them and their work ethic, this nation would never have gotten off the ground. The majority within this group eventually realize that it is highly unlikely that they will ever become wealthy themselves, but through their love of country and their appreciation of the results of hard work, this nation has become the most unique collection of people to ever populate this Earth. They are what America is really all about! Included within this group are those who understand and cherish the traditions that have made this nation strong, those who fight and die in our wars, and those who do not want to see this country turned into something our founding fathers would not be very proud of.

The third group of Americans neither create the wealth nor work for those who create the wealth, but they have become convinced that they are nevertheless just as entitled to an equal share of this wealth as those in either of the other two groups, simply because they were lucky enough to have been born here or to have immigrated to this country from somewhere else. This is the group that will depend upon government to provide for their everyday existence and who makes up the voting bloc sought by those in government who have lost sight of what it means to be true Americans. Ambition, initiative, and the strong desire to succeed are traits that are rarely found within this group. Occasionally, some within this group will find that they are not happy being dependent upon someone else for their survival, and they learn how to move themselves into the second group, and on a very rare occasion, a few even elevate themselves into the first group. Once they realize the beauty and uniqueness of America, they are no longer satisfied or content with just an existence, and they take advantage of the opportunities found nowhere else in this world but in America.

Those who think America should take care of everyone's every need obviously give little or no thought to who is going to pay for all of this. Entitlements do not come cheap, and if liberals want to kill all the ambition and incentive of those who have funded all of the growth and prosperity this nation has enjoyed since 1776, then they better take a quick "reality check" to see where this money is going to come from. Liberals do not see themselves as the ones who will be paying the taxes necessary to fund and support these entitlement programs for their utopian world, but then, liberals have rarely allowed their thoughts to drift very far into the direction of the real world anyway.

Yes, this nation is indeed made up of multiple groups; economic, ethnic, and otherwise, and with each clinging to its own set of values, rules, and guidelines. The first two groups have known and understood their roles within civilization almost since the beginning of time. However, the third group, the one that liberals like to describe as the *perpetual victims*, could not possibly survive without the first two. .

THE LIBERAL MAINSTREAM MEDIA

Americans have looked to the various forms of our media—newspapers, radio, TV, and now the Internet—to deliver the news and to keep us informed. In the early days of this nation, the media could be counted on to provide the news with a large degree of truth and honesty. But, as has become the case with many things in modern times, truth and honesty have lost out to the almighty dollar, and where the mainstream media is concerned, also to the liberal, socialist agenda of those who would see this nation turned into a carbon copy of a socialist Europe.

Following the old saying "The squeaky wheel gets the grease," the past several decades have seen America become increasingly bombarded with the socialist demands of the squeaky wheel of liberalism. In keeping to the idea that the strange, the odd, the crazy, the weird, and the unreasonable is what sells news, the American mainstream media has transformed itself into the loyal guardian of liberal socialist ideals. In doing so, they have chosen to forsake the long-held values and traditions that made this country great, all in the interest of selling stories and promoting socialism, and not necessarily in that order. Today, the mainstream media will promote liberal socialism every time at the expense of family values and Christian principles and will try to bury anything that attempts to get between them and their cause.

Like many Americans, I had become increasingly disappointed with the mainstream media, but I mistakenly thought that they would present the truth if only it were revealed to them; that is, until I submitted a letter to the editor of my local newspaper, and saw how they distorted it to fit their agenda. The purpose of my letter was to question why so many people would vote for any Democrat candidate on the ballot, regardless of his or her qualifications or stand on the issues, simply because that was the way their parents and grandparents had voted before them. My letter was direct and straight to the point, beginning with my title, "What's in a Name?"

I checked the "letters to the editor" section in the newspaper each day, hoping to find that my letter had been printed. When my letter, or what had started out as my letter, appeared in the paper on the Sunday just before the 2004 general election held on the following Tuesday, I almost missed it until I started to read the letters in that section and saw one that vaguely resembled mine. The first thing that caught my eye was the title, which definitely was not the title I had given to it. The editor of that newspaper had taken it upon himself to change the title from the fitting and descriptive one I had given it to "Democrats Don't Deserve Support." I found out that not only had he changed my title, but he also had left out much of the content of my letter, the combination of which totally changed its meaning and intent. The one thing he did not change, much to my dismay, was that my name still appeared as the author of this letter. This was very misleading, because after he made his changes, this was no longer my letter.

After I calmed down, I rationalized that this must have been just an unfortunate example of a typographical error. The next morning I called the editor to inform him that the letter I submitted had been printed with several errors, and that I would appreciate it very much if he would check the original letter I sent to him and reprint it as it was submitted. He arrogantly informed me that it was his prerogative to edit or make any changes he so desired to any letter submitted to *his* newspaper, and that the changes he made to my letter had been done to better express *my* intent. His attitude left me with the feeling that the term *freedom of speech* pertained to his rights as a journalist, and had nothing what-so-ever to do with mine. There would be no retraction, no correction, and nothing that even resembled an apology. This included, but was not limited to, the title and content of any letter to be printed in *his* newspaper. I told him that when he arbitrarily made *his* changes to *my* letter without *my* permission, this letter was no longer *my* letter, and I did not want it printed showing *me* as its author. He said that all letters printed would be done so with the name of the person submitting the letter, and that my only choice was "to send or not to send" a letter. At that point I was convinced that there would be no more of *my* letters submitted to this editor.

I had been a regular reader of the *letters to the editor* section for some time, and I now started to wonder how many other letters this liberal editor had altered to fit *his* own agenda. I had noticed a couple of occasional contributors to this column who seemed to have views somewhat similar to my own, and I called them to see if anything like this had ever happened to them. To my amazement, they shared similar experiences they had with this editor, and each had also complained to him, but without success. They said that they were upset at first, but became determined not to allow this liberal editor to keep them from expressing their views. They said it appeared that the more letters they submitted, the fewer alterations he made. It was almost like the more acquainted he became with their views, the more leeway he would allow them. After a few months, I decided to try again. To my great surprise, this time my letter was printed exactly as I had submitted it. During the next several months, I became a semi-regular contributor to the "letters to the editor" section, even to the point where I would receive phone calls from readers thanking me for letters I had submitted, and even encouraging me to submit more letters.

Thanks to this liberal editor, I had been taught a lesson in real-world politics, and I finally began to realize and understand the significance of the term "liberal media." From that point, the phrase *power of the press* took on an entirely different meaning for me. What I had once thought was an honorable profession had proven itself to be a phony and manipulative weapon of the liberal socialist movement to convert the United States of America into a socialist state. After my first personal experience with the "liberal media," I was determined to find out to just what lengths these people would go to distort the truth and to do whatever it took to transform the views and opinions of their readers into what they determined it should be. They conveniently position themselves within the protective blanket of the U.S. Constitution, and they use this wonderful document in an attempt to brainwash the public. This tactic is shared by each segment of the media, including TV and radio, and apparently has been in operation for a much longer time than I was aware.

Fortunately, thanks to the efforts of Rush Limbaugh, Sean Hannity, Glen Beck, and others, these sleazy tactics of the anti-American mainstream media have been exposed to a large segment of the general public. As certain real events were found to have been totally ignored by the mainstream media in an effort to hide the truth from the American people, it became apparent what their true intentions and objectives were, and the battle to save America from liberal socialism, was on! The weapon of choice to use against this enemy of the true American spirit is very simple, and its components are the same ones used by that great American comic book hero Superman: *truth, justice, and the American way.*

Those who are part of the liberal media try to reinforce a false sense of guilt in the white community, and they have made a concerted effort to assign labels to the enemies of their movement and place them into specific target groups. They promote the necessity of big government—one that relies upon large numbers of people who are comfortable with the label of *victim* and are content to be totally dependent upon government for their existence. To reinforce the need of these people to remain dependent upon government for their total existence, any possibility that they might become ambitious and successful, thereby overcoming their dependence upon government must be eliminated. The specific targets of the liberal movement are: white males, the Christian faith, education, big business, and anything that closely resembles initiative or ambition. Also to be thrown under the bus are; family values and those long-held principles that were encouraged by our founding fathers, which are recognized by liberals as the real enemies of everything they stand for.

The Christian faith itself provides an inner strength for mankind that is virtually impossible to acquire without it. Once we understand exactly what these liberals are proposing, the picture starts to become much clearer. As with any group that promotes liberal socialism, these old values are indeed major obstacles to achieving their goals of mind control and maintaining the ignorance that imprisons their followers. When the qualities that these liberals fear most are truly examined, the pieces of their socialist puzzle finally begin to fall into place.

As was true in the days of slavery, education is the one and only thing that combats ignorance. Ignorance does not necessarily mean stupidity, but it means an absence of the factual truth. Education teaches one how to acquire and understand knowledge, and knowledge combats ignorance. The success of big business is imperative to the economic success of any nation, as it provides the jobs that feed the growth of a nation. Initiative and ambition are similar, but they work hand in hand to achieve one's individual success, and those individual successes in turn translate into the success of this nation.

Strong family values are the foundation of any successful nation, and the erosion of these values has become a major factor in the decline of the United States of America. This nation has long been the emotional powerhouse of the world, and without the United States leading the way, this planet will become a pitiful and empty shell. Those principles and values that our founding fathers saw as vital to the success and survival of this nation must never be compromised. If these values are allowed to evaporate, and liberals are obsessed with the goal of making this happen, we will witness an even further deterioration of the morals, values, and traditions this nation was founded upon.

Polls have shown that a majority of Americans believe in God, family, and country, and pretty much in that order. We take exception when the liberal media endorses the theory that everyone must learn to accept the gay lifestyle and same-sex marriage, and that we must turn our heads to illegal immigration. But, what really gets our goat is when we see organizations like the ACLU remove the Ten Commandments from public places, attack Christmas programs in public schools, and fight for the right of Muslim immigrants to have a footbath built in airports funded by taxpayers' money. We can put up with a lot of things, but when organizations that have proven themselves to be un-American and unpatriotic cesspools do everything within their power to destroy the things we hold dear, we can no longer sit idly by and do nothing.

How could *we*, the patriotic citizens of this great country, have allowed this liberal media to become so bold and callous when presenting its version of the news according to its own biased agenda? It represents the evil, the lazy, and the discontented as the pride of our country, while ignoring those who put their lives on the line to protect the rights that allow the liberal media to distort the truth. They label anyone who tries to preserve our long-held traditions and values as fanatics, while portraying those who cling to abnormal and unacceptable lifestyles as unfortunate mistreated victims. They portray patriotic Americans as having joined the military only because they cannot qualify for anything else, while encouraging an invasion of illegal immigrants to take advantage of liberal, socialist entitlement programs.

GUTLESS LEADERSHIP

One by one, the gutless leadership of the Democrats in Congress backed off when asked to denounce the slanderous and idiotic article about General David Petraeus printed in the *New York Times* and paid for by Moveon .org, the treasonous and despicable slime Web site funded by George Soros. In their attempt to steal for themselves some measure of credibility, these unpatriotic cowards now collectively hide themselves behind the banner of a once-proud political party that refers to itself as the Democrat Party. Democrats of times past would not have dreamed of allowing their own personal political ambitions to jeopardize this nation's national security, as have the candidates offered up by this Democrat Party today in their quest for the office of president of the United States of America.

But this group of self-centered leadership pretenders could not hide their true colors when they quietly supported and defended this disgraceful attack upon General Petraeus, a real leader whom this group unanimously approved to lead our military operations in Iraq just a few months earlier. I can only hope that enough followers of this group, intent upon weakening and giving away this once-great and once-proud nation to anyone and everyone who feels that he is owed something for nothing, will wake up and see these pretenders for what they truly are.

DISGRACEFUL HOLLYWOOD VALUES

Many of us who were around in the late 1940s and early 1950s can still remember when we saw our first TV program. We had just two or three channels then, and at first, programming would not start until around 2:00 in the afternoon, but it would then run its schedule to include the 10:00 news and maybe a late-night movie. Programming included movies, comedies, sports, and news, all suitable for family viewing and enjoyment. We learned several things from TV, most of them good, such as how other parts of the world and our own wonderful country lived, places most of us would likely have never seen had it not been for TV.

Commercials told us of the many products available to us, what they did, and where we could find them. They showed us what the new-model cars looked like and how they performed, and we could almost see ourselves sitting behind the wheel. Newscasts told us what was going on in our local communities, our state, our nation, and in the rest of the world. They told us of medical advances, new businesses moving into the area, and the weather conditions we had in store.

Television itself isn't bad today, but those who make the decisions about what the public wants and needs to watch have definitely had a very strong impact upon the moral decay of this country. Commercials once consisted of informing us of what cereals tasted best, or what washing detergents out cleaned the others. We still see the same type of products advertised today as in commercials of years past, but now commercial airtime is also devoted to the different brands of male-enhancement products, or ladies trying on an array of the different bras available, or credit-card offers that will allow us to buy almost everything our hearts desire and with no apparent consequences should their use cause us to fall deeper and deeper into debt.

Movies that were primarily family-oriented comedies, musicals, mysteries, or dramas have been replaced by movies featuring weak and empty plots, extreme violence, vulgar language, and bloody gore, not to mention unbridled sex scenes that leave absolutely nothing to the imagination. Modern sitcoms expose adults and children alike to lifestyles and situations that previously were locked behind closed doors.

It is sometimes hard now to imagine that we were once satisfied with having only three channels, considering that today we have hundreds of channels available to us on satellite or cable. Back then, on any given weekend, and depending upon where we lived and which season we were in, we could choose between a couple of football, baseball, or basketball games to watch during the weekend, and a movie was usually available on a couple of nights. I can still remember watching the first-run showings of *I Love Lucy, Bonanza, Gunsmoke, Perry Mason, Andy Griffith, The Beverly Hillbillies*, and what I consider to be some of the very best comedy ever seen on television, *Amos and Andy*, a program outlawed after pressure and protests by the *NAACP*. Today our choice includes watching programs featuring gay couples, infidelity, and foul language, and shows where kids and parents alike have no respect at all for authority of any kind.

ROLE MODELS

We do not need to look very far to understand how the morals of our country seem to have gone down the drain. Look at the sorry excuse for role models that today's young people have to choose from. Take sports, for example. Instead of positive role models such as Joe DiMaggio, Bart Star, Bill Russell, Willie Mays, Yogi Berra, and Hank Aaron, today's young people try to pattern themselves after the likes of Barry Bonds, Jose Conseco, Allen Iverson, and Terrell Owens. Many sports heroes of past generations played their sport for the love of the game and would actually earn their reasonable salaries, which in many cases were considered to be upper middle class or just slightly above. Except for those few in the top income echelon, many professional players would take off-season jobs in retail stores or other businesses to supplement their incomes. Many of today's spoiled athletes play only when they feel like it, place very little value upon the integrity of their sport, collect their obscene millions for average or below-average performances, and then hunt down their personal drug dealers to supply their "social" needs. What some of today's generation will try to pass off as our jealousy toward these prima donnas is in reality our disappointment with their distorted and warped value system.

Is there anyone who can honestly mention the names of today's generation of so-called entertainers such as Sean Penn, Brittany Spears, Paris Hilton, Snoop Dog, and Tom Cruise in the same breath with real stars such as Jimmy Stewart, Cary Grant, Irene Dunn, John Wayne, Gary Cooper, Claudette Colbert, and Myrna Loy? Once, talented performers and real-life believable story lines were all that were needed to fill seats in movie theaters. Today the emphasis is upon blood and gore, unbridled profanity, and displaying as much nudity as possible without being arrested, which no longer seems to be a threat. Is it any wonder why today's young people have a problem trying to distinguish between reality and the immoral world of Hollywood? Granted, Hollywood of times past would often drop subtle hints to suggest that things were happening behind the scenes, but this would only add to the mystique of the story line. Today, however, Hollywood blatantly and unashamedly leaves absolutely nothing to one's imagination.

We could once actually look up to athletes and movie stars, because they actually led by example. Today we see those in the entertainment community collecting (not earning) their obscene paychecks, flaunting their immoral lifestyles, and thinking that their obnoxious behavior entitles them to be our political and moral spokespersons. If we allow these trends to continue, just what can we expect from our future generations?

Lucky Democrats

A wonderful vision appeared to me recently concerning the events leading up to and during General Petraeus's report to the congressional committee about progress of the surge in Iraq. Many, if not all, Americans are aware that this brave American hero was unmercifully attacked, first by Moveon .org (the slimy ultraliberal website funded by its un-American benefactor George Soros), then by the various Democrat members of the committee who repeatedly questioned this general's integrity before he had even uttered a response, and again during the presentation of his requested report.

The idea that made its way into my thoughts was how those leadership pretenders should thank their lucky stars that they had pulled their childish antics on a gentleman such as General David Petraeus, and not on a "blood and guts" general such as George S. Patton. I can just picture General Patton listening in disbelief as this stupid bunch tried to act important. When he had taken all of the foolishness he intended to take from these clowns, he would arise from his chair, tuck his helmet securely under his arm, pick up his papers, and walk around his table and across the room to where these morons were sitting, confident that they were safely out of his reach. He would then walk up and down directly in front of their table, shaking his head in disgust as he sauntered by each one. Then, picking out the leader of this group, he would position himself squarely in front of this person, put his fisted hands on his hips, bring his nose to within two inches of the nose of the person directly across the table from him, and then proceed to tell them in no uncertain terms, "Just who in the hell do you clowns think you are talking to?" I can just see this bunch trembling violently in stunned disbelief. Patton would then slowly move his gaze from side to side until he had made piercing visual contact with each and every one of these clowns. He would then turn around and stalk out of this den of thieves, with his every footstep echoing throughout those hallowed halls like a cannon shot, until he had disappeared from sight.

Oh, for a chance to have witnessed such a grand spectacle. General Patton would have given this bunch the level of disrespect they so rightly deserved. If this event had actually happened, General Patton would have most assuredly been charged with *contempt of Congress;* a charge General Patton would be in total agreement with, since he obviously held such strong contempt for this cowardly bunch.

THE GREAT AMERICAN GARAGE SALE

The liberal plan of rewarding the total lack of responsibility and accountability has just taken another giant leap forward, and the selling out of America is now well under way! It has long been known that unaccountability was the watchword endorsed by liberal Democrats in Congress, but it now appears that they have been joined by a group of turncoat Republicans who have abandoned their conservative principles after drinking from the same liberal poisoned watering hole.

Living by their true liberal guidelines that say certain groups can never be responsible or accountable for their own actions, liberals pushed to make mortgage loans available to those who, due to questionable credit histories did not qualify for loans through the conventional markets. This liberal Congress has just now passed legislation to bail out many borrowers to whom credit shouldn't have been extended in the first place, along with risk-taking lenders and speculators who participated in this subprime mortgage loan market. Forgiveness is a wonderful Christian principle, but forgiveness of irresponsibility is both dangerous and contagious. Many of these loans were made to "house flippers," who bought properties to remodel for resale, with little or no investment in these properties. Many of these lenders and speculators took advantage of these risky loans, reasoning that a liberal Congress would likely bail them out if the loans did go bad. After seeing this plan backfire, this liberal Congress now plans to replace one mistake with an even more disastrous mistake by bailing out those who participated in these risky mortgage loans. Perhaps the most bizarre move of this liberal Congress came when they appointed Barney Frank and Chris Dodd, two of the primary instigators of this blatant act of legislative irresponsibility, as members of the committee to investigate why these same financial institutions they strong-armed into making these ridiculous loans did so. This bailout legislation is a slap in the face to anyone who has purchased property and fulfilled the conditions of his or her mortgage, and also to those who previously could not fulfill the conditions of their mortgages and lost their property as a result. How long are we going to continue rewarding stupidity and incompetence and expect different results?

Liberals encourage the lack of ambition and business savvy by rewarding that same behavior over and over again. By observing the continuation of these horrible policies, is there any wonder that certain groups are satisfied with little or no success? As long as there are enough people who are willing to exchange their votes for a lifetime of government subsistence, why then would liberals ever try to encourage those people to take control of their destiny?

FOR SALE: OFFICE OF PRESIDENT OF THE UNITED STATES OF AMERICA

(After watching how the 2008 presidential election was conducted, the following represents what Democrats might have considered doing when they selected their candidate to run for president. As witnessed by the way they have treated George W. Bush and other Republican presidents in the past, and by their

own choice in the 2008 election, is it any wonder that liberal Democrats hold the office of president of the United States of America in such low regard?)

Successful candidate can obtain position either through purchase or by qualifications.

Duties: Leader of the free world, protector of our national security, commander-in-chief of our military

Location: Washington DC

Purchase Price: $500,000,000 (provided through contributions in return for promises)

Salary: $400,000 plus expenses

Job Benefits: Residence furnished, company jet, company car with driver, personal security guards, company-paid health care and pension

General Qualifications: Must have the ability to study polling information, prepare political responses that promise to do exactly what public wants, and then conduct official duties after elected in a manner that will deliver exactly the opposite of what was promised; previous experience as a carnival barker, used-car salesman, junk-bond salesman, or community organizer a definite plus

Specific Qualifications: If position is purchased, no executive, leadership, or military experience is required, and on-the-job-training will be provided; associations with known terrorists, convicted felons, and racist, bigoted ministers will be ignored; spouse's hatred for this nation will be condoned; political contributions from terrorist groups will be welcomed. Political party affiliation with unscrupulous members of Congress preferred. You must have the ability to be evasive when asked specific questions about your background; ability to conceal pertinent medical, educational, birth, and citizenship records if believed to be questionable or nullifying; courage to ignore orders of federal judge to produce said birth and citizenship records without fear of penalties; ability to avoid questions dealing with suspected fanatical religious connections; and ability to raise political contributions by delivering promises that are contradictory to intended performances

All qualified and unqualified applicants should apply in person to Underworld Employment Agency, Chicago, Ill., Attn: Midnight Collections Mgr.

Stealing America

Many of us will wake up one day and realize that we have bought a pig in a poke, or that we have been sold a "bill of goods." Real Americans, who once risked their own lives to establish a nation unlike any other this world has ever seen, are slowly but surely being replaced by a group of phony Americans who are more intent upon giving this country away than they are in doing whatever is necessary to help it grow stronger and become more self-sufficient. To even consider supporting a candidate who proposes taking the wealth of this nation and distributing it among all the people suggests that we have become so blind or so gullible that we will believe anything, regardless of how unrealistic it is.

The best way to ensure that this nation not only survives but prospers is to allow those who actually understand how to develop the resources of this nation, to prosper themselves. This will allow every segment of our society to have an opportunity to grow, even those who hold no interest in actually becoming successful. There is nothing wrong with being a member of the working class, and even to suggest such an idea is an insult to the intelligence of the American people. After all, the working class describes the majority of the American people, and a role in which we are most comfortable.

To explain the goals of these phony Americans in common, yet everyday language, we might say that they are a classic example of those who would have us believe that we can strengthen the weak by weakening the strong, which just happens to be a basic premise and the primary goal of a socialist society. Socialism is an economic system that punishes initiative and ambition while at the same time rewarding the absence of those very same virtues within its people. In reality, the leaders of this movement are not so stupid as to believe this wild assumption themselves, but they see this as the best way to steal enough of the votes of those who do buy into this farce, which will help them regain the dominant place in government, which they feel is rightfully theirs, and return them to the seat of power which they so vainly covet.

More "Political Correctness"

Here we go again. Male students at Harvard University will now be forced to relinquish some of their scheduled gym time, which they paid for as part of their expensive tuition, to a group of Muslim female students who feel that their modesty is being compromised by sharing gym time with males. Bit by bit, and piece by piece, we are losing control of *our* very own country. These Muslim women came to *our* country, so it is *their* responsibility to adapt to *our* way of life, not the other way around. If they truly feel that they cannot accept the way Harvard University has been scheduling gym time for decades, they should have their own mosque finance the building of their own gym, and then they can set their own rules.

I, for one, am getting fed up with seeing my tax money used to build things like footbaths in airports for people to use as part of their religious practices, while at the same time seeing my *Ten Commandments* removed from those very same airports because they might offend those same foot bathers. Something is very wrong with this picture. Our ancestors did not sacrifice, fight, and die to build this nation just to have it given away a couple of hundred years later by groups of "politically correct" liberals who are afraid of offending someone.

Enough is enough! We have become so brainwashed with buying into this "political correctness" hogwash that we are willing to give away this entire nation to anyone who we fear we might have offended. Just in case the people of the United States may have forgotten, this is *our* country. If *you* come to *our* country, it is *your* responsibility to conform to *our* way of life, not the other way around! *You* abide by *our* laws and traditions. *You* learn and speak *our* language. Don't try to make *me* speak yours!

The traditions of this nation are barely hanging on by their fingernails, and would have surely have been lost except for the few who still realize that we have something here worth fighting for! During the past few decades, we have become aware that we are quickly losing, by death and old age, those real American heroes who did not hesitate when the call came to defend their country. Unfortunately, those real American heroes are being replaced by un-patriotic freeloaders whose motto is "Take everything you can, but give nothing back in return." Wake up, America!

WHAT IS WRONG WITH DEMOCRACY?

Today we have many people asking what is wrong with this idea we call democracy. They feel that since they have not become successful in America, then there must be something wrong with America, but not with them personally.

During the tumultuous era that gave us the *Declaration of Independence*, the *Articles of Confederation*, and finally the uniquely magnificent *U.S. Constitution*, good friends and even brothers have been separated by their feelings about how these things were created. Now, over two hundred years later, we have been living under the laws and guidelines of this same wonderful document, but there are at least as many arguments today challenging what it means to live under democracy as there were over two hundred years ago.

If our founding fathers could come back today and tell us what was guiding their thoughts while drawing up this document, I think they would tell us that although this document was not perfect, it was and still is the closest thing to perfection that has ever been devised by mankind.

Democracy does not promise that every man, woman, and child will become wealthy simply by living here. What it does promise is that every man, woman, and child will have the opportunity to do the things that are necessary to become wealthy. If they are not willing to do so, then they have no one to blame but themselves. We are not guaranteed that our attempts will lead to riches, but we are promised that if we have a burning desire and pursue our dream with a never-say-die attitude, the chances for achieving riches are much greater than if we just sit back waiting for a handout.

Our constitution allows us to apply this same logic to everyday life: if we want something badly enough to work for it, then we have an opportunity to achieve it. Democracy in this country offers people an opportunity to work toward success, but it does not guarantee success itself. Success in this country is available to those willing and motivated to work hard and study how success is achieved, but those who are inclined to let government take care of them can be equally as confident that riches will not likely come their way. This does not mean that those without ambition and desire do not deserve to be successful, but the chances for success are greatly multiplied for those willing and able to pursue success.

In any society or economic system, there will be those who have achieved success, but there will also be those who are not successful, and their existence is always going to be affected and controlled somewhat by those who are successful. This is simply a fact of life, and all of the entitlement programs in the world will never change that.

What is wrong with democracy? Nothing, absolutely nothing! The real problem is that too many people do not understand the difference between the availability of an opportunity, and taking advantage of that available opportunity. If they do not truly understand the difference between the two, then they will continue to ask, "What is wrong with Democracy?"

WHAT AMERICANS CANNOT ALLOW TO HAPPEN

In recent years, real Americans have watched as several of the leadership pretenders in our government have set out to transform us from being a nation where hardworking and God-fearing people depend upon their own resources to supply their needs, into one where it is the role of government to supply those needs, as in a socialist state. We have seen anti-American groups like the ACLU fight to eliminate many of the values and traditions we have long held dear, while seeking rights for illegal immigrants, pushing for acceptance of the gay lifestyle and same-sex marriage, and taxpayer funding for religious traditions of Muslim immigrants, while at the same time moving to destroy and eliminate our own religious traditions and beliefs.

We have seen attempts by liberal legislators, and also by some who campaigned under the conservative banner, to endorse the passage of programs that would reward failure, nonconformity, and a lack of ambition by providing those people with government entitlements that would carry them from the cradle to the grave. We see liberal justices try to transform our constitution to fit their liberal agenda, while ignoring their own constitutional duty to judge laws according to that same constitution.

We have allowed real Americans to be ridiculed for defending our nation, for honoring their own true Christian values, for supporting family values, and for acknowledging the importance of a good education. Several real Americans, after watching liberal groups of American pretenders attempt to steer America in the same socialist direction of surrender as adopted by our European neighbors, have even lost some of their own enthusiasm to fight for what is good and right about this country. We seem to have lost our will to fight to preserve and protect our true American history, and the American way of life.

It is sad to acknowledge that the last war this nation can point to with overwhelming pride is World War II. Something strange happened to this nation after our great victory over the Japanese and the German war machines in World War II. We seem to have lost much of our patriotism, and the young people of today seem to feel little or no responsibility to defend this country against those who are jealous of our freedom and democracy. Doing away with the military draft was one of the most dangerous things to happen in this country. The draft provided manpower for our military, but it also taught discipline, responsibility, and direction to our young people. Many of our young people today show little or no appreciation for our history, the true history of this nation, and would likely turn their back on our way of life if called upon to defend it.

We have allowed "political correctness" to replace common sense and responsibility, and this has caused an evaporation of patriotism. We have allowed our own Christian beliefs to be discounted and the traditions and beliefs of immigrant religions to become more acceptable than our own.

THE RAPE OF AMERICA

We are justifiably appalled when we read or hear about the brutal rape of one of our citizens, whether male, female, young, or old. But it seems that we have become much less concerned or bothered when we learn about what has become the virtual rape of the assets, values, morals, resources, and the very history and tradition of the United States of America.

Major factors in the rape of America are the conciliatory removal of God and our own Christian values and traditions, de-emphasis of the teaching of the real history of this nation in public schools, disrespect for all authority within this nation, total lack of pride in what it means to be an American, loss of control and respect in our schools, loss of respect for our military and the need for a military draft, young people's lack of a sense of responsibility, lack of the ability to prioritize, a total absence of pride in one's appearance, the willingness to give away the resources of this country to anyone who wants something for nothing, misunderstanding the meaning of national security, suggesting that equality means taking from the rich and giving it to the poor, and politicians who will say and do anything in return for a vote.

Our laws are designed to punish those accused, tried, and convicted of the rape of another human being. What are we going to do to punish those who are engaged in the rape of our nation? The difference in these two crimes is not as great as we might think.

ONCE UPON A TIME IN AMERICA

Long, long ago, in a land that now seems so far away, a wonderful dream found its way into the minds of a determined group of visionaries. They set out to create upon this Earth a nation that was totally unlike anything ever seen before. Amid the rubble of a world that had catered to its royalty, but at the expense of a meager middle class and a huge peasant class, this new nation would become the beacon of democracy and a fertile breeding ground for those with ambition, drive, and initiative.

But, with mankind being what it is, what once was a wonderful country known as the "Land of the Free" has evolved into a country that has become the "Land of the Freeloader," thanks to the twisted notions of a group of insecure liberals who feel that this world owes them a living simply by having been born. This group of do-gooders sees political value in perpetuating the idea that government provides for everyone's existence from the cradle to the grave. We now have seen several generations born into this world with one or both hands extended at birth in hope of accepting anything that can be donated to them. One of the best ways of guaranteeing that these dependent groups of people remain dependent is to instill within them and their offspring the understanding that they are now, have always been, and always will be *victims*! These people are further indoctrinated with the idea that they do not possess the common sense necessary to provide for themselves, and thus they will always be wards of the state."

Oh Lord, please save us from ourselves.

GETTING OUR PRIORITIES STRAIGHT

Regardless of how we may personally feel about the war now being waged in Iraq, we cannot and must not do anything that will in any way enhance the danger that our brave men and women in uniform now face over there 24/7. These brave young American heroes voluntarily joined our military at the risk of their own lives and careers. They went into this foreign land to put down an insurgency by a group of fanatical Islamic murderers who will most assuredly soon find their way to our own doorsteps if left unchecked, especially if we continue to follow the lead of the so-called liberal leadership now in control of Congress, who have chosen surrender over victory. Whether we agree with this war or not, we must understand that we are right smack in the middle of it, and we must not allow anything to compromise our troops' chances for success or for their very safety while they are there. There cannot be any room for discussions that would in any way jeopardize the safety and well-being of our brave troops while they are in harm's way!

This being said, I must also confess that, like many who have fervently supported President George W. Bush in his plans for the successful execution of this war, I have grown very weary of the lack of progress in putting down this insurgency. As we were taught in high school history class, if we do not learn from our past mistakes, we are destined to repeat them, and this fact is very evident where this Iraq war is concerned. We obviously did not take to heart the lessons learned from our many mistakes in Korea and Vietnam, and many of the same mistakes have reappeared in the Middle East. The only way to properly and successfully execute a battle plan is to attack the enemy with the most overwhelming force possible, get the job done as quickly as possible, and bring our troops home. The longer this war goes on, it becomes more and more apparent that we did not use this rationale and that this has created a situation that has become much more difficult to work with or to correct. Had we followed the early advice of Colin Powell and other military leaders who urged that we double the number of military personnel than were originally sent to this region, this war could have been successfully concluded, our troops brought safely home, and our attentions directed toward other pressing problems now facing this nation, such as that of securing our borders.

Contrary to the shameful declaration of surrender proclaimed by the liberal Senate majority leader Harry Reid, this war can still be won; however, if we continue to follow the same plan of strategic mismanagement by this administration, it will only serve to prove that the coward Harry Reid was correct. With my own son in the heat of battle on a daily basis in Iraq, I am much more interested than most people in bringing this war to a quick and satisfactory conclusion and bringing our brave, young men and women home. But I also understand that this problem reaches much deeper and is much more involved than just the specific territory of Iraq. Whether we realize it or simply choose to ignore it, the world as we know it is now in an undeclared war between freedom and fanaticism, between democracy and intolerance, and between civilization and total destruction! We can continue to bury our heads in the sand and ignore reality, or we can stand up and tighten our belts and get ready to fight this true and real enemy of humanity. The choice is still in our own hands, but time is quickly running out!

We have given far too much attention to those who insist upon a philosophy of being "politically correct" in anything and everything we do, to the extent that this philosophy has proven itself to be a major obstacle to maintaining our position as the most dominant, compassionate, and powerful nation this world has ever seen. We have become so concerned about not insulting or making one group or another feel uncomfortable that we have weakened the very fabric that once was the foundation of this nation. Are we going to follow the same path of appeasement that our European neighbors implemented when they chose to ignore long-proven historical facts such as the reality of the Holocaust in hope of not offending members of the Muslim religion? Are we going to follow the lead of the New York City public schools and use taxpayer funds to build a separate school specifically for the education of Arabic-speaking children? Are we going to continue to allow immigrants, whether legal or illegal, to come into this country and not be required to learn our language, our customs, and our history? After all, we assume that they are coming to this country because it offers them hope for a much better life than they would have experienced in their home countries. If we are fooled into allowing them to make this country just another version of the country they left, what advantage has been gained by anyone in doing so?

My fellow Americans, we are quickly approaching a very serious crossroad in the history of this nation! The direction and even the very future existence of this nation will depend upon which road we will take. At one point in our nation's history, we were perfectly willing to take the tougher road to get a job done, if it meant that in the long run the best interest of this nation to grow, prosper, or survive depended upon us doing so. But, it seems that our very own success and prosperity has allowed many to lose the will to fight for a cause that once would have been accepted without question as being in the best interest of this nation.

Do you remember the old saying "The squeaky wheel gets the grease"? Somehow, a lackadaisical attitude by a majority within this country has allowed the wishes and demands of the "squeaky" minority to take priority over those of the majority. People in the minority make the most noise; therefore, they receive the most attention. We have been led to believe by certain bleeding-heart liberals in this country that we should feel guilty about the hard-earned success we have enjoyed as a nation, and that in order to correct this perceived injustice, we must do everything possible to hand over our hard-earned abundance to those less fortunate countries of this world. The fact has somehow become lost that most, if not all of these so-called less fortunate countries have occupied their place on this Earth for thousands upon thousands of years before our nation was even founded. But for a lack of will or skill, or for some other reason, their ancestors, who could have achieved the same level of success as our ancestors did, chose not to do so, thus sealing their own fate.

The election of November 2006 was viewed by some as a majority of the voters preferring Democrats over Republicans. But what is much more likely is that many who would have voted Republican were finally disgusted by the way this same group of Republicans had promised to do so much but had actually done so very little to justify returning them to Washington. This vote was more intended as a message rather than a mandate. We now find that Washington is home to a group of socialists who want to tax us to death and give away the assets of this once-great nation as entitlements to anyone who will agree to hand over his or her vote in return.

Have we really placed our priorities in the right order? Can we truly remember what it means and feels like to be a *proud American?* While there is still time, maybe we can return to our senses and again take on the role of *true Americans.*

God bless our troops, and God bless this nation!

FINALLY, A PERFECT WORLD (SATIRE, OF COURSE)

The Democrat presidential debates have enlightened conservatives to the fact that we have been supporting the wrong political party for years. We were so caught up in our own selfish ambition to influence world politics that we have lost all touch with reality concerning what is truly in this world's best interest. Fueled by our false illusions of a world living in peace and harmony under the misguided concept of democracy, we have made the entire world mad at us. We now have an opportunity to correct these mistakes!

Liberals have promised *change*, and although we have not been told exactly what those changes are, or just how America will pay for those changes, we can surely trust liberals to come up with a plan that will be fair and equitable for everyone. From the context of the Democrat debates, these are some of the changes we might expect to see.

1. An immediate, total withdrawal of all American military forces from Iraq, and possibly from the entire Middle East region as well. This should allow the government of Iran time to complete and implement their misunderstood and much maligned nuclear program, which everyone now understands is intended strictly for peaceful purposes.

2. Government entitlement programs will be implemented to provide free medical care, free education, housing, food stamps, and full employment for those who wish to work, while providing complete subsistence to those who would rather not suffer the indignities of employment. Our government will now take care of our every possible need from the cradle to the grave, and we can soon eliminate the need for and expense of a free public education, because there will no longer be a need for anyone to learn how to do anything.

3. Islamic Sharia Law will be incorporated with equal standing into our own system of laws, which will allow Muslims to concentrate upon their religious duties to convert the infidels. These peace-loving nomads respond so much better to diplomacy rather than to military retaliation, and this could eventually encourage them to even abandon their purely self-defense tactics of bombing our transportation systems, skyscrapers, and government buildings, which liberals have convinced us are simply capitalist icons of evil and intolerance. Who are we to question the true motives of this tolerant and peaceful religion? After all, hasn't our own history taught us just how dangerous it can be to even consider granting any degree of equality to women?

4. Liberals will remove any and all obstacles to the safe and free movement across our borders by anyone wishing to come into the United States for any purpose. Some of these visitors might require government assistance during their undocumented visits to this country, but they will promise to abide by all of our laws, learn our language, and pay their fair share of taxes.

How wonderful! Isn't this exactly what we have been wishing for? We have finally achieved Utopia. Bless you, dear liberals. Bless you.

POLICEMAN OF THE WORLD

What is the reason for the conciliatory demise of this country, whose people once showed so much promise of finally becoming the nation that could pull it off and not become like all of the other nations of the past? Among other things, we have simply been allowed and even encouraged to forget our nation's history. The blood, sweat, and tears shed by those tough-spirited souls who led the way, almost two and a half centuries ago, to put this dream into motion are now deemed to have been unimportant and unnecessary, and are now even being forgotten. Just as the Christian religion is based upon faith in something that happened thousands of years ago, faith in the American spirit is based upon the actions of the brave pioneers who took it upon themselves to build the very foundations of a nation, the likes of which had never before been seen in the history of mankind.

Now we are allowing the uneducated, undisciplined, unpatriotic, unmotivated, non-Christian, and un-American illegal immigrants to dictate to the lawful and dedicated citizens of this nation just how they are to be governed and how we are to live our lives. We have been taken in by group of *career politicians* who have no concept of what it is like to bring home a paycheck earned as a result of a hard day's work, something most Americans do routinely. This group includes a Muslim delegate from Minnesota in the House of Representatives who will likely do everything he can to change American customs and traditions. We also have at least one gay delegate from Massachusetts in the House of Representatives who is allowed and encouraged to defend and rationalize his immoral lifestyle and impose it upon the men, women, and children of America.

Under the masquerade of *political correctness*, we have allowed many liberal members of our Congress, with the help of their own private legal team from the ACLU, to remove the observance and display of articles and traditions of our own Christian faith, while at the same time encouraging—and even funding through taxpayer money—Muslim and other non-Christian religious traditions to be displayed and observed in public places. How much longer will it be until we follow the cowardly lead of our European neighbors in banishing our own national customs and traditions because they might insult the growing numbers of Muslims now taking up space in our schools and other public places? If these people really want to come to this country, then it should be their responsibility to assimilate our values, customs, and traditions instead of imposing their values, customs, and traditions upon the people of this country, which has opened its doors to them.

I am reminded of a situation in small rural community in south Arkansas, where a group of Hispanic immigrants, some legal but also some likely illegal, had been allowed to use a vacant local church building for their own religious services after the former congregation had built and moved to a new larger building. The former occupants of this church building had always displayed the American flag and the Christian flag on the stage at either side of the pulpit. A member of the church that had allowed this Hispanic congregation to use their former church building was asked by the new congregation to spray the building for bugs. When this man arrived at the church building to spray, he observed that the Christian flag and the American flag had both been thrown in a corner at the rear of the building, and the flag of Mexico was now proudly displayed in their place. This is not an isolated case, for this is how far too many immigrants repay the generosity of this country that has taken them in after they have left countries where they could not even make a living for their families. They show their gratitude by displaying the Mexican flag, while tossing out the flag of the country that has taken them in and given them opportunities only dreamed of in their former country.

We cannot continue to be the "policeman to the world" and the one nation that rushes to help even those countries who will take our help, but then turn their backs upon us and attack everything we have stood for.

Only in America

The very fact that Ahmadinejad, the terrorist-supporting president of Iran, was allowed to speak at Columbia University shows how tolerant the American people are of those whose goal in life is to kill us. I wonder what would happen if our President Bush were to ask to speak at a college, university, or to any venue within Iran? Would our president have been allowed to speak there, and if so, how much of what he said would have been edited or even totally eliminated?

Political Noise

Barack Hussein Obama wants us to believe that all of the uproar about his relationship with his minister Jeremiah Wright is simply "political noise" and should be cast aside and not allowed to confuse the focus of his message. I have two problems with Obama's approach to this Jeremiah Wright time bomb. First, people want to know why and how Obama could sit in this church for twenty years, listening to Jeremiah Wright's anti-American bilge, and just now become so offended that he would cut all ties to this racist minister. He now says that he will find another church that is more representative of Middle-American values than those expressed by this disgraceful excuse for a minister.

Second, just what exactly is the message he wants us to focus on? We know he says that he represents *change*, but what does he want to *change*, and how?

It is becoming more and more apparent that the thing that worries Barack Obama most is what will happen if even the most hard-line Democrat voters should want Obama to explain what he plans to do if he is elected president. We are now watching as the disguise Barack Obama has been hiding behind for so long begins to melt away. What we now see is a very transparent politician who can sell ice to Eskimos but has no clue what to do when the time comes to make the hard and tough decisions necessary as leader of the most powerful nation on the face of the Earth. How will he react as commander in chief (oh, what a scary thought) of our armed forces when the time comes for him to launch an attack upon a Muslim nation, a nation that believes in the same religious philosophy into which Obama was indoctrinated as a young boy? Where is he going to find the money to pay for the socialist programs he wants to saddle the American taxpayers with? Obama knows, but he hopes that you and I don't find out until after the election. Who is going to pay for his socialized health-care programs? We are! Who is going to pay for his welfare programs? We are! Who is going to pay for his expanded public-housing programs? We are? Who is going to pay for his educational programs, which will replace the truth about how this nation was founded with his more *politically correct* version? We will, you and I, in the form of higher taxes!

Finally, the one question I would ask Barack Obama is, "What is your position, your honest position, on the payment of slave reparations?" If Obama is going to legislate that the American taxpayers must pay *slave reparations* to descendants of slaves, this will tell us volumes about who this guy is and how he will govern. The American people deserve answers to this question before he charms his way into the White House.

BIRDS OF A FEATHER

Barack Obama can't understand why the ABC debate commentators used the first forty-five minutes of the recent Democrat debate between himself and Hillary Clinton to inquire about his twenty-year association with the minister he refers to as his mentor, his relationship with Weather Underground terrorist bomber William Ayers, Michelle Obama's comments about not being proud of this country, his reasons for wanting to increase the capital gains tax, and his reasons for not wearing an American flag lapel pin, before moving on to what he refers to as "the real issues." This is just another link in the growing chain of examples showing that Barack Obama just doesn't understand why the American people want, need, or even deserve to know the truth about his questionable past. Many are indeed interested in his association with his America-hating, racist minister and his Pentagon-bombing friend. Obama and his supporters have tried to spin any questioning about these matters as being racist, but these are justified concerns about real issues. Obama and his supporters try to spin any criticism toward their untouchable candidate as racist, off-limits, and unfair. To those citizens who see these as real issues, they are very real issues, and any attempt by the Obama camp to ignore them is being very unfair to the voters!

Many indeed want to know why he remained as a member of a church, whose racist minister indoctrinated the membership into hating America, and preached to them that our government was responsible for 9/11, and had also infected the black race with AIDS. Many indeed want to understand his association with the self-confessed and unrepentant bomber of the Pentagon and other government buildings while a member of the Weather Underground terrorist group. Obama dearly hopes that these do not become real issues, but it is too late. These are real issues, and Obama must give true, open, and honest answers to these questions or accept the consequences.

We are known by the company we keep, and Obama has certainly shown a propensity to associate with some very un-American company. Obama must remove all doubt about his true and honest feelings for this country by pledging his love for this nation, or these will remain real issues as long as he is a candidate for the office of president! If he is too ashamed to proclaim his love for and devotion to America, then America should be too ashamed to proclaim its love for and devotion to Barack Obama. If Obama will not sever all ties with these people who have openly expressed their hatred for this country, then there should no question that he is not qualified to hold the office considered the most powerful one in the world.

You Miss It When It Is Gone

Have you ever heard the old saying "You never miss a good thing until it is gone"? I truly hope this is not what our children, grandchildren, and great-grandchildren will be saying down the road if the good ol' United States has become only a fond memory.

Except for a few left-wing radicals like Hillary Clinton, Ted Kennedy, Nancy Pelosi, and Harry Reid, I don't think that there is really very much true difference between the Democrats and Republicans in what they would like to see as the future of this nation. The fatal plans of these radicals for the destruction of this nation could be accomplished if the voters do not kick them out of office and place leadership into the hands of people who truly love this country and have no intention of destroying it. For some reason these radicals cannot bring themselves to accept or understand the unprecedented success this great nation has enjoyed for almost two and a half centuries. They seem to have an overriding guilt complex; one they feel can only be satisfied by destroying the very fabric of this nation and turning it into one where government controls every aspect of its people's lives. The only way they can achieve this is by winning over those who insist upon receiving something for nothing, and who will give their vote in return for entitlements.

The United States has been a world power for less than two and a half centuries, a much shorter time than most of the other countries who claimed world supremacy throughout Earth's history. The success of this nation has taken place in large part because our founding fathers recognized the unique idea that people must possess certain freedoms not granted by rulers of other countries. These freedoms would in turn encourage ambition and initiative among its people, thereby leading to discoveries and inventions that could not be realized or even dreamed of under suppressive and tyrannical kingdoms and dictators.

The irony in all of this is that the left-wing radicals found in our government are trying to make changes that will ensure that this great nation reverts to the practices of kingdoms and dictatorships of centuries past. Personal freedoms will vanish; all power will be kept protectively in the hands of the government, thereby killing any incentive for ambition and initiative, the jewel within the human mind that makes things happen. By pushing for the passage of entitlement legislation such as free (?) and mandatory government health care for all, $5,000 baby bonds, and 401(k) retirement plans for everyone, not to mention food stamps and subsidized housing, the plan of this group is to turn us all into a collection of dependent taxpayers and not ambitious, imaginative, and innovative entrepreneurs. They want us to be dependent upon government for everything rather than to actually be the government, as America was originally designed.

THE FUTURE OF AMERICA

What do we truly want America to look like in the future? Are we honestly satisfied with the direction in which we are currently headed? Are we confident that we will be happy and content with what this country looks like five, ten, twenty, or fifty years from now? Do we want America to be a land where our cities and communities are safe places and where we and our families can go downtown, or to shopping malls, or to parks, and feel perfectly safe in doing so? Is America now a place where our schools can dedicate their time, energy, and resources to the task of educating our children? Do we want America to be a place where our children can grow up in the traditions and values we hold dear, and where we can worship our *God* in the way we so choose? Is this what America is like right now? If our founding fathers were to come back to see what has become of the nation for which they laid the foundations, would they be proud of what they see?

I am afraid that we all know the true and honest answer to these questions. The real question, however, is, "What are we going to do about it?" Our cities and communities are not safe! Our schools cannot dedicate their efforts to education! Our tax revenues are spent on building jails and prisons and hiring additional police officers, instead of building parks and schools and hiring teachers. Americans are being compelled to forget their own traditions and values and to become more open and receptive to the traditions and values of those who came here from other places.

When we speak of race, there must be only one race that concerns us, and that is the *human race!* Black, white, brown, red, or yellow, it doesn't matter. If we continue to allow lawless thugs, punks, and gangs to rule the streets of our cities, no one of any color will be safe. Do we want our cities and towns to look like Memphis, Washington DC, Detroit, Philadelphia, or inner-city Los Angeles? Those cities have become war zones with no one willing to identify and attack the real problems. We have become so afraid to make any comment that might be seen as racist that we are allowing the lack of corrective action to destroy this nation from within. This is exactly what Russian Premier Nikita Khrushchev was referring to in the early 1960s when he said that Russia would not need to lift a finger to defeat America, and that we would destroy ourselves from within.

Political correctness is quickly becoming the weapon of our own self-destruction.

Wake up, America!

A Socialist America

The United States of America, this most unique government experiment ever devised by mankind, deserves a much greater fate than to be relegated to the doldrums of a socialist state. America was built upon the ambition and initiative found within the hearts and minds of special people, both rich and poor, blue blood or common heritage, and where the desire to succeed became its very heartbeat.

We are now told by Obama and his liberal counterparts that the wealth and the best things in life must be shared equally by everyone, including those who constantly take but give back nothing in return for the betterment of this nation. We are led to believe that simply by being born, all are entitled to the same benefits as those who saw the same basic opportunities available to everyone in this country, but who also realized that they must take advantage of those opportunities in order to become successful in this nation of unlimited potential.

If we are content to sadly allow this unique economy and society to fall into the same disarray and ruin as demonstrated by some of our European neighbors, then socialism just might be all we deserve. If, however, we are determined not to allow the United States of America to suffer the indignity of surrendering its heritage, traditions, and values to anyone who wants to invade these borders and selfishly partake of the many blessings America has to offer, then we must stand up and fight for our principles!

The true America is not simply the land upon which we settled; it is the spirit beating within the hearts of its people, or to be more precise, the spirit beating within the hearts of those people who sacrificed their blood, sweat, tears, and even their lives to make America like no other nation upon the face of this Earth. If we continue to allow unprincipled fortune hunters to systematically dilute and break the true American spirit, that spirit will totally disappear within the next two generations. If we feel that the inventors and creators of commerce are the real enemies of this nation, then we have lost our true understanding of what America is all about. The American spirit is found deep within the hearts and minds of its people, not in the entitlements freely handed out by liberal destroyers.

Is America really worth fighting for? If so, when are the real Americans going to stand up and fight for her? Time is quickly running out. We will soon see the passing of those generations whose members never questioned their duty to fight for America. Who, then, will take their place?

AMERICA UNDER SOCIALISM

What can we expect America to become under a regime of the liberal, socialist, Democrat Barack Hussein Obama as president? Since the mainstream media continues to turn its head away from any evidence of Obama's questionable associations and his lack of qualifications, we likely will not know much about this mysterious politician until we find ourselves in the suffocating socialist clutches of the most liberal administration in our history.

We will surely see the Bush tax cuts be allowed to expire and personal income taxes increase. But, contrary to what Obama promised during his campaign, not only will the wealthy see tax increases, but Americans of all tax brackets will see their taxes go up. We will see corporate tax rates increase and, as a result, funding for research and development within corporate America will be diverted elsewhere.

We will see an attempt to use taxpayer funds to pay reparations to descendants of former slaves, which will likely cause even the most lackadaisical Caucasian to say, "Enough is enough!" We will at some point see a strong effort to take wealth away from those who earned it by building their businesses, and distribute it among the people of this nation, many of whom have never made a positive contribution to this country. Studies have suggested that if all of the world's wealth were divided equally among the world's people, within ten years the majority of this wealth would have found its way back into the hands of those who know how to create it. The results of this study have sadly been validated by many winners of the various lotteries. Once the unaccustomed wealth has been squandered away, the winner is often left in a much worse financial condition than before they won the lottery.

SOCIALIZED MEDICINE

A lot of people in this country have been brainwashed into believing that a government-sponsored health-care program is the best way to go. Liberals would have us believe that socialized medicine would be more equitable for the majority of American citizens, but they fail to explain the long wait for treatment and even diagnosis that the citizens of countries where socialized medicine has been in place for years now must endure. Ask Senator Ted Kennedy if he is glad that his plans for socialized medicine had not taken effect at the time his brain cancer was discovered. Would he expect to receive the identical treatment under the same system of socialized medicine which he and his liberal Democrats in Congress have been advocating? How would he deal with being forced to wait for weeks or even months to receive the same degree of treatment that he received almost immediately after his medical condition was diagnosed? Someone of Senator Kennedy's financial means could and would surely pay any amount necessary to travel to a foreign country for the necessary medical attention, and thereby avoid the same long delays that would be forced upon the rank-and-file patient under socialized medicine. How might Senator Kennedy explain the special considerations he received compared to those the average American citizen would be forced to endure? Would he suggest that he was not given preferential treatment due to his wealth and political standing? Would someone from the poverty class, which he and his liberal buddies claim to be looking out for, receive the same prompt attention that Senator Kennedy did? I think not!

If he were perfectly honest, even Senator Kennedy might acknowledge that he received preferential treatment for his condition because of who he was. But, if he had been forced to abide by the same rules of socialized medicine as the average American citizen would be subjected to, he would very likely not be alive today. How confident would Senator Kennedy be of his fate if he had to rely on the same system of socialized medicine that he and his liberal cohorts have been trying to push down our throats for the past sixteen years? I would venture to say that Ted Kennedy secretly feels like he is the luckiest person on the face of the Earth because his system of socialized medicine had not yet been implemented, and his medical care was provided by the privatized medical system he has appeared so eager to replace. Senator Kennedy greatly benefited from the very system he claims to be unfair to the majority of Americans today.

What do you think about socialized medicine now, Senator Kennedy?

A WOMAN'S RIGHT TO CHOOSE

I don't think anyone will disagree that our constitution gives each one of us certain inalienable rights, and a woman's right to choose is certainly one of those rights. My position on this issue may at first be confusing to conservatives and liberals alike, but I am totally in favor of a woman's right to choose. The issue should not be whether the woman has a right to choose, but instead, at just what point this choice is to be made.

Why is this even an issue? Anyone who cannot see that a woman does indeed have a choice in this matter is being totally unfair to all women. Again, the question here is not whether the woman has a choice, but instead at what point this choice is to be made. To put this matter in its simplest terms, the woman's choice should be made before the possibility of conception has taken place, not afterward. Once this choice has been made, the possibility of another life having been created should be given paramount consideration and equal value. Among things to be considered is the fact that this possible new life should also have certain rights, and among those is the right to life itself, which must be respected and honored. The facts of life most of us learned during our formative years give us the knowledge of just how new life is created, and once a woman has made her choice in this matter, she must also consider the possible consequences of this natural act, and take precautions accordingly. *The new life we create also deserves a chance at life!*

THE MORTGAGE CRISIS

The American people are not as stupid as Barack Hussein Obama, Barney Frank, Chris Dodd, and Chuck Schumer think we are. They are trying to blame George Bush for the current mortgage crisis, when, in fact, it was the liberal Democrats who pushed for making home loans available to many people who did not qualify under customary mortgage requirements. Liberals insisted that these mortgage seekers should receive financing, even though many of them had poor credit histories, were without jobs, and some even had no Social Security numbers. In fact, as it turns out, many of these loans were made to illegal immigrants who should not have been in this country in the first place.

The names of congressional liberals, who pressured banks into making loans available to those who did not fit the traditional mortgage qualifications, are well-known to everyone. Barney Frank, Chris Dodd, and Chuck Schumer are just a few members of this liberal political circus who, in return for accepting huge political contributions, have played leading roles in causing the huge financial crisis this nation now finds itself mired in. They have also brought into their little group, the likes of Franklin Rains and Jim Johnson, those forced-out heads of Fannie Mae and Freddie Mac who took millions out of these financial institutions before driving them into the ground. These less-than-honest scoundrels have attempted to deny their own obvious involvement in pressuring banks to make these bogus loans to unqualified borrowers, and have even blocked attempts by John McCain, George W. Bush, and others to investigate the extent to which Barney Frank and Company were actually involved in the creation of this unethical entitlement scam. However, as is their usual tactic, they again tried to shift all blame to Republicans.

What is it about socialism that presumably smart people just cannot recognize or understand? If they have become so gullible during this election that they actually try to defend this stuff, I cannot see much hope for them returning to reality! The blame for this financial crisis sits squarely in the lap of Barney Frank and his liberal Democrats. Their desire to push us into socialism is so strong and arrogant that they have even brainwashed and transformed formerly clear-thinking people into accepting this rubbish.

What would George Washington, Thomas Jefferson, John Adams, Andrew Jackson, Abe Lincoln, and all of those other great Americans—who fought with everything within them to make this nation the strongest nation ever seen upon this Earth—have to say about what is going on today? What will we do if this liberal, socialist Obama administration plans to convert America to socialism actually comes true? I fear that regardless of whether an Obama administration is a success or a failure, what remains of this once-great nation will be only a mere shadow of its former self.

PATRIOTISM

Remember ...

... when the first calendar day of the week meant going to church on Sunday morning, and then back again on Sunday night?

... when young boys would gather at a popular vacant neighborhood lot for a baseball game on a summer morning, and then head back again for another game in the afternoon?

... looking forward to sitting in a folding chair or on a blanket spread on the ground for a concert at the local bandstand during warm summer afternoons?

... when getting cooled off meant going inside to stand in front of a window fan rather than an air conditioner? (You see, many of us really didn't know what an air conditioner was back then.)

... when we picked out our nicest casual dress clothes to wear to school each day, regardless of how well-off our family was?

... when going shopping meant riding with your parents or taking the bus to the downtown department stores?

... when doing something out of line in school meant a trip to the principal's office for a possible paddling, and then getting it again at home once your parents found out?

... when school teachers' careers spanned twenty, thirty, and even forty years, and they were deservedly looked up to as pillars of the community?

… when professional athletes played their sport for the love of the game, were not insulted by being offered six- and even seven-figure incomes, and made most of their news on the field of play instead of in the gossip columns or court dockets?

… when movie stars could make movies in which they actually kept their clothes on and scripts contained little or no profanity?

These and many other wonderful memories actually took place, and it doesn't seem to have been so many years ago. These memories belonged to a time that seems so embarrassingly innocent by today's standards, but allowed people to appreciate one another without being labeled as odd or different in doing so.

Those memories were made during a period when time seemed to move at a much slower pace when compared to today. Even words such as "gay" and "making love" had much more innocent meanings than they do now.

Just like in the movie classic *Gone with the Wind,* where the world Scarlet O'Hara knew while growing up was vastly different from the one transformed by the Civil War, the world in which my generation grew up now seems so far removed from the world of today that it almost seems like a fairy tale.

Every generation seems to fondly remember its formative years as being much simpler and less threatening than later generations, and those sentiments have prevailed today. The main difference between the younger generations of today and those of yesteryear is that the same degree of patriotism does not seem to have been passed down to today's young people.

UNIQUE AMERICA

What does it mean to be an American? Many would consider this to be a very simple question to answer, but the real answer to this question has been totally misunderstood by many who call this wonderful land their home. The real answer to this question is so obvious that it is very often overlooked.

Our forefathers brought a unique vision to this country that was entirely different from anything this world had ever experienced. For those of us so fortunate to have been born in this wonderful land, it seems so easy to just take everything for granted. How different would our lives be if we had been born somewhere other than America, like the mountains of Afghanistan, or the deserts of Africa, or the frigid lands of Russia? It takes a very special individual to totally grasp and appreciate what it means to be an American. The main difference between a real American and everyone else can be found in one's mind-set. The mind-set of a real American is fueled by ambition and a burning desire to succeed. A real American will not accept dependency upon anyone or anything.

Some want to see this country become a mirror image of our European cousins, where they would have access to so-called free health care and have their every need provided by their government. What they do not understand is that the United States is not France, and it is not even England. To appreciate the uniqueness of America, one must understand the difference between capitalism and socialism, between capitalism and communism, and between democracy and dictatorship, barbarism, and totalitarianism. The total concept of America is so unique that many people just cannot comprehend or appreciate what we have.

Occupants of this country can be divided into two very distinct categories. We have those who are perfectly willing and eager to take whatever this nation has to give to them, but who feel no obligation to give back anything in return. Then we have true Americans, who appreciate and love this nation so much that they are willing to make the necessary sacrifices to ensure our survival as a nation. The sad hard truth is that all of our enemies are not to be found outside of our borders.

The definition of what it means to be poor in this country is very different from what it means to be poor in almost every other country in this world. The financial resources of those considered to be poor in the United States would place them in the middle or even upper middle class of many other countries on Earth. But the harsh truth, which is very difficult for many to accept, is that a large portion of those who consider themselves to be poor in this country would also find themselves being poor in the other countries, simply because they cannot or will not grasp the reality of what it means to be an American.

It takes a very special person to understand and appreciate what it means to truly be an American. This beautiful and unique land that has been placed into our care asks so very little of us, but it does ask that we preserve, protect, and defend our way of life against those who would try to destroy it.

What Is This America?

What is this country we call America? How and why is it different from any other nation ever forged upon the face of this Earth? What kind of person did it take to make this nation strong, and what kind of person will it take to make sure that America survives and prospers into the future?

To better understand America, we must first acquire an understanding of the meaning of the word "unique." *Webster's Dictionary* defines "unique" as "One; Single; Sole; Being without a like or equal; Very rare or uncommon; Very unusual." Although many countries have unsuccessfully attempted to do what America has done, it is impossible to compare America with any other country or nation upon the face of the Earth, because as the definition of the term "unique" suggests, there simply is no other country or nation like America!

What type of person makes the realization of the American dream possible? First, we must envision what the American dream means to us and actually see ourselves having the opportunity to live it! The American dream is possible when there are people who do not accept dependence upon government for their very existence. The American dream is possible when there are people who understand that nothing worthwhile comes cheap or free. The American dream is possible when we have people who are willing to lay their lives on the line to protect and defend liberty. The American dream is possible when there are people who take every advantage available to them to improve their way of life and to make a better life for their own families and others. These are the people who do not feel that big government is the answer to the success and survival of this nation, but who see the role of government as a supporting one for our national security, commerce, enterprise, and one of encouragement to ambition and initiative. Entitlements should only be made available to those who cannot provide for themselves because of illness, injury, or conditions totally beyond their control.

Just as there are other countries that have tried unsuccessfully to compare themselves with America, there are also people, even within America itself, who consider themselves "Americans" but who have never been able to grasp what a true American really is. To be truly American, one cannot be selfish, self-centered, uncommitted, unpatriotic, or undedicated to achieving the American dream. A true American cannot possibly look at the many opportunities this country offers and not make every effort to take advantage of those opportunities. Unfortunately, we have within this country those who would take advantage of the opportunities, even to the point where they assume that the rewards of these opportunities might even be worth working for, but who have no interest whatsoever in taking the steps necessary to reach the ultimate destination to which these opportunities could lead them. They are not willing to take advantage of the educational opportunities this nation provides. They are not willing to make the necessary sacrifices to ensure that the American dream not only survives, but prospers. And they are not willing to serve America when called upon to do so.

A PROUD AMERICAN WITH MIXED EMOTIONS

I write this letter with very mixed emotions. I am torn between my feelings as the proud parent of a member of our nation's armed forces, and my feelings as a citizen of the most wonderful and prosperous nation this world has ever seen.

On one hand, as a parent I fear for the safety and well-being of my son, who is into his second deployment in Iraq. He has volunteered to fight for and protect the way of life that we as Americans are privileged to be a part of and enjoy. On the other hand, I share the same fears of losing our way of life to this group of Islamic terrorists we are fighting today, as our ancestors must have also felt when they had to fight to protect their way of life against the likes of Adolf Hitler.

History teaches us that our greatest leaders are not always the ones who make the popular decisions, but are instead the ones who make some unpopular and tough decisions that later turned out to have been the right decisions. Skeptics have questioned every move FDR and George Bush had to make on a daily basis, decisions that must have been very gut-wrenching for both men. These were decisions that each of these men knew would surely cost the lives of many of the best and brightest young men and women of their generations. But they also knew that these were tough decisions that had to be made for the preservation of our freedom and democracy. They were decisions that could not be passed on to later generations simply because that would have been the popular or easy thing to do.

Americans are different from the majority of the rest of the world. Even though it appears that much of this world hates us, they hate us because they are so jealous of what we have. Americans make hard and tough decisions that the rest of the world is either unwilling or incapable of making. This has made us different from, and more successful than, others who refused to make those decisions. This is likely the *one and only* reason we can still call ourselves Americans today, instead of suffering under the flag of conquerors who would have subjected us to unbearable tyrannical conditions, just as these present-day terrorists will surely do if they are allowed to prevail.

Throughout history, true Americans have made these tough decisions, even in the face of the slander and ridicule that has confronted President Bush. I hope and pray that the dissenters within future American generations can look back and realize that their right to dissent was protected by the decisions made by our brave leaders of today, those people who had the courage to make tough but unpopular decisions.

Advice from the Baby Boomers

To all of my fellow baby boomers out there, do you ever wonder just where the time went? It seems like only yesterday when we were school kids without a care in the world, and time moved ever so slowly. We wondered if the time would ever come when we would be treated like adults and would no longer have to put up with what we perceived to be the pains of adolescence. Those days now seem to be just a fading memory, but we still wonder where the time went.

Now that we are looking our golden years square in the face and are considering the prospects of our own retirement, some of us might wish that we had done things a little differently. When our parents and all of those we looked up to as youngsters tried to forewarn us that this time would surely come, we might have politely agreed with them, but inside we were thinking that whenever we reached that time in our lives, we would do things our own way. By that time, we would surely have it made! Sound familiar? Isn't it funny how a little *maturity* really can make people a little wiser?

Most of us baby boomers have, from time to time, found ourselves in that role of adviser to our own children, or to those of the younger generation who would seek our advice, or to those who would just listen to us when we tried to favor them with our vast experience. The problem here is that most of these younger people will pay no more attention to our free advice than we did to those willing to bestow the knowledge of their years upon us. It is so true that hindsight is 20/20, but how are we now going to convince these younger generations not to make the same mistakes we made? The only thing that bothers me about the younger people of today is that so many of them have little or no ambition, but then I guess our elders said the same thing about us. For the most part, a majority of our generation did not abandon their values, but that is not something I see in today's generation. Today's youth seem to be very bright, but I wonder if they understand what it is that actually made this country great, because if they have not learned this, then those values will not be passed on to future generations. If that happens, what might the future hold then for the rest of us?

Passing It On

What are we really passing along to our children that will help this nation grow and prosper? When looking around at the young people of today, I am afraid that in many cases, we are not giving our children the necessary foundations that will successfully carry them and this nation into the future. Things like pride in and love of country, a strong work ethic, self-discipline, strong family values, respect for authority, and primarily a love of God. These are things that our parents, grandparents, and great-grandparents passed along to their children, and they are things that served as the backbone of this great nation's previous generations.

During my years of teaching school, it became apparent that in many cases, these values had not been passed down. This great nation was built with and nurtured by the blood, sweat, and tears of great men and women of years past. The prosperity of this nation was entrusted to the care of future generations who hopefully would continue to build upon the values and beliefs their ancestors had handed down to them. The future of this nation was not to be left to a bunch of indifferent people who would allow it to be squandered away, or to people who would take what this nation had to offer them but give back nothing in return. I am afraid that many of the people to whom our ancestors have entrusted the future of this great nation would allow it to disintegrate into a second-class nation that has lost not only its direction, but also its will to continue to be the bastion of democracy.

Hopefully, it is not too late for the true patriots of this nation to retake it from those who have never appreciated what they had. They never could see the efforts of the people of past generations who had visions of this most wonderful icon of freedom extending like a thread, endlessly into the future. While we are still in the majority of this great nation, we *must* rise up and defend the values and beliefs upon which this great nation was founded. We *must* start electing leaders who share and promote our core values, and not those who are willing to sell out our nation for the sake of getting a few more votes. We definitely do not need leaders who will legislate according to the dictates of the Koran instead of the U.S. Constitution. We have allowed certain groups within this country to convince many Americans that being a Christian is too old-fashioned and outdated, while at the same time encouraging the belief that abortion is just an acceptable method of birth control, and that the homosexual lifestyle is totally acceptable and normal.

We have but a short time to work to secure the election of someone who will return us to the core values upon which this nation was founded. The first step *must* be taken by each and every one of us.

Honoring Our Past Generations

There seems to be so much emphasis upon improving relationships between the races, when maybe we should be at least as concerned with honoring relationships with our past generations. History has shown us that life certainly is not easy and was not meant to be. The simple act of being born does not guarantee anything, especially the right to a life nestled in the lap of luxury, or to be given the very same opportunities as those who were born rich. One thing that many of us fail to appreciate is the fact that regardless of the circumstances into which we were born, there are always many more people out there who were born into much worse circumstances than our own.

We have become a nation that has allowed its average citizens to be dragged down by the underachievers among us, instead of encouraging those underachievers to raise their expectations. The generations that built this great nation, including those who grew up during the Great Depression and shortly after World War II, had left us with wonderful examples upon which to build and continue the growth of this nation for many generations to come. But somewhere along the way, the prosperity that came as a result of the efforts of those generations that defended our nation during World Wars I and II was allowed to drift into complacency and a feeling of satisfaction with the status quo, and the once-great United States of America hasn't been the same since. We are allowing ourselves to go quickly from being the great beacon of democracy to being a group of uninspired and unmotivated underachievers. If we ever allow ourselves to finally lose sight of what made this nation totally different from any other nation that has ever occupied space on this Earth, we will most assuredly lose our will to remain that one bright ray of hope this world must have in order to survive, or even to exist. If we ever stop understanding that we are different from all of the other nations on this Earth, including those European cousins who also appear to have forgotten this same fundamental truth, then this world that has prospered tremendously over the most recent four centuries will likely cease to exist.

This nation now known as the United States of America rose above a group of nations and countries that were established on this Earth for a period far longer than the that enjoyed by this nation. There is absolutely nothing wrong with being proud of what was achieved by our forefathers. God surely must have taken the best from all of the other nations and put those seeds here to grow into what became the United States of America. He embodied in our ancestors a resolve to build this nation into a place where freedom and democracy would be allowed to grow and thrive, to show the other nations of this world the possibilities that could also be achieved by them, if they were only willing to pursue these values.

Look at how long, and in most cases how unsuccessful, the previous world powers had tried to achieve some degree of perfection in this world. They apparently were more interested in gaining power and territory than they were in promoting harmony. Some of these countries look today much as they have for centuries and centuries, while other countries have come to their rescue time and time again.

Consider the issue of slavery and the one thing that many people fail to understand about this issue. Suppose the ancestors of those in this country who continue to refer to themselves as African-Americans had managed to avoid capture by their own people for the purpose of selling them into slavery in this country. As a result of avoiding capture, their ancestors would have remained in Africa for these past four to five centuries. What would their lives be like today, and would they be better-off?

No one can argue that the institution of slavery was not cruel in most every respect; however, knowing what we know today about life on the African continent, would an existence spent in slavery have been any crueler than a life spent in sub-Saharan Africa? Despite being one of the oldest civilizations on the face of the Earth, in many ways the Africa of today is not greatly different from the Africa of thousands of years ago.

The ancestors of many European descendants who now call the United States of America home were themselves impoverished serfs or slaves, but when the opportunity presented itself, these people took every advantage of their situation, thus changing their destiny forever. There were no laws that made it possible for our European ancestors to receive any entitlements like those available to many in America today. Likewise, these same entitlements have also been one of the main reasons why people accepting them have become totally dependent upon them as their only means of existence, both now and into the future.

There is plenty of blame to be passed around, if that is truly what we want to do. But if we continue to follow the lead of those who propose that government take care of our every need from the cradle to the grave, then we deserve a life of mediocre existence in which incentive and the burning desire to achieve will have evaporated. Within a very few generations, and I fear that it will be much sooner that we might think, this nation will become no better than any other nation which is totally dependent on their government for survival.

We have spent hundreds of years trying to find the answer that will fix the perceived problem of racial injustice. In fact, the only answer that will ever work is for each of us to look deep inside ourselves and find the drive and determination that once transformed past generations from poverty and mediocrity and into achievement and accomplishment. We cannot and will not find any degree of success by expecting relief from a government that is designed either to protect the interest of the privileged class or to be all things to all people, which common sense tells us is totally impossible.

Since most of us were not born with silver spoons in our mouths, we attained what levels of success we have achieved through our own initiative. We worked hard by the sweat of our brows, realizing the importance of getting everything our educational systems had to offer us, or possibly knew someone who could help open a door for us. Those who were born into circumstances where it appeared that they already had four strikes against them at birth, either chose to accept the plight that life handed to them, or decided to rise above those obstacles and take control of their own destiny. Regardless of what had happened to other members of their families in the past, they chose simply not to accept what life handed them, but instead used those same negative circumstances as incentive to control their own destiny, and not be dependent upon anyone but themselves.

AMERICA, OUR AMERICA

Unfortunately, it appears that many members of our most recent generation seem to have lost sight of the fact of what it means to be an American. This unique nation is so different from any other nation on Earth that it is imperative that we understand this fact in order for the United States to survive. This nation does not operate like any other nation, and never has.

What kind of legacy are we leaving for those who come after us to carry on after we are gone? When we look back at how previous generations protected those legacies that were entrusted into their care, our own track record leaves a lot to be desired. It appears that far too many of the values and traditions proudly handed down by our ancestors for us to preserve, protect, and strengthen have become forgotten or diluted to such an extent that those who passed them down would hardly recognize them today.

The one thing we must understand and appreciate is that this nation is indeed unique among all other nations on this Earth. With that fact in mind, we must realize that although it certainly was not the intent of our founding fathers that there would be a national religion, neither did they intend for us to abandon the very spiritual values that helped to make this nation strong and unique. Many of our earliest settlers came here to practice their own religious beliefs without government interference. Although many of their traditions and beliefs were somewhat strict and demanding to their own followers, they understood that those beliefs should not be forced upon everyone else. It also was not the intent of our founding fathers that our religious values and beliefs be cast aside under the pretense of allowing the beliefs of others to be observed. There is now a very dangerous movement underway by a group of left-wing, liberal legislators and judges who do not understand their role as being to preserve, protect, and defend our constitution. Instead, they apparently see their role as a mandate to change the very intent of our founding fathers and reinterpret our constitution to fit their own liberal agenda.

One very important fact that any visitors to this nation must recognize and appreciate is that this is *our* nation, and if it is their desire to become a part of *our* nation, they will be welcome. But, if it is their intention to turn this nation into a carbon copy of the nation from which they came, they will find us to be a very suspicious and inhospitable people.

POWER TO THE PEOPLE

When did the people of this nation relinquish the real power found in our constitution to this group of political ambitionists? We, the people, have allowed Ted Kennedy, Nancy Pelosi, and Harry Reid to turn Congress into their own personal playground sandbox, and at the expense of what is really in the best interest of the American people. There are also some Republicans who can be included in this group, but their names are not as well-known due to their lack of backbone in speaking out. These political power brokers would rather indulge in their childish games of political infighting than working in the interest of cooperation across party lines, even when it comes to defeating this nation's enemies. They see investigating drugs in professional sports as more urgent than issues involving our national security. The voters need to send people to Washington who will place the best interest of this nation ahead of anything else, especially those juvenile political games played by jealous liberals who will make sure that they find nothing good in the actions of President George W. Bush. They are allowing their childish games to rip apart the very soul of this nation, and they should be recalled and made to answer for their despicable actions.

We are in the midst of very trying times in America. We found ourselves caught up in a presidential election in which neither party offered a candidate who represented what this country really needs. We are being asked to compromise the real qualifications for the office of president and substitute a veiled attempt to absolve ourselves of guilt by promoting race or gender over leadership. We must forget race and gender, but we must also not place the power of political parties above interest of the American people. This nation's very survival is at stake, and the power of political parties must be totally dismissed, even as a consideration. This was a very odd election in which we were forced to focus upon which one of these less-than-desirable candidates will do the least amount of damage to this country. If we are fortunate enough to survive the next four years, there will hopefully emerge a legitimate candidate by 2010 or 2012, one which can finally bring the people of this great nation together.

Regardless of our political party affiliations, we must put this Congress on notice, and in no uncertain terms say that this political bickering for the sake of a power struggle is destroying this nation and must cease immediately! We must notify the leadership of both parties to stop playing their childish games, or we, the people, are going to send them packing! It is time that the people stop being pawns for these ambitious *career politicians* and return the real power of this country to where it rightfully belongs, into the hands of the people!

The "Political Correctness" Monster

Real Americans who truly care about the future of this nation must step up very soon and retake control of this country; otherwise, this nation as we have known it will cease to exist! "Political correctness" is the vehicle used by phony Americans in their quest to destroy, from within, the most unique nation mankind has ever seen.

Other than national security, perhaps the next problem needing immediate attention is the immigration issue, both legal and illegal. First and foremost, if people are in this country illegally, they must be sent back to where they came from, period! If they are caught in this country illegally a second time, there must be mandatory jail time imposed at hard labor. I cannot understand how or why construction of the border fence was halted, while at the same time allowing so many ridiculous and unnecessary pork-barrel items to slip through. This speaks volumes for the necessity of a presidential line-item veto. One of the most sensible ideas to come out of Congress lately was the border security fence, a measure that due to an absence of cooperation from the Mexican government to help control these illegal border crossings, is a vital necessity. Individuals in Congress responsible for halting the construction of this border fence should be immediately brought up for a recall vote, and the completion of this fence, which a large majority of the American people overwhelmingly support, must be restarted and completed with the utmost urgency! There also must be *no entitlements, no scholarships, no free medical care, no driver's license, and no nothing,* except for a *one-time, one-way trip home* for all illegal immigrants and their families!

Communities within this country which have become home to illegal immigrants and their families must be placed on notice that all transactions involving governmental, educational, medical, or business-related issues will be conducted in the English language only. The creation within this country of a satellite mirror image of Mexico should not and must not be allowed! Any member of the U.S. Congress trying to enact legislation that would assist in the *Mexicanization* of the United States must be immediately recalled and removed from office as quickly as the law will allow.

This is *our country*, a fact that many within this nation have totally lost sight of. Anyone planning to come here illegally, *stay out*! Anyone wanting to come here legally must understand and be required to adapt to our customs and traditions, and not be encouraged or allowed to impose theirs upon us!

DISTORTING THE REAL TRUTH

Have you read any good books lately? When you think about it, many good books we grew up reading for various reasons—such as to feel good about ourselves, for religious enrichment, or to learn about this great nation—have been relegated to a status of unimportance. Perhaps the most targeted of all of these wonderful books is the good book itself, the holy bible.

Just ask yourself when was the last time liberal segments of our government encouraged anyone to read the bible, or self-improvement books, or books about the real honest-to-goodness U.S. history. The very sources that revealed to us what made this nation great have been shoved to the back shelf. Liberals now tell us that promoting anything having to do with the Christian religion should be de-emphasized because it might make certain groups of people feel uncomfortable. We are told that many parts of our history should be removed because they show certain groups in an uncomplimentary light.

Do we really want to forget that which is real in the interest of being "politically correct"? If we do not put a stop to this nonsense, and quickly, we will not be able to recognize this country in the very near future.

HAVE WE REALLY LOST OUR MINDS?

Look around you. Is it so hard to find things in this country that are worth protecting? If we do not come to our senses, and very soon, this nation will have the life expectancy of an ice cube in a hot frying pan.

We have evolved from a nation whose people loved it so much that when the Japanese attacked Pearl Harbor in 1941, the lines at military induction centers stretched for blocks. Young men lied about their age so they could join up to fight our enemy. Women traded in their brooms, mops, and aprons to fill the factory jobs vacated by the men who went off to war. There were paper drives and scrap metal drives, and people accepted food and gas rationing as normal sacrifices of a wartime economy.

Today, there seems to be very little evidence of the abundance of patriotism that was found everywhere during World War II. This patriotism was found among the young, the old, the rich, and the poor, and for many, nothing was going to keep them from defending their country. Americans enjoyed living the good life, and Americans were not going to let anyone or anything keep them from defending their country!

Many people today have redefined what "the good life" means. To some it means "If it feels good, do it," or "It isn't cheating if you don't get caught." Too many of our younger generation have turned their backs on pursuing a good education, and instead they spend their time in and out of trouble. Some people feel that going to work means going downtown to pick up their welfare check or food stamps. The idea of finding a real job that can feed their families with their pride intact is simply not part of their agenda. To many young people today, the thought of serving in the military is beneath their dignity. They are willing to take whatever this country has to give to them, but they feel no obligation at all to defend their freedom and our way of life, if called upon to do so.

Is there really anyone in this country that would rather live somewhere else? The only real threats to America are the disrespectful and ungrateful attitudes of those who have failed to appreciate what this unique nation has to offer. It would not take long for most people to realize that the grass is not always greener on the other side of the fence. It takes a very special person to appreciate America, but unfortunately, not everyone who calls themselves an American understands what it really means to be an American. If someone does not understand or does not care what a lot of good people had to go through to establish this nation, then they will never understand what it means to be an American, and they do not deserve to be called an American! They want to enjoy the abundance of opportunities this nation offers, but if they are called upon to defend this nation by serving in its military, they quickly lose sight of what being an American truly means. Real Americans never question the call to defend their country. Phony Americans never answer it.

This is America: love it or leave it!

HOW DID WE GET HERE?

When studying the history of America in our schools today, we have the advantage of knowing what actually happened. Our situation is somewhat the reverse of that of our forefathers. They knew where they wanted to go, but they weren't sure just how to get there. On the other hand, we think we know where we are, but far too many of us don't have the slightest idea how we got here.

This land was not unlike most any other land on this Earth at the time our forefathers settled here, but it was what they did after they arrived that proved to be the difference, and made America what it is today. Most of us could not begin to describe or appreciate what our ancestors went through to give us the freedoms we now enjoy, and even with our many faults, this is still the best nation on the face of this Earth. We can only hope that what we leave for our future generations is at least as good as that which our forefathers and ancestors left in our care. They deserve nothing less.

Too many Americans are so lackadaisical about what it really means to be an American. We complain that the millions of illegal immigrants come into this country to take advantage of all of the free programs that the United States has to offer; but in all honesty, far too many present-day Americans are here for that very same reason, and are unwilling to give anything back in return. Could it be possible that these immigrants, both legal and illegal, have a better understanding about what we really have here than do many of our own citizens? We can all look at a great athlete and long for the chance to trade places with them, but most of us have no clue as to what that great athlete had to do to get to where they are. It most assuredly did not take place overnight, and certainly did not happen without a great deal of dedication, work, sacrifice, and pain. And, it most assuredly did not come as a result of some government entitlement program.

Thanks to the liberals in charge of today's educational system, who now see the real history of America as being *politically incorrect*, the majority of today's young people may never know or appreciate what really happened to get us where we are. They haven't been introduced to what it means to be a real American, and if they don't have the right stuff inside of them, they will never recognize it when it is introduced to them. It isn't any wonder that they feel no true allegiance to this country, or that they feel any urgency to put on their nation's uniform to defend our way of life. They do not understand the opportunities to be gained through obtaining an education. All they are taught is the *pie in the sky* dreams offered by today's liberal politicians.

The right to be an American is something that not everyone appreciates or deserves. Let us hope that we don't wake up one day to find ourselves under the oppressive rule of some tyrannical dictator, and then innocently ask ourselves, "How did we get here?"

WHAT HAPPENED TO THE TRUTH?

There is no doubt that this nation is not perfect, although regardless of just how short we may have fallen in our attempts at perfection, the United States is the closest thing to perfection this old world has ever seen, or likely ever will see. Sure, we have our problems, but many of those problems are a result of someone trying to make life a little better for someone else, whether it is to benefit the wealthy, the poor, the men, the women, the children, the elderly, the majority, or some minority. Even to its own detriment at times, this has always been a nation that has tried to help others, but as we have all too often seen, those we are trying to help often show their gratitude by trying to destroy us.

What is it about the wonderful history of this great nation that makes the younger generation of today feel that it is no longer important to learn how we got to where we are? Are we going to follow the lead of some of our European neighbors and stop teaching the real history of this nation, or quit celebrating some of our own religious holidays because that might go against the traditional religious teachings of certain other groups who have recently migrated to the United States? Don't look now, but this is already happening here.

This is a nation where people from less-than-royal bloodlines can become leaders in government, education, business, or industry. This is a nation where a wealthy plantation owner from Virginia, or a backwoods young lawyer from Illinois could ascend to the office of president. This is a nation where a young black educator from the South could experiment with various uses of the simple peanut that would radically improve agriculture within this nation forever. This is a nation where a grade-school dropout could become the greatest inventor that the world has ever seen.

Many of the blessings this nation has enjoyed throughout its history can be easy to understand, while some seem to have been hidden behind the disguise of the institution of slavery. While no one can reason that slavery itself was anything but an evil institution that was utilized to satisfy the enormous agricultural demands of this rapidly growing young nation, it allowed many people who would have otherwise spent their entire lives in the heat, hunger, and genocide of sub-Saharan Africa to eventually become American citizens. Many people will not allow themselves to look at this statement as being anything but racist, but that narrow-minded viewpoint itself is one of the major reasons this nation either cannot or will not resolve the issues of race. But, if those citizens of this country today who are of African ancestry were to give an honest and well-thought-out answer to one question, it would go a very long way toward helping resolve many of the racial issues this nation faces today. That question is, "Are you better-off living as you are today in America, or living the lifestyle of those who call one of the sub-Saharan African nations their home?" What we refer to as living in poverty in this nation today would be considered a very good lifestyle in many other nations of the world.

What is so bad about the United States of America that has caused certain segments of our society to attempt to turn this great nation into a mirror image of those weaker countries of this world? Why should we want to unconditionally open our borders to the thousands or even millions of people who are so desperate to flee their own homeland, but who at the same time want to remake the United States into an identical likeness of the very country from which they are fleeing? If this nation is so much better than the one they are running away from, why then would they not want to learn and adopt English as their language; or learn all about the history of this great nation they are about to call home; or agree to honor and follow our laws; or to do everything that they possibly can to blend into our American society? Perhaps an even more important question would be, "Why are some so-called Americans willing to allow the United States to become North Mexico?" If they are so unhappy living in the United States, they should go somewhere else where they can feel much more comfortable.

Has the true American "silent majority" finally decided to give up this great nation to anyone who thinks he or she is entitled to it just because they are here? Have we finally decided to allow the *Church of Political Correctness* to dictate how we must turn our backs on our own traditional values and beliefs, and become more concerned about not upsetting the traditions of outsiders? Have we finally decided that all of the hard work and bloodshed, which our ancestors endured to establish this great nation as the only true democracy this world has ever seen, was useless and should be thrown out like yesterday's dirty bathwater?

Surely not all of the people who call themselves Americans have lost their true sense of pride in actually being Americans. Have we decided that it is time to turn over the many riches of this great land to those who place no value on education, hard work, or preserving the traditions and beliefs upon which this great nation was founded? What will this nation look like in the next ten to twenty-five years? Will this nation cease to exist? If so, this world is doomed to the fate of all those other nations that allowed their values and beliefs to become compromised.

The United States of (Un-Hyphenated) America

The thought has often occurred to me that the only ones who pay any attention to what I might have to say in these letters to the editor, is me. I do feel, however, that if I have an opinion about an issue, and if I feel strongly enough about that issue, I should express my opinion. Using this thought as my inspiration, I would like to voice my opinion on a matter which I have felt very strongly about for a long, long time.

As citizens of this great nation, we are all Americans—first, last, and always! We are not *British-Americans, French-Americans, Italian-Americans, Irish-Americans, Chinese-Americans,* or *African-Americans.* We are, and should very proudly be, *Americans,* period! It is long overdue that we drop the descriptive terms that have done much more to separate us as a people than they ever did to bring us together or unite us. We will never achieve our true strength as a nation if we continue to show descriptive individuality instead of acknowledging that we are one nation, and cease giving in to those who would keep us forever divided and separated. There will always be certain things that separate us. Whether it is ancestry, wealth, occupation, education, physical or mental abilities, or beauty or the lack thereof, the most important thing for the continued survival of this great nation is for each and every one of us to proudly proclaim that we are *Americans,* pure and simple.

Our ancestors who first came to these shores did so for various reasons—some good, and some not so good. We are all different, each and every one of us, but regardless of the reasons for our being here, we are here, and this is our home. If there are those who feel that life for them would have been so much better if they had never lived in this wonderful country, or if they wish to return to the land of their ancestors, then maybe they need to exercise their right to do so. For those of us who do understand and appreciate just how fortunate and lucky we are to call ourselves Americans, while at the same time understanding that there are many others in this world who would gladly do so if only given the chance, we should thank whatever god we worship that we were indeed chosen to be Americans, not hyphenated Americans, but Americans, one and all!

The Meaning of Success

Success evidently means different things to different people. In the formative days of this nation, decisions were commonly made with both the immediate and the long-term welfare of the nation as major considerations. On the other side of this coin, success to some means *profit at all costs.* The greed of our own American oil companies has allowed our position as the world energy leader to become that of a follower; a follower of China, Russia, Mexico, and Venezuela, in addition to the Middle Eastern countries. We have watched as American oil companies such as Exxon-Mobil continue to resist investing the bulk of their enormous profits back into research and development of alternative fuel sources. Their leadership seems to live by the creed that since they will likely be long gone by the time that the petroleum supply finally runs dry, they will take their share of the profits now and leave the solution to these problems for those who will be in charge when that time finally arrives. While the foreign oil kingpins have been working long and hard in their efforts to overtake the United States as leader of world energy markets, it appears that our own oil company executives have chosen to sell out, not only the future of our children, but also the future of their own children and grandchildren, for the sake of their own immediate personal financial gains.

There is plenty of blame to be passed around here, and oil company execs are not the only ones guilty of selling America down the river. Environmentalists and liberal politicians must accept a huge portion of the blame for this, but sadly, the lion's share of blame for this travesty falls directly into the lap of the naïve and lackadaisical Americans who have sat back and allowed this to happen.

Success should not be dictated solely by immediate rewards, but also by the promise of the future security of one's nation, and that of civilization itself. Although the meaning of success is different for different people, I cannot imagine a definition that is more fitting than "those lucky enough to be called Americans."

WHAT IS A CITIZEN?

What does it mean to be a citizen of this or any country? Far too many people residing in the United States see citizenship as a one-way street, and in doing so have missed out on one of the true pleasures of knowing what it means to be a true citizen of America. It is easy to accept all of the benefits and privileges that come with living in this wonderful land, but too few residents of America today are willing to do their part to see that this nation continues to be able to provide those same benefits and privileges that they have long enjoyed. Part of being a citizen is enjoying the feeling of pride in knowing that you have done something for your country, whether it be serving in the military, or just being a good citizen for your community. At some point in the history of any nation, there comes a time when it becomes necessary for all able-bodied citizens to take the bat into their own hands and step up to the plate, and start swinging. Those who answer their nation's call in the defense of liberty share a common bond that cannot be understood by those who do not accept that same responsibility. Some of those patriots have given their lives to protect our freedom and our way of life, and those who do not appreciate or honor those sacrifices do not deserve to be called Americans.

What is so terribly wrong with doing whatever is necessary to defend this country and our way of life? One thing that has become abundantly clear is that far too many people have fallen into the trap of listening to and following the advice of misguided *career politicians* who do not feel that this nation is worth defending. Many brave American patriots have given their lives to defend the values and beliefs that this nation has held dear for almost 250 years, and this is a fact that those liberal legislators have missed all along. Americans who see our way of life as truly worth defending deserve much better than to have their principles attacked by those who would display their false pride in this nation. Those politicians have lost touch with, or never learned in the first place, what it means to be a real American. Very few, if any, of these politicians have ever worn our nation's uniform, and they cannot even begin to understand the deep, abiding feeling of pride that only a true patriot can enjoy.

A true American citizen understands that along with citizenship comes certain responsibilities. Among these is recognizing the importance of abiding by our nation's laws. A true citizen knows the value of obtaining an education. A true citizen understands that unless he takes part in the political process, if only to vote, at the very least he has weakened or even forfeited his right to complain when things do not go as he would like. A true citizen recognizes the fact that paying a fair tax is a privilege of living in a free country, and that it is his responsibility to try to elect legislators who share his goals. A true citizen recognizes the legal rights of other citizens, even if those rights seem to be in contrast to his own goals. A true citizen understands his responsibility to raise and support his family. A true citizen understands his responsibility to defend his country if called upon to do so. A true citizen understands that the well-being of the nation comes before the well-being of the individual, and that within a system of true cooperation, these work hand in hand for the benefit of all.

Citizenship is a privilege, and not an entitlement. Real citizens understand that fact, while phony citizens never will. Be truly proud to be an American.

THE OVERLOOKED DUTY OF CITIZENS

The Declaration of Independence was, in a manner of speaking, a *Dear John* letter to the King of England. It served as justification by the patriots and inhabitants of the British colonies in North America to divorce themselves from what they felt was their harsh and unjust treatment by Great Britain. This very same rationale should be applied to our own government if it totally ignores the wishes of the majority of its people.

The fourth paragraph of this great document reads as follows: "But when a long train of abuses and usurpations, pursuing invariably the same Object evinces a design to reduce them under absolute Despotism, it is their right, it is their duty, to throw off such Government, and to provide new Guards for their future security." In plain and simple language, it states that when we send someone to Congress, we intend for them to perform in a way that will benefit the majority of the people. If they lose sight of this objective, then it becomes our duty to throw them out and replace them with someone who will do what we send them there to do! This could mean by a method as simple as our vote, but it could also mean that it may become necessary to take other measures to achieve the desired results. These people are elected to be *servants of the people*, and when they lose sight of this, it is time to send them home. Somewhere along the way, this presumption has been lost in translation, and our entire government has become a dysfunctional bureaucracy. To find evidence of this, just look at how the Democrats react when the commander in chief is a member of the opposition party. They whimper, cry, and constantly look for ways to belittle the president of the United States. What happens to a person once they have been elected to the U.S. Congress? They are originally consumed with the noble idea of helping and improving the circumstances of their own constituents who sent them there. Unfortunately, those who become long-standing members of this very select and elite fraternity develop into something that is not very productive to the majority of the general public. After butting their heads against the proverbial stone wall while trying to introduce or support legislation that would be beneficial to their own constituents, they discover that in order to achieve any success at all, they must learn how to "play the game," and before they know it, they have become just like all of those other members of their hallowed fraternity. The very insightful Declaration of Independence can also be applied to what many citizens consider to be a completely nonfunctioning government in our own country. The fourth paragraph of the Declaration of Independence states that it is the duty of the people of a government to remove that government, or a member of that government, if they do not perform their duties as directed by the people.

As is the case with most documents describing a nation's laws and the rights of its people, the U.S. Constitution is open to many different interpretations. However, it is the duty of a citizen to become familiar with those government documents, because if we do not know and understand what our rights are, we are fair game to the interpretation of anyone.

OUR NATION'S DESTINY

Who will control the destiny of this nation? Studies indicate that if current trends continue, within the next twenty to thirty years the population of this country will be dominated by Hispanics and/or Muslims. By that time, one or both of those groups will have the population numbers necessary to vote into office the president of their choosing, and one who no doubt will propose laws needed to advance their own agenda. Those within this country who are of European or African ancestry could easily find themselves part of fading and persecuted minorities.

Consider what these changes would mean for the country that we and our ancestors have called home for centuries. What will become of freedom and democracy? Will the Congress in place at that time listen to the majority and legislate a national language, perhaps Spanish rather than English? Will our constitution be amended to mandate a national religion—Islam, for example?

In the interest of our very survival as a nation, we must recognize that the true definition of *political correctness* has become "the conscious effort by a nation's people to replace proven traditions, values, and beliefs with meaningless and hollow substitutes that promote a false atmosphere of good feeling among its people." *Political correctness* is quickly proving itself to be the long-anticipated but much-feared self-destruction of this nation.

We Americans have long turned our heads while a deliberate but clouded transition has been taking place right under our very noses. We have allowed such villainous organizations as the ACLU to diminish the role of Christianity, while at the same time throwing open the doors to religious movements such as Islam to gain an ever-increasing foothold within this country. While many have remained silent, the ACLU, sometimes referred to as *Satan's Law Firm*, has become the greatest enemy to the true American spirit we have ever encountered. They have masqueraded as a watchdog for minorities, the poor, and the misunderstood, while at the same time fighting to eliminate the very principles, values, and traditions that have made this nation strong. I wonder if the ACLU has ever given any thought to their fate under Muslim rule.

So who really controls our destiny? Our destiny is still very much within our own hands, but only to the extent that we quickly recognize who our true enemies really are and immediately put plans into place to destroy those whose intentions are to destroy us. Some will criticize those of us who would even suggest such possibilities, but to be honest, this is one time when I truly hope my suspicions will indeed be proven wrong.

AMERICAN PEOPLE AREN'T STUPID

Why does our government feel that the American people are grossly incapable of taking care of themselves without the heavy-handed interference of a bumbling government bureaucracy? American know-how has proven, time and time again, to be much more efficient than government in getting things done, so why do we continue to allow our government to interfere in every step of our lives? By the same token, our government has proven over and over that the best way to destroy a good thing is to turn it over to our government to operate. Examples are numerous, but just to mention a few, look at how government control has almost single-handedly destroyed our educational system, Amtrak, and has squandered billions upon billions of American taxpayer dollars in its attempt to *fix* everything.

Our government feels that it can better operate big business, such as financial institutions, oil companies, U.S. automakers, and other members of our free-enterprise system. But when we take a closer look at problems within those industries, it becomes apparent that massive and outrageous government intervention was the cause of the majority of their problems to begin with. Just ask yourself this very simple question: Would you feel more comfortable if your government had total control of your family's everyday life, or would you prefer control being left to your discretion? Government was originally intended to help in times of natural disasters, and later for our national defense. Over time the role of government became expanded to what we see today, where government wants to control every single aspect of our lives. Big government does not necessarily mean better government. When given too much authority, government tends to suffocate human initiative and ambition, and the nation's productivity becomes stagnated.

During the most recent 250 years or so, this land we call America has been witness to many changes. Many of these changes have been good for the majority of the people of this nation, but some of them were actually intended to destroy the very ideals and principles upon which this nation was founded. From the time our founding fathers began to put their ideas on paper (first as the Articles of Confederation, followed shortly thereafter by the U.S. Constitution, the most wonderful document ever devised as a design for government, and followed almost immediately by the Bill of Rights), this nation has evolved into what has become known as the beacon of democracy. Our people enjoy a vast array of freedoms never before seen in any other nation. Why, then, does it seem that we have so many enemies wanting to destroy our American way of life, not only from abroad, but also from right here at home?

Over the centuries of our existence as a nation, we certainly have endured more than our share of growing pains, but we have also enjoyed an economy whose strength has never been equaled by any other nation. We have been eager to share our discoveries and technology with the rest of the world, and we are usually the first nation to come to the aid of our neighbors during times of natural disasters or when they are attacked by hostile enemies.

This nation was originally populated by groups of people from very different backgrounds. Most of them were, in a manner of speaking, discards from their countries of origin. Some were farmers, some were merchants, some were laborers, some were poor, and there were even some who could be described as wealthy. Most of them, however, not only had talent and skills, but they also had a burning desire to succeed. Collectively this was a group of people who saw coming to this new land as their one chance in a lifetime to accomplish their dreams, something that had proven to be impossible in their homelands. These were the original Americans, and they were to be followed by many others who had the same goals and dreams. For these pioneers, this country was very special to them. They understood that this wonderful land would deliver its many riches to them, but in the form of opportunities, not as handouts or entitlements.

The question now becomes, how do we put America back on track while fighting attempts of those who feel no allegiance to this great nation, and who, if allowed to continue on their present course, will destroy this country? Believe it or not, the answer to this question is very simple. We must not allow the liberal minority in this country to dictate the course of this nation!

This nation is always going to take care of its people, and without government entitlement programs as proposed by liberal legislators. Those who cannot take care of themselves due to physical or mental disability could be helped through certain government programs. Many of these can receive help from within their own communities, from business, civic, or religious organizations, for instance. If businesses were allowed to function within their own parameters, our economy could grow in ways only dreamed of previously.

Our educational system would develop and produce leaders in every field under the direction of leaders within the education community itself, if allowed to do so free of the heavy and burdensome hand of incompetent government intervention. Our health-care system could work in cooperation with the insurance industry to ensure that the world's best medical care was made available to all of our citizens at reasonable cost, and again, without government interference. The American people are the envy of the rest of the world, whether they will admit it or not.

TAKE BACK AMERICA

Remember the Revolutionary War, the War of 1812, the Civil War, World War I, World War II, Korea, Vietnam, and Iraq? Many brave Americans fought and died on these and other battlefields, both here and abroad, to preserve democracy and the unique American way of life. Many American colonists risked their own lives to help establish this nation. Early legal immigrants to this nation brought their trades, skills, and a strong desire to become part of this unique new nation. When and where did things start to fall apart and change?

Remember burning draft cards; running off to Canada to avoid the draft; street riots with burning vehicles and buildings; giving the drug culture a try; Jane Fonda going to Hanoi to support the enemy; becoming an American Taliban; Hollywood's obsession with vulgar, violent, and immoral movies and lifestyles; radical educators promoting un-American ideologies; sanctuary cities harboring illegal aliens; refusal to allow ROTC on campuses; condoning gay insults at Christian ceremonies; ordering the removal of the Ten Commandments from public facilities; banning Christian celebrations of Christmas during holidays; allowing government-funded non-Christian religious customs and practices in public schools and facilities; belittling Christian principles under the pretense of appearing to be *politically correct*; feeling guilty for insisting that immigrants coming into this country do so legally instead of illegally; saying that you support our troops, while at the same time condemning the very values and principles for which these troops are fighting; and mistakenly giving credibility to the idea that you can strengthen the weak by weakening the strong. Although some of these actions might arguably be considered by some to be an attempt to prove a point, the majority of these actions are nothing more than veiled and cowardly attempts to undermine conservative American traditions and values. In short, we have turned our backs upon the very things that made this nation strong in the first place!

What does it mean for someone to be a true, dyed-in-the-wool American? Just as it is not intended for everyone to be wealthy and successful, or a great athlete, or a genius, it is also obviously not intended for just anyone to be a real American, and there are numerous people in this nation proving this point to be true every day. Many people do not seem to realize or even comprehend that this nation is indeed unique among all of the other nations this world has ever seen. It takes a special individual to appreciate and accept what it means to live the Great American Dream. It is very easy for anyone to just sit back and be the recipient of the many advantages that comes from living in this most wonderful of all nations, but to be the type of person that will assume that role and responsibility of a *true American patriot* is what separates real Americans from the fair-weather Americans.

I am not trying to say that someone is not a true American just because they believe differently than me, but if someone constantly turns his back upon the traditions, values, and beliefs that originally made this nation strong, then yes, I am saying that they are not real Americans. These people would not be loyal citizens no matter what country they called home. Many of these people are willing and happy to take whatever this nation has to give them, but they are anything but willing to accept the responsibility that goes along with doing those things that are necessary to be a real American, especially if that means making any personal sacrifices. Those wonderful young men and women serving in our military, both now and in times past, are prime examples of what it means to be real American heroes.

In this country we have far too many people who see no advantage in working for a living or holding down a real job; those who feel no responsibility to support and become parents to children they bring into this world; those who feel no shame in using, buying, or selling illegal drugs; those who do not feel a certain pride when they see our nation's flag; those who see no value in obtaining an education, and who interfere with those students who are trying to learn; and those who have the warped idea that the true enemies of this nation are actually their heroes. Those at best are fair-weather Americans, and at worse traitors who will call themselves real Americans when it is convenient for them to do so, but who will back away when the situation actually calls someone to step up and get the job done.

Believe it or not, there are still those in this nation who appreciate the tradition and responsibility of military service to their country. They respect the office of the president of the United States of America even though they may not agree with the current office holder's political views. There are still many who feel pride in putting their hands over their hearts and repeating the Pledge of Allegiance, or reverently uttering *The Lord's Prayer*. We still have some legislators, although there are far too few, who see their role as working within the intended framework of our constitutional government, and who understand the meaning of "separation of powers," and who will work to ensure that our government functions in the best interest of its people.

Are there still very many real Americans around? Yes, fortunately for those who are fair-weather Americans, there are still a lot of people who live their lives daily as real Americans, although not as many as this nation will need in order to survive in a world that seems bent upon its own destruction. Although it is true that radical Islam is definitely a dangerous enemy of democracy and to any nation that embraces democracy, those within this country who do not take this threat seriously present just as much of a danger as does radical Islam.

Contrary to a popular belief, there certainly is no shame in being a real American, just as there is no shame in being a real Christian, and it is time that all real Americans and all real Christians stand up for what they truly believe in. When the rank-and-file American citizen finally realizes the importance of these facts and accepts their own personal responsibility to this unique nation as a real American, then, and only then, will the United States of America return to its rightful place as *the* dominant nation on Earth.

Then, and only then, can we *take back America*.

OUR LAST CHANCE

Have we gone too far toward anarchy to correct this mess? Has crime gotten so out of control that a strong policing effort cannot rein it back in? Have our entitlement programs become so firmly entrenched as a way of life in this country that reestablishing a strong work ethic cannot replace dependency with ambition?

We are quickly losing the uniqueness of this nation, which was what once set us apart from any other nation on this Earth. The things that once made America great have become so compromised that we are in grave danger of becoming just another country, with a government that seeks total control over everything, an economy whose leadership has lost sight of what makes an economy strong, and a people who have replaced ambition and the human spirit with dependence upon government as their way of life. How long until we more closely resemble those Second or Third World countries than the strongest nation on Earth, which we once were? We may soon reach the point of no return where that once-great American spirit could be lost forever.

There are some very hard and sensitive decisions that need to be made. First, we must return to the strengths that made us unique and build upon them until they are once again important to us. In the beginning, this nation received its inner strength from a strong belief in God, and when we lost sight of that, we started losing our core values and became so tolerant of everyone else's beliefs at the expense of maintaining our own. The guilt-induced theory of *political correctness* must be totally and permanently removed from our vocabulary! We must understand the importance of such terms as education, ambition, drive, emotion, pride, nationalism, and patriotism to our history. Returning to these values will be a very important step toward becoming the nation we once were.

The next phase will be very difficult for some; because it is going to force many of us to perform a *reality check* within our hearts and minds, which some of us will likely not be capable of doing. We must be willing to recognize those things that have weakened us as a nation, looking at both the strong and weak points within each one of us and within each race of our people, and we must do so without feeling hurt or intimidated by what we find. We can no longer allow guilt of the long-ago institution of slavery to dictate a large portion of our social and economic policies. We must get over past history and come together as one great people with a common goal. There are both strengths and weaknesses within each person and each race of people within this nation. If we cannot recognize what those strengths and weaknesses really are, build upon those strengths and work to eliminate those weaknesses, we may lose our final chance to once again be that great and unique nation our forefathers envisioned.

THE GREATEST PRESIDENTIAL SPEECH

I received by e-mail this message of how wonderful it would be if we were to hear our American president, Democrat or Republican, deliver the following speech. Do we have anyone who has the intestinal fortitude to make such a profound announcement? Wouldn't it be great if we did? Every time I read this, it sends chills up and down my spine to think of the possibilities with a leader such as this. To here our American president deliver this speech would indeed be truly wonderful!

My fellow Americans,

As you all know, the defeat of the Iraqi regime has been completed. Since Congress does not want to spend any more money on this war, our mission in Iraq is complete.

This morning I gave the order for a complete removal of all American forces from Iraq. This action will be complete within thirty days. It is now time to begin the reckoning.

Before me, I have two lists. One list contains the names of countries that have stood by our side during the Iraq conflict. This list is short. The United Kingdom, Spain, Bulgaria, Australia, and Poland are some of the countries listed there.

The other list contains everyone not on the first list. Most of the world's nations are on that list. My press secretary will be distributing copies of both lists later this evening.

Let me start by saying that effective immediately, foreign aid to those nations on List 2 ceases immediately and indefinitely. The money saved during the first year alone will pretty much pay for the costs of the Iraq war. Then, every year thereafter, it'll go to our Social Security system so it won't go broke in twenty years.

The American people are no longer going to pour money into Third World hellholes and watch those government leaders grow fat on corruption.

Need help with a famine? Wrestling with an epidemic? Call France.

In the future, together with Congress, I will work to redirect this money toward solving the vexing social problems we still have at home. On that note, a word to terrorist organizations: Screw with us, and we will hunt you down and eliminate you and all your friends from the face of the Earth.

Thirsting for a gutsy country to terrorize? Try France or maybe China.

I am ordering the immediate severing of diplomatic relations with France, Germany, and Russia. Thanks for all your help, comrades. We are retiring from NATO as well. *Bonne chance, mes amies.*

I have instructed the mayor of New York City to begin towing the many UN diplomatic vehicles located in Manhattan with more than two unpaid parking tickets to sites where those vehicles will be stripped, shredded, and crushed. I don't care about whatever treaty pertains to this. You creeps have tens of thousands of unpaid tickets. Pay those tickets tomorrow or watch your precious Benzes, Beemers, and limos be turned over to some of the finest chop shops in the world. I love New York.

A special note to our neighbors. Canada is on List 2. Since we are likely to be seeing a lot more of each other, you folks might want to try not pissing us off for a change.

Mexico is also on List 2. Its president and his entire corrupt government really need an attitude adjustment. I will have a couple extra thousand tanks and infantry divisions sitting around. Guess where I am going to put 'em? Yep, border security.

Oh, by the way, the United States is abrogating the NAFTA treaty—starting now.

We are tired of the one-way highway. Immediately, we'll be drilling for oil in Alaska—which will take care of this country's oil needs for decades to come. If you're an environmentalist who opposes this decision, I refer you to List 2 above; pick a country and move there.

It is time for America to focus on its own welfare and its own citizens. Some will accuse us of isolationism. I answer them by saying, "Darn tootin'."

Nearly a century of trying to help folks live a decent life around the world has only earned us the undying enmity of just about everyone on the planet. It is time to eliminate hunger in America. It is time to eliminate homelessness in America. To the nations on List 1, a final thought: Thank you, guys. We owe you, and we won't forget.

To the nations on List 2, a final thought: You might want to learn to speak Arabic.

God bless America. Thank you, and good night.

If you can read this, thank a teacher. If you are reading it in English, thank a soldier!

MILITARY

Rarely are we asked to speak before a group to honor those fallen veterans who made the ultimate sacrifice in defense of this nation. The following is the text of the speech I delivered to a gathering of Cherokee Village, Arkansas, residents and guests at the Memorial Day celebration on May 28, 2007. This was one of the proudest moments of my life.

MEMORIAL DAY, MAY 28, 2007

It is truly an honor for me to speak to you today as we honor our fallen heroes of all wars and conflicts, both past and present.

Memorial Day is a time for Americans to reconnect with our history and our core values in honoring those who made the ultimate sacrifice by giving their lives for the ideals we all cherish and hold dear. Who can forget the inspirational challenge of President John F. Kennedy, during his one and only inaugural address, when he urged Americans to "ask not what your country can do for you; ask what you can do for your country." More than a million American service members have died in the wars and conflicts this nation has fought since the first colonial soldiers took up arms in 1776 in their fight for independence, and each and every one of these brave Americans we honor today has fulfilled JFK's request to the maximum. Each person who died during those conflicts was a loved one cherished by family and friends, and each one was a loss to his or her community and to this nation.

The first observance of this special day was born out of compassion and empathy in 1863, amidst the anguish and turmoil of our own Civil War. While this war was raging, grieving mothers, wives, and other loved ones in Columbus, Mississippi, were placing flowers on the graves of their own fallen Confederate soldiers when they noticed that the nearby graves of Union soldiers were dusty, unattended, and overgrown with weeds. Even while grieving for their own fallen soldiers, these compassionate Confederate women understood that these dead Union soldiers were also the cherished loved ones of their own families and communities far away. They then began to clear the tangled brush and mud from those graves as well as from graves of their own soldiers, and they laid flowers on them too.

Soon the tradition of a Decoration Day for the graves of fallen soldiers began to spread. On May 5, 1866, with the Civil War finally over, Henry Welles of Waterloo, New York, closed his drugstore and suggested that all other shops in town also close for a day to honor all soldiers killed in the Civil War, both Union and Confederate alike. This was a gesture aimed at healing and reconciliation in a land that had been ripped apart by this conflict. Sixteen years later, in 1882, the nation observed its first official Memorial Day, a day set aside to remember and honor the sacrifice of those who died in all of our nation's wars.

For decades, Memorial Day was a day in our nation when stores closed and communities gathered together for a day of parades and other celebrations with a patriotic theme. Memorial Day meant ceremonies at cemeteries around the country, speeches, the laying of wreaths, and the playing of *Taps,* all done in honor of those who had given their lives in service to their country. In some places, these ceremonies continue, as we see here today. Those of us present at this event today remember and recognize the true meaning of Memorial Day as we gather to honor our fallen heroes. We also understand that on Memorial Day, we honor the ideals and values those fallen heroes stood for and died defending.

Today, America is busy finding new ways to pleasure itself, new ways to avoid responsibility, and new ways to destroy the family and isolate and marginalize those who call for morality and personal responsibility. On this most solemn holiday, we must stop and consider the great sacrifices that others have made so that we may enjoy the freedom and prosperity we have experienced for so long. Let us consider what those valiant warriors were fighting for ... and let us honor each and every one of them with a prayer and a pledge to restore to this nation the honor, the morality, the values, and the love of God for which they so willingly and unselfishly gave their lives. Our true memorial to them will be the nation and the culture we create as a result of their sacrifice. We must ask ourselves, are we really giving them the recognition they deserve?

The words of JFK should resound loudly in the hearts of all Americans, but somehow, they seem to have become lost, not only on some of our recent generations, but also upon some of our legislative leaders who sadly appear to look down on our military, including those now serving in Iraq. Where did the idea come from that military service is not necessary? I honestly believe that one of saddest days in the history of this nation was the day the military draft was abolished. We have seen the young people of today disregard and even disdain the idea of serving in the military. Military service should be viewed as a privilege—no, an honor—for our young people of today. Many of the political issues of this Iraq war today can be traced to the abolishment of the military draft. Problems such as the lack of numbers of our military personnel, the length of each deployment, and the time at home between deployments all could have been solved with a military draft. Is there any reason that those of us here today who have served in our country's military would have been more obligated than the young people of today to serve our country in a time of need? I would hate to think that past generations were more loyal and dedicated to the security of this nation than today's generation might be, because if that is true, then the future of this nation is in serious jeopardy! No one wants to go to war, but if and when the time comes that war is the only option, then if the same pride and love of country does not beat passionately in the hearts of those young people of that day, then that nation is doomed!

Sadly, many Americans have lost their connection with the history of our nation. All too many Americans today view military service as an abstraction, as images seen on television and in the movies. Many even in our own Congress today try to minimize and downplay the important role of our military in a world where ruthless and fanatical murderers would have freedom and democracy totally disappear from the face of the Earth. For a growing percentage of the American people today, Memorial Day has come to mean simply a three-day weekend or a major shopping day. Families might still gather for picnics, but for many of them, the patriotic core—which is the spirit of remembrance—is absent and has long since vanished.

Memorial Day, like the military itself, has been largely cut off from its historic meaning for many Americans. They have forgotten what the military really stands for in our nation's history. Many Americans have no experience with or connection to the military. There are many reasons for this disconnect. We have fewer and fewer veterans to share their stories, and many of our older veterans, especially those from World War II and Korea, tend to be reluctant and do not like to talk about their military experiences. Unlike past periods in our history, the majority of members of Congress today have not served in the military. Many Americans do not have any relatives or even neighbors who serve now or have ever served in the military. In fact, many Americans today have never even met a soldier.

We are living in a time of economic prosperity when threats are not well understood, and when many young people have no personal connection to the military. Today, fewer young people are drawn toward military service. In fact, all services face challenges in reaching their recruiting goals. Nine out of ten high-school students surveyed say they have no interest in serving in the military. ROTC programs in our colleges and universities struggle to sign up cadets to fill the officer ranks, and some of the more liberal colleges and universities have even abolished the ROTC curriculum from their campuses.

We all have heard the stories of our heroes and legends of the past, who did not outwardly seem to be destined for greatness, but whose patriotism come forth when duty called. That was the spirit found in all of the great American heroes that we honor on this special day, and I hope and pray that this same spirit beats in the hearts of those generations upon whom the future of our nation may someday depend.

Memorial Day should not be about swimming, picnics, or ball games. But neither is it an unqualified endorsement of American society as we know it today. These brave soldiers, sailors, airmen, and Marines died protecting their country and what it stood for. They died defending a way of life that they felt was worth dying for ... including their families, children, freedom, morality, values, and responsibility. Each and every one of us should take a moment and look into our own souls to see what we are doing to honor this bloodstained legacy they have left behind. Did those valiant Marines on Iwo Jima make their sacrifice so that the very definition of marriage itself could be altered to include same-sex couples? Did our Revolutionary War heroes who desired independence go into battle for rights that would allow the killing of unborn children? Did men die in the trenches of the Argonne Forest to ensure that any and all mention of God would be forever removed from schools or other public places? Did those who perished at Pearl Harbor on December 7, 1941, do so with the intention of allowing undocumented aliens the same rights and privileges as the citizens of this nation, or those who came here by lawful and legal means?

The picture is not totally bleak, however. Margaret Mead once said, "Never doubt that even a small group of thoughtful and committed citizens can change the world. Indeed, it is the only thing that ever has."

You may not realize the significance of your attendance here today, but in doing so, you are making a statement and doing a very important thing. You are making a difference. You are not forgetting the sacrifices of our military heroes. Let me share with you some other ideas and examples of what people have done to make a difference—to reconnect Americans with their military, past and present.

In May 1996, Carmella LaSpada met a group of schoolchildren on the Mall in Washington DC. She asked them what Memorial Day meant to them. They all paused and then said, "That's the day the swimming pool opens." Ms. LaSpada decided to show these children and others like them just why they are free and who paid for their freedom. She started the "Moment of Remembrance" campaign, her goal being to put the meaning of the word "memorial" back into Memorial Day. She challenged all Americans to observe one minute of silence at exactly 3:00 PM on Memorial Day, as *Taps* plays, to honor those who sacrificed their lives for us.

You know what? That first year, one thousand shopping malls in this country did exactly what she asked on Memorial Day. They announced the moment of silence at 3:00 PM; so did several baseball stadiums, including Yankee Stadium; transportation centers, such as Chicago's O'Hare International Airport, Amtrak, and bus lines; and several amusement parks.

We can all make a difference by our individual acts. And it is important that we do act! It is very important that those of us who do understand the importance of our history, who understand the importance and value of our military, that we act to reconnect the American people to the role our military has played in the astonishing history of this most wonderful nation!

Let us remember and never forget those we are honoring with our presence here today, the airmen, sailors, Marines, and soldiers whose ultimate sacrifice has made this country the greatest nation this world has ever seen. Listen to these words by Charles M. Province as he proclaims the soldier's role in protecting the many freedoms we have long enjoyed:

> It is the Soldier, and not the reporter,
> who has given us Freedom of the Press;
>
> It is the Soldier, and not the poet,
> who has given us Freedom of Speech;
>
> It is the Soldier, and not the campus organizer,
> who has given us the Freedom to demonstrate;
>
> It is the Soldier, and not the lawyer,
> who has given us the right to a fair trial;
>
> And it is the Soldier—who salutes the flag,
> who serves the flag, and
> whose coffin is draped by the flag—
> who allows the protester to burn the flag.

I would ask that we not forget those brave young men and women who are serving in our military service today, and their many sacrifices to make this world a safer place in which to live. Some of you here today have loved ones now serving our country in the name of freedom and democracy, including my own son who is now in his second deployment to Iraq. Let us make sure that these brave men and women do not suffer the same fate as those Vietnam-era veterans who, thanks to an uncommitted and indecisive administration and a liberal media, came home to jeers and threats instead of cheers and fanfare. Some of these brave warriors still hurt very deeply today from the lack of appreciation and respect cast upon them by a misguided and misled public.

Please join me in a moment of silence as we remember all of those who have made the ultimate sacrifice.

In closing, I would like to ask that you please continue to make a difference with your words and actions, and I thank you very much for coming here today!

May God bless our soldiers and this nation.

To Fight or Not to Fight, That Is the Question

Many Americans have honestly struggled with this question: Should we be involved in a war or not? To justify a decision on this matter, we must answer a few basic fundamental questions.

1. Is our national security at risk?
2. Have American lives been lost or endangered due to the deliberate actions of some other person, group of people, or nation?
3. Would the actions of others that would cause us to make a decision to go to war prevent physical or economic damage to the people of this nation should these actions not be responded to?

Assuming that there is justification to take action, what must be done to ensure our best chances for success? The military must be properly funded, trained, and supplied with ample equipment and manpower, even if this means implementing a draft. The military must be ready to confront the enemy with an overwhelming force to complete the objective, destroy the enemy's will to fight, get the job done, and then come home. Once the decision has been made to fight, all bridges to retreat or surrender must be burned! It is victory and nothing else! Anything less is totally unacceptable!

WARS HAVE NO WINNERS

As I read the recent letter to the editor written by one of our World War II veterans, my first thoughts were that he was just another person who hates George Bush. But as I read further, I began to realize that, like my own father, this veteran was one of those proud American heroes who laid his life on the line during World War II, and having survived that war, he understandably hates to see the death and destruction that results from any war. Thanks to that wonderful group of patriots who risked their lives to defeat the true enemies of mankind that threatened the world during their time, we are reading his letter today in English rather than in German or Japanese. I would like to offer a special thank-you to all of our veterans for their service to our country!

Like many reading my letter today, I have also experienced firsthand the feelings of helplessness as I watched my own son deploy twice to the battlefields of Iraq. Although I truly understand and share the frustrations of many others as I watch the events of this Iraq war unfold before my very eyes through daily news accounts, I also realize that this enemy we are fighting in Iraq is every bit as real and every bit as intent upon destroying this nation as were Adolf Hitler and leaders of Japan during World War II. Just as there are reasons to suggest that we are fighting the wrong enemy on the wrong battlefield in Iraq, there is also ample evidence to support the fact that we are the ones who chose this battlefield instead of those radical Muslims who would surely bring death and destruction to our shores. Maybe this war would have been more politically correct and acceptable to the general public had it taken place in the mountains and caves of Afghanistan or Pakistan, but the fact remains unchallenged that since 9/11 these battles have been fought exclusively in the distant lands of those Muslim extremists rather than on our own soil. We now have the luxury of historical documentation to learn what our fate would have been if Adolf Hitler had been victorious in World War II, and from what we have been able to piece together so far about the fate of the unlucky conquests of these radical Muslims, life under Hitler would have been like a walk in the park by comparison.

THE DRAFT, GOOD OR BAD?

For many people, a required military draft is a very divisive issue and summons up nothing but bad thoughts. But when we sit back and honestly look at what the draft did for the many people whose lives were directly affected by it, then maybe, just maybe, it wasn't as bad as many people might think. In a time of war, the value of a military draft is enormous and obvious, but a peacetime draft also has many positive aspects. To what extent this might be relevant would be difficult to determine, but our prison population began to grow at about the same time the military draft was abolished. The cost of maintaining our prisons today might be much less if a significant number of inmates had spent time serving in our military rather than roaming the streets of our cities and towns as unemployed vagrants. A lack of true purpose in life or the need to support a drug habit just might have been replaced with a sense of satisfaction and accomplishment if their time had been spent in the military instead of prison.

To today's young people, the requirement to register for a military draft has negative connotations. The one thing they do not consider is that there are many positive aspects of serving one's country in the military, whether as a volunteer or a draftee. Many men would not have experienced military life except for the draft, and in some cases, certain strengths that had been hidden within them began to surface, strengths that might not have appeared otherwise. Self-discipline, self-esteem, courage under fire, leadership, a willingness to sacrifice for others, patriotism, and a deeper love for one's country are just a few of the strengths that might have remained hidden had it not been for military service. Many relationships, some temporary and some longer lasting, are established as a result of one's time in the military. Many professions in life were a direct result of relationships began while serving in the military.

On a more patriotic note, many people today who do not feel a need to protect or defend their country feel this way because they did not serve in the military, which tends to nurture such feelings. Many men who would not have experienced military life except for the draft would not trade their military experience for anything, even if given the opportunity to do so.

In today's political climate, a large percentage of young people have never served and never plan to serve in their country's military. As a result, many of the same young people show an absence of such traits as self-discipline, patriotism, a sense of belonging, and a feeling of accomplishment that comes from military service. All young people in Israel, both male and female, are required to serve in their country's military service. As a result, a strong sense of love of one's country seems to be somewhat lacking in the youth of America when compared to the youth of Israel.

Just as we seem to have lost some of our strong family values when women left the home for the factories to replace men who had gone off to war during World War II, we also seem to have lost a portion of our once strong tradition of patriotism when required military service was abolished. Many of our leaders today became the people they are as a result of their military service. It is entirely possible that lack of leadership in our government is because very few of them have spent time serving in our military. The direction of our nation during the past fifty years has evolved from one of patriotism into one that is more concerned about being "politically correct." In doing so, we not only have become less respected around the world, but we have also lost some of our *self-respect* as well. We seem to have lost the mental toughness that results from military service, and we very likely will not get it back again until we once again return our national priorities to where they should be: to the defense of this nation.

WAKE UP, AMERICA

This real-life wake-up call may be too realistically violent for young viewers, so you may choose not to allow them to read this article. Real life can be brutal at times, but avoiding the truth can be even more brutal.

In his role as our commander in chief, there is no doubt that George Bush has made mistakes, and perhaps many mistakes, in executing his plans to bring the Iraq war to a successful conclusion. My main complaint about George Bush's approach to fighting this war is that he waited far too long to put his "surge" into action and his plans do not go far enough. Unfortunately, it may be at least two or three years too late, but he has finally put a general in charge who knows what it takes to go after this enemy. If the president and the secretary of defense will allow this man to do what needs to be done, our objective to *win* this war *will be* successfully accomplished. If we are honestly going to use this "last and final" effort to do whatever is necessary to go after and to break the backs of these fanatical Islamic militants, then we must do so with all of the military might and strategic genius we possess! Remember, whether you agree with this war or not, we are not the ones who sent those murderers to our country, to learn to fly our own planes into our own buildings on September 11, 2001, and killing over three thousand innocent Americans.

First, we must forget trying to appease those who are content to remain on the sidelines and spout their *politically correct* slogans, because many of these are the very same ones who have long been systematically giving away our country to anyone and everyone who thinks they are owed something for nothing. Second, President Bush's plan to add 21,000 troops to our forces on the ground in Iraq is like sending twenty-five dollars to the BMW dealership, thinking that this will buy us a brand-new, top-of-the-line BMW. This just won't get the job done. Instead of sending 21,000 troops, why not deploy 100,000 to 150,000 additional troops? Storm in, attack, bomb, and totally annihilate this slithering snake of an enemy whose only goal in their miserable existence is to kill anyone who does not bow down to their barbaric ideology. This is war; it is not a tea party, as some people seem to think. Unfortunately, people do get killed in war, but we must be totally committed to winning this war *over there*, or I promise you, these Islamic fanatics will certainly bring their deadly attacks right here to our doorstep! If anyone really thinks that these murderers will show mercy to anyone after they move their attacks over here, all you need to do is to look at the news every day, and you can see the extent to which these killers will go in carrying out their plans. They don't care if it is women, children, or their own countrymen; they will kill anyone who doesn't follow their warped beliefs of how people should live their lives. They want your life and my life to be as miserable as their own pathetic existence is.

Wake up, America!

DEAR SENATOR PRYOR

This is a letter I sent to Senator Mark Pryor, Democrat from Arkansas, about his position on the *troop surge*.

Dear Senator Pryor,

Thank you for your April 20, 2007 letter replying to my e-mail. If I am reading your letter correctly, it is not the usual form letter, but the message it unfortunately conveys is the typical Democrat-choreographed response to very serious concerns. After reading your response, I ask that you help me to better understand your positions described in this letter, paragraph by paragraph.

Senator Pryor, if your honest position on these issues is as you claim them to be in this letter, I too share your admitted concern for our brave men and women serving in Iraq, as my youngest son is now serving his second deployment there. My problem, as is the case with many Americans who follow the more traditional approach, is that you appear to say one thing, but your support tends to reveal that you follow the beat of a totally different liberal drummer!

In the third paragraph, you repeat the usual Democrat song and dance that you *"Do not support the president's surge plan."* To make your statement more completely honest, you could have also added that you *don't support any plan this president introduces, either now or in the future.* I do agree with you that we must work to turn over responsibility for security and military operations to the Iraqi government ASAP, but that should not include the traditional Democrat *cut and run* tactic, and we must not turn over these operations until the Iraqi government has been given enough time to successfully prepare to handle this role. You also mention in this paragraph that "*The president has decided to move forward with his surge plan despite the will (?) of Congress.*" The last time I checked, the United States Constitution does not require a president to seek the *will of Congress* to execute and implement his operational plans for a congressionally approved war. This Democrat-controlled Congress has consistently shown that it will not support anything this president does, regardless of the nature of his plans or programs. With the president constantly butting heads with a totally uncooperative Congress, he has no alternative but to avoid wasting time on this totally misguided and untrustworthy group, and proceed according to the advice of his trusted military commanders in the field! Put yourself in his place, and ask if you would *not* do the same thing if faced with a totally antagonistic Congress.

In paragraph four, allowing for some necessary safeguards, you and I are in total agreement. I agree that the president should lay out measurable goals for stability in Iraq and provide his plan to achieve those goals, but to a very select and bipartisan Congressional committee that was *under oath* not to *reveal* or *leak* any of this information under penalty of *treason!* But I feel that there are some aspects of wartime preparations that do not need to be, and should not be, made known to unauthorized members of Congress, or to the general public. As the parent of a soldier in Iraq, I am very interested in bringing our troops home as soon as reasonably possible, but not at the risk of compromising our mission and the lives of our troops simply to satisfy the thirst of certain *power-hungry* members of Congress so they can feed their enormous egos. I also feel that there is no need for me to be made aware of certain plans or programs being designed to execute this or any war!

Paragraph five really allows your uncompromising allegiance to the liberal wing of the Democrat Party to come to the surface. You admit that you do not support attempts by this Congress to impose a public timeline on troop withdrawal, using as your reasons the testimony from military commanders in the field and the personal pleas from the families of our brave young men and women that are actually in harm's way. You also mention in paragraph six that you are opposed to public timelines, but then you go on to declare that you supported this bill because it features a montage of funding, which was obviously included to trick the American people into thinking that President Bush, by vetoing this two-faced bill, is turning his back on our troops. How could you offer up this bold-face lie and allow your blind allegiance to this disgraceful group of liberal Democrat traitors to contaminate your duty to your constituents? This president will sign this funding bill once this cowardly and disgraceful *timeline* nonsense is removed, and you know it. The people are much smarter and less blind than liberal Democrats give us credit for being.

If you are indeed opposed to this public timeline, then for once, vote your conscience instead of following the insane and destructive commands of your liberal snake charmers. No one should be opposed to funding our troops; at least no one except the cowardly liberal Democrat traitors in Congress who wave the white flag of surrender disguised behind this *timeline*. Be a man and not a liberal puppet!

ABANDONED/UNATTENDED VEHICLES

I may be missing something, but as the parent of an American serviceman in Iraq, it appears to me that there is a simple solution to a very dangerous problem that faces our brave, young military personnel in Iraq every day. Many injuries and deaths among our military in Iraq are caused by IEDs, or improvised explosive devices. Many of these IEDs are planted and detonated in the large number of abandoned vehicles that line the streets and alleys of Iraq.

My suggestion to help with this problem is to make a public announcement that all vehicles left unattended will be destroyed if not removed, and then give the deadline for this ordinance to be complied with. After this imposed deadline, any vehicles not removed will be destroyed by tank fire, and the debris will be pushed aside to an area that would not be a threat to our troops. If the Iraqi people are not willing to cooperate with our military in dealing with this problem, then they must suffer the consequences. If these vehicles are important to their legitimate owners, then hopefully they will recognize the problem and will see how they can help reduce the violence this way. If the legitimate owners of these vehicles are not willing to help in this situation, then maybe the loss of their vehicles will help them to understand the importance of their compliance.

POLITICS

What do followers of Barack Obama, the Stepford wives, and the citizens of Germany just prior to World War II have in common? Think about it.

THE ONLY ISSUE

Regardless of one's political preference or what any candidate in this presidential race may suggest to be the most important issue of our time, there is only one issue that if not given absolute top priority, no other issue really matters—not health care, not the economy, and certainly not global warming. That issue is our national security!

We can listen to the political jargon from any of these presidential candidates, but as we have learned from past experience, most politicians will say or do anything they feel will get them elected, whether they agree with it or not. The only candidate to put into that hot seat of the White House is the one who will stand firm and not back down in the face of any terrorist threat to this nation. We must ask ourselves if the candidate we support can and will make this tough decision without any hesitation when that time comes.

There is one question we must ask Barack Hussein Obama, and demand that he gives a straight answer instead of his usual dancing-around-the-issue rhetoric, and that question is, "When the time comes, will you have the courage and resolve to pull the trigger on any Islamic government, any rogue terrorist, or any entity representing the ancestral Muslim indoctrination of your childhood, should they pose a threat to this nation?" Although many want to keep this issue totally in the background, this is still a very relevant issue for many people.

For Hillary Clinton the question is, "In the face of an impending attack upon this nation, will you, with conviction, commit our military to action against

127

any threatening enemy without first testing the winds of public opinion before you act?"

The question for John McCain is, *"How will you, as president, order the extraction of urgent, vital, and time-sensitive security information concerning an impending attack upon this nation from a captured terrorist who you are convinced has this information?"*

None of these candidates have yet indicated that they are willing to make these necessary but unpopular decisions while the clock is ticking. Talk is cheap! Courage and action are indeed very rare!

Without our national security in the right hands, *nothing else matters!*

GIVE DEMOCRATS A CHANCE

Now that the 2008 election is finally behind us, the time has come for people of both parties to do something that hasn't been done in this country during the past six years. Members of both parties need to put aside their political differences and work together for the well-being of this nation. Democrats say they are now willing to reach across the isle and work with Republicans, but as Democrats have proven many times, their definition of bi-partisanship is, *when Republicans give in and allow Democrats to do exactly as they wish.*

If members of the Republican Party will show the Democrats that good things can happen when members of the minority party actually put out an honest and sincere effort to work with the majority party, our political process can work in the way it was intended to work. Then we will not be the laughingstock of the rest of the world, as President-elect Barack Obama seems to describe us. During the past six years, while Republicans held the majority, Democrats tried to move heaven and earth to find fault with anything and everything the Republican Party did, regardless of whether Democrats actually agreed with it or not. Politics has become so dirty and ineffective because one party was afraid that the other party might look good if their plans actually worked out well.

We are one nation, and we need to work together instead of looking at the other party as the enemy. Both parties share equally in the blame for this nonsense, and our country has suffered tremendously because of the childish antics of these politicians.

Enough is enough! It is time for all politicians to grow up and start acting like the mature adult leaders we hoped we were sending to Washington when we voted them into office, or it will become the duty of the voters to send the entire bunch packing, just as was done to the Republicans in the 2006 election.

This election was not a win for the Democrats as much as it was another wake-up call to *all* politicians. The message was clearly intended to let them know that the real citizens of this nation are totally fed up with their poor performance, or the total lack of performance, by all of these politicians.

CONGRESSIONAL PRIORITIES

We elect people to Congress in the hope that they will sponsor and pass laws for the benefit and protection of the people of this nation. How, then, can this Congress justify spending its limited, valuable time investigating drug usage in professional sports, while not allowing the time necessary to consider extending legislation that would allow for the early detection of possible terrorist plots against this nation? I, for one, think that advance knowledge of any terrorist plots against our country would carry a much higher priority than whether or not Roger Clemens took HGH, or an investigation into the termination of federal prosecutors, which, by the way, was well within the authority of a president who has spent his entire time in office in the crosshairs of this liberal-Democrat-controlled Congress. The priorities of today's legislators are so far out of whack that they defy reason. Their objectives are so transparent that they no longer even attempt to conceal them. It should also be noted that some so-called conservative legislators seem to have forgotten why they were sent to Washington, and have become just as big a part of the problem as have these liberals.

Will it take another national catastrophe for us to finally realize that we are allowing liberal concepts to weaken the very fabric of this nation? Cal Thomas's recent column describes how this very thing has been taking place in England and several European nations for years. They are trying to appease their Islamic invaders by allowing the integration of Islamic Shari law into their own national laws, which is like trying to mix oil with water. He compares this to British prime minister Neville Chamberlain's 1938 conciliatory pact with Adolf Hitler, who agreed not to invade Britain in return for Britain turning its head while Hitler invaded Czechoslovakia, a move only intended to buy more time to build up his own illegal war machine. Chamberlain's appeasement led to World War II. Will modern-day appeasements to Islamic demands bring about similar disastrous results?

The time is long overdue for our Congress to get its priorities straight and stop leading us down this path of false security, and into the arms of the Islamic menace.

Congressional Agenda

Are we getting our money's worth from those we send to Washington? Hindsight seems to expose a real and urgent need for a class designed especially for incoming congressmen and congresswomen, and it probably wouldn't hurt if we required those who have held office for a while to sit in on a refresher course from time to time. It doesn't seem to take very long before they forget what they were sent there to do.

I am not sure just who sets the agenda our Congress will follow, but whoever has this responsibility has been dangerously neglectful in their duties. Look at the rock-bottom negative approval rating for this Congress, which is probably at its lowest in recorded history. Just what exactly does the oath of office taken by members of Congress require them to do? When Congress was spending its time investigating drug usage in professional sports, maybe it should have checked out the effects of those same performance-enhancing drugs for their own use. If anyone needs to have their performance enhanced, it is definitely the members of this Congress.

The voting public needs to find a way to force these legislators to answer questions it has about certain issues; questions that seem to have either been ignored, or responded to with empty or scripted form letters. It seems that once these people ascend to office, they close their doors to direct inquiries by their constituents, and join in playing those political games that take up so much of their time. Once they are forced to actually listen to their constituents, we seem to keep giving them the benefit of the doubt in the hope that their real job will become important to them again. Who knows, maybe they just might start doing the job we sent them there to do in the first place.

Just Who Does Congress Work For?

In the scheme of the typical employer-employee relationship, just who is supposed to work for whom? Does the janitor actually work for the company president, or is it the other way around? Does the private work for the General, or is it the General's place to take his orders from the private? With this thought in mind, should the voters tell our senators and representatives in Congress what we want done, or is it the role of our legislators to tell the voters how they are to live their lives? Get the picture?

As far as Washington DC is concerned, the cart has been before the horse for a long, long time, and as anyone with any common sense can tell you, this just will not work! For years, we have allowed under-performing, undisciplined, and totally out-of-control legislators in Washington to control almost every aspect of our lives. During this time, these legislators have been assuming that they are not accountable to anyone for their actions. Even in such wacky places as our nation's capitol, the inmates are not supposed to be running the asylum, but this is exactly what has been going on. We have Barney Frank and Chris Dodd setting themselves up to investigate why our financial institutions are failing under the weight of bad mortgage loans to unqualified borrowers. What Mr. Frank and Mr. Dodd fail to reveal is that they were the ones who forced those financial institutions to make those bad loans, in the hopes of receiving votes from these unqualified borrowers. To make matters even worse, many of these bad loans were made to illegal immigrants who should not have been here in this country in the first place, and was done so with the blessings of Frank and Dodd.

This nation can no longer afford the insane luxury of allowing out-of-touch *career politicians* to make our laws and tell us how we must live our lives! The inmates have been running the asylum far too long, and it is time for their real employers, the American voters, to take matters into their own hands and correct this travesty of justice.

CONGRESS AND OIL PRICES

High oil prices and political finger-pointing have much more in common than this Congress is willing to admit. While Congress has been conducting hearings to ask oil company executives about their record profits, Congress continues to ignore their own significant role in creating this problem. As has been customary with this Congress, a solution is sitting right under their noses, just waiting to be put into motion, but they seem to be more concerned with who might get credit for solving this problem than they are in actually helping the American people.

Congressional pandering to the *politically correct* crowd has been killing America's economy and hurting its people during these trying times. Congress has ignored one opportunity after another to ease the pain at the pump by not allowing American oil companies to drill in Anwar or resume drilling in the Gulf of Mexico and the Pacific Ocean, just off the California coast. They see no problem with China, Venezuela, and other countries drilling for oil just off our coasts, but they are allowing pressure from environmentalists to justify forbidding American oil companies to drill in these same areas. Building new refineries and allowing for the construction of nuclear power plants would also be a tremendous help in easing the pain at the pump. This Democrat-controlled Congress continues to deny any real help with high gas prices for the American people, as evidenced recently when they voted down bills to allow new drilling and refining projects. Newly discovered oil deposits in New York contain several decades' worth of available oil supplies, and even reopening capped oil wells within the United States would help alleviate the current shortage and result in lower prices at the pump.

However, once they found out during the heat of the presidential election that the American public was strongly behind new drilling measures, they softened their stance on blocking new drilling. Once their liberal candidate Obama had secured the White House, liberals in Congress let it be known that they would submit a bill that would again block any future drilling. Even with firsthand knowledge of how phony and unscrupulous this liberal Congress operates, the voters sadly again returned this den of thieves back to Washington.

This Congress just does not understand or appreciate the value of using common sense in its decision-making process. Until it does, the American people will continue to suffer as a result. Unless, of course, we wise up and kick them out!

THE CAREER POLITICIAN

How often have we elected a new voice to Congress, only to watch as that well-intentioned newcomer eventually becomes just like the rest of them? By the time they learn what games they must play to get their own bills passed, they have become exactly like those *career politicians* who have become so comfortable in their self-perceived role of really *knowing what is best for us better than we do ourselves*. The actions of this group of *career politicians* present the best argument yet in favor of *term limits*.

I must admit that I have mixed feelings about term limits. First, let me say that the reason I do not like term limits is because it limits the voters' right to choose the candidate they really want. But, neither do I like to see the same *career politicians* who view their position in Congress as an entitlement, or even their birthright to continue to roam these hallowed halls. Once they have been in office for awhile, they have become so politically powerful that it is almost impossible to vote them out. In today's political climate, becoming a political newcomer is almost impossible, unless they are already wealthy. The faces change from time to time, but since the new ones have learned the ropes from the same old crew who think that the general public isn't smart enough to know what is really good for them, the game never changes.

Is it any wonder that the general public feels that Congress doesn't listen to, or understand the problems of the people? How can anyone like Ted Kennedy possibly understand what it means to go to bed every night worrying how you are going to feed your family, or pay your bills? Career politicians have learned that to keep getting elected, they must promise to help those who either cannot or will not help themselves. They rationalize that if they actually live up to their political promises, they might no longer be needed, so it becomes vital that those problems get some relief, but are never corrected to the extent that their bloc of voters want them corrected. For liberal politicians, this has been the carrot they will dangle before their constituents. This has been their basic political philosophy for decades, and this is also how they have managed to continue buying the votes of certain groups. If the day ever comes when the voters finally realize and understand this, the liberal movement will become ancient history. The success of the liberal movement depends upon exploiting our weaknesses, rather than developing our strengths.

POLITICAL GAMES

Like many Americans today, I have become totally frustrated with our Congress and the dysfunction of our entire political system. We have watched as Harry Reid and Nancy Pelosi, the comical Democrat leadership of the Senate and the House respectively, has used their positions to play their political games at the expense of our national security, and our economy. Regardless of what our president says, according to these two hypocritical clowns, he is always wrong. They act like the public cannot understand what they are doing as they play their childish games, but the only ones fooled are those zombie-like robots who continue to blindly follow their lead.

The rank-and-file American feels totally helpless as they watch these *career politicians* go about destroying this country. Those things that are truly in the best interest of this nation are way down on their list of priorities, as they spend the majority of their energy doing everything within their power to make the opposition party look bad. The time has come for us to send these childish buffoons back home. The American people deserve much better than this un-patriotic bunch!

THE CHILDREN'S GUIDE TO UNDERSTANDING POLITICS

Should we be spending any of our time trying to give our children an introduction into the grown-up world of politics? Why not just allow them to play on the swing, slide down the slide, climb the jungle gym, play chase, and enjoy all of the innocent playground games that children often indulge in?

Should we really expose little Johnny or Mary to the adult games that make grown people express their hatred for anyone who believes differently than they do, or which divide generations of families and races, and destroys lifelong friendships over differing political views? If they have a better understanding of what politics is really like, will they become better able to handle these political differences than their parents have done?

My original reason for wanting to include this small section into this book was to show children how the world of politics really works. The problem with this idea is that maybe politicians need to grow up before they try to teach anything to anyone. Maybe the children should be teaching the adults about politics instead of the other way around.

IMAGINE THAT

Surely there must be a more fitting way to determine who will be chosen to ascend to the high office of president of the United States of America. While we are supposedly choosing the person who is traditionally recognized as the most powerful person in the world, we are instead left with the feeling that we have been watching recess at the kindergarten playground. The one thing that is apparently missing in this electoral process is dignity. Is there anyone out there who will not be absolutely thrilled and relieved to see this seemingly never-ending political campaign come to an end?

What a horrible way to show our impressionable young children how those who hold our highest leadership roles are supposed to conduct themselves. Is there any wonder why they grow up thinking that this is the proper and correct way to participate in our political process? How is it that we continue to wonder how this world keeps getting crazier and crazier from one year to the next, and then get upset when our children can't seem to get along together?

The following letters were written at different stages during the 2008 presidential primaries.

WHAT IS IMPORTANT

We are quickly approaching decision time in our quest to select the next president of the United States. When the dust finally settles, we hope that there will be some very real and distinct differences to emerge between these candidates, differences that will reveal someone who will not be afraid to act when real leadership is required.

While John McCain understands the importance of protecting our national security, he falls short when it comes to being a true conservative. In the current political campaign, which more closely resembles a popularity contest than a true, soul-searching exercise to determine a candidate's leadership abilities, modern-day conservative voters turned their backs on three candidates with successful and proven leadership experience. Mike Huckabee and Mitt Romney ran state governments that were dominated by opposing liberal values, while Rudy Giuliani ran the world's largest city at a time when it came under attack by the forces of evil and world terrorism.

For the first time in American political history, Democrats will choose between two minorities—a female and a black—to be their presidential candidate. Each of these two candidates boasts of their valuable political experience, but facts do not bear out these claims by either of these two office-seekers.

Hillary Clinton has consistently referred to her vast political decision-making experience, but when pressed for specific examples, she ignores those questions entirely. It appears that her self-proclaimed experience consists primarily of looking on as her husband ran the offices of president of the United States and governor of the state of Arkansas, or she improperly (or possibly illegally) assumed an administrative role of authority to which she was neither elected by the people nor confirmed by Congress. Her time in the U.S. Senate has been totally consumed by her self-perceived destiny to become the first female president of the United States, instead of concentrating on her defined senatorial duties of sponsoring bills into law.

Now let us look at Barack Hussein Obama. No one will argue the fact that Mr. Obama is young, energetic, charismatic, and can charm the paint right off of the walls. But, eight undistinguished years in the Illinois state legislature, and a largely absent and unproductive first term as U.S. senator from Illinois do not exactly provide the type of leadership experience necessary for running the most powerful nation on the face of the Earth. Charming his audiences into swooning in the aisles or applauding his nose-blowing talent is one thing, but charm alone will not likely convince an unfriendly world leader to back off during a threatening showdown. This requires a totally different kind of leadership ability, one that Mr. Obama has shown no evidence of possessing. Perhaps the most troublesome quality that appears to be absent in Mr. Obama is a deep and abiding love and passion for this nation. The wrong choice here could prove to be a disaster.

WHAT CHOICES?

Regardless of the time period in question, when it comes to the election season, "change" always seems to be the mandate. *Change* this, *change* that. This is wrong; that is wrong. Candidates proclaim, "The people want change, and I am the agent of change." It goes on and on. Political candidates continuously insist that we need change, but they seldom tell us specifically what they are going to change, or if they do, how they will go about making their changes. We must be very careful, because time has proven that *change* simply for the sake of *change* is rarely in the best interest of this nation.

What are we as Americas really looking for in our president? Are we looking for a diplomat who can please all of the people all of the time, or one who can successfully run a big corporation, or one who is a skilled military leader? Might it be possible for us to find one who encompasses all of these talents and skills? If we are expecting to elect the perfect president, then I am afraid we will never achieve success. The one we elect must have the best interest of this nation as his or her number-one priority, because the worst thing that can happen would be to elect someone who has an ax to grind, or one who has a selfish political agenda to advance. National security must be the ultimate objective, because if this is not protected, then nothing else really matters anyway! Political agendas mean nothing if presented to a nation under siege. Fighting for or against a woman's right to abort a live fetus comes up empty when compared to protecting this nation against an enemy whose sole purpose in life is to destroy us. Proving or disproving the likelihood of global warming becomes meaningless when a rogue enemy is rushing to develop a nuclear weapon that can destroy all of mankind.

This upcoming presidential election is looking more and more like a no-win situation for the citizens of this nation. Democrats will choose between two firsts as their candidate: a female or a black. The Republican choice has obviously been orchestrated by the liberal media, and John McCain, who defeated other more conservative candidates, will now be wearing the Republican banner. Many conservative Republicans are not convinced that they can, in good conscience, vote for him.

On the Democrat side, Hillary Rodham Clinton, the ex-first lady and currently junior U.S. senator from New York, claims to be the most qualified and experienced candidate on either side, though she will not back up these claims with evidence. She has also exposed herself to be ruthless, less than honest, and having a win-at-all-cost mind-set.

Barack Hussein Obama brushes off all requests for him to reveal the qualifications and experience he claims to possess in vital areas. The only thing he has proven so far is his Pied Piper ability to hypnotize people into blindly following him. Although some claim that they no longer question his early Muslim indoctrination, he still has failed to convince many how decisive he would be if called upon to launch all-out military strikes against Islamic countries or governments. His plan to kill the Bush tax cuts and increase income and capital gains taxes on the wealthy clearly demonstrates his lack of understanding of how to energize the economy. The most obvious and damaging challenges to Obama's ability to lead this nation are his close ties to his racist and anti-American minister Jeremiah Wright, his relationship with Weather Underground bomber William Ayers, and his association with Chicago slum lord and convicted felon Tony Rezko.

REAL ISSUES

In Barack Hussein Obama, we have one of the most impressive campaigners we have seen in the history of American politics. However, does being a good campaigner automatically translate into being a competent president and leader? After listening for months to Obama's flowery speeches and watching his Muhammad Ali bobbing and weaving impression when asked revealing questions, we are still asking the same question as in the Wendy's hamburger advertising campaign: "Where's the beef?"

Obama claims to have a mandate for *change,* but he still has not revealed his plan for what he will do as president. If, as according to Obama, his association with Jeremiah Wright and William Ayers are not real issues, then just what specifically does he consider the real issues to be? Does he not see one's character as a real issue? Is it not important that his spiritual adviser and mentor preaches hatred of America, specifically white America? Is it not important that his friend and neighbor just happens to be someone who bombed our Pentagon and other government buildings, and held a fund-raising event in his own home for Obama?

What are his specific solutions to the specific issues? As far as I can see, the only issue Barack Hussein Obama claims as a real issue is *change* itself. What is change? What does he want to change? What does he propose to do to make this change? Exactly what are his specific ideas for economic change, and how would he go about doing it? What is his specific vision for our military and the war on terror?

EXPECTATIONS OF OUR PRESIDENT

When did we decide to compromise the qualifications for the office of president of the United States of America so much that we have allowed for the possibility of a weak and inexperienced candidate to assume that office? Should he not be required to make available his legitimate birth, medical, and educational records to verify his qualifications to hold this office; qualifications specifically outlined in the U.S. Constitution? We are allowing an effort by liberals to re-energize white guilt over the institution of slavery (which ended 150 years ago) in hopes that it will influence the outcome of the 2008 presidential election. The people of the United States of America have proven that they will vote for qualified candidates for office, regardless of race or gender, if their qualifications are valid.

In light of the many unanswered questions about Barack Hussein Obama, why are we so understanding and accepting of the fanatical efforts by liberal Democrats and their liberal media cohorts to promote a candidate to the office of president whose judgment of character is at best very questionable; whose experience consists of occupying a seat in the U.S. Senate for a two-year time period, which has been almost exclusively devoted to seeking the office of president, instead of fulfilling his duties as the paid representative of his constituents; whose Muslim name and background are a slap in the face to every red-blooded American; whose obvious lack of patriotism and devotion to this nation are laughed off and even treated as nonexistent, or even racist issues; and whose loose-cannon wife strongly professes her dislike, and possibly even hatred for this nation? There is no question that there are many members within the black community who have the qualifications and integrity to become outstanding candidates for any office they so desire. Obama obviously realized early on that the assumed guilt over slavery would become an issue that would work well to his advantage, and could even be used as his own personal excuse to not answer any question about any subject as he so chooses. There is no need to promote a candidate whose questionable background discourages his honesty and openness with the citizens of this nation, simply to satisfy someone's self-imposed guilt about slavery.

BEWARE OF WHAT YOU WISH FOR

Have you ever wished that the United States was more like England, France, or Canada? Well, if you vote for Hillary Clinton or Barack Obama, you just might see your wish come true. The sad truth is that we all may wake up one day and realize that we have been sold a bill of goods.

Since it now appears that Hillary is starting to pull away from her Democrat opponents in her quest to become that party's presidential candidate, maybe we need a crash course on what to expect from a Hillary Clinton White House. For starters, just look at the type of people she surrounds herself with inside her political machine. One would be that world-famous fund-raiser Norman Hsu, who never met a scam he didn't like. Another is good ole' Sandy Berger, whose idea of protecting our sensitive national documents is to steal them from the National Archives, stuff them down his socks and underwear, and then look for the nearest paper shredder.

As details of Hillary's political agenda are starting to come to the surface, we can now see parts of her plan for transforming this nation's economic system from capitalism into socialism, a dysfunctional economic system practiced by many of our European neighbors, and supported by suffocating taxes upon its people. One major difference between these two economic systems is that under capitalism, ownership of land and wealth remain in the hands of private individuals, like you and me. Under socialism, ownership of this very same land and wealth would eventually be transferred to and controlled by the government. While capitalism rewards ambition and initiative in its people, socialism actually punishes people who display those very same attributes.

To further explain the goals of socialists like Hillary Clinton, in common, everyday language, she is the classic example of someone who would have us believe that we can strengthen the weak by weakening the strong, which just happens to be a basic premise and a fundamental goal of a socialist society. How does Hillary propose to accomplish her agenda? For starters, she plans to take private wealth and property away from those who have created it, and distribute it in the form of entitlements, among all of the people of this nation. This idea might sound great to someone who has never owned any property, but this wealth and property that Hillary intends to take just might include *your* home, *your* business, or any property that *you* may own, either now or in the future. But in her ever-present rush to further divide the people of this nation into opposing groups (this time the *haves* versus the *have-nots*), the one thing Hillary seems to have overlooked is the fact that both she and her husband Bill are themselves now members of that illustrious group she refers to as the *haves*, those whom she plans to separate from their wealth as she gives it to the *have-nots*. Another example is her idea for a national health-care plan. Then comes her idea to give every child born in America a $5,000 bond, which could also include children of illegal immigrants. Yet another example is for everyone to have access to a government-funded 401(k) plan—for retirement, don't you know. Are you starting to get the picture?

Now, all of this really sounds great, but there is one overwhelming but intentionally not discussed problem. *Who is going to pay for all of this?* The answer is that *we are, you and I, through higher taxes.* In all fairness to her intelligence, Hillary is not so stupid as to really believe this nonsense herself; however, she and her political machine have long realized that by promising things such as this, they can steal enough votes of those who will buy into this farce, thereby allowing her to gain that seat of power she so vainly covets.

These ideas are so irresponsible that to even consider supporting a candidate who proposes such ideas only proves that far too many people have become so blind or so gullible that they will believe anything, regardless of how unrealistic it may be.

It's All About Money!

It is very hard to understand how my home state of Arkansas could vote for John McCain for president, but re-elect the three of the four House seats held by Democrats to Congress, and for the most part unchallenged? After learning that there would be no Republican opponents for the Arkansas senatorial and First District congressional races in the 2008 election, I began to make inquiries as to why this was happening. I can somewhat understand how it might be hard to run a successful campaign against Senator Mark Pryor, because he is from a family with long Democrat political ties in Arkansas, and he has not always followed the dictates of the liberal wing of the Democrat Party.

But, I cannot understand why the citizens of the First Congressional District have allowed themselves to remain content to be represented (and I use that word very loosely) by the likes of Marion Berry. Around election time, he will occasionally do something for an area of this district to justify another vote, but overall he is both blind and deaf to the needs of the people of this district.

Mr. Berry and his Arkansas Democrat senatorial counterpart, Blanch Lincoln, have proven themselves simply to be puppets of, and liberal mouthpieces for the likes of Ted Kennedy, Nancy Pelosi, Hillary Clinton, and Harry Reid. Arkansas sadly has become a Southern state represented by these two homegrown legislators who take their marching orders from Ted Kennedy in the Senate and vote with the same convictions as his gay liberal Massachusetts sidekick Barney Frank in the House. How could we have allowed our standards to fall to such a level? I can answer that question in one simple word: *money!* In recent news accounts, Marion Berry boldly has touted the fact that he has a war chest containing over $500,000 but no political opponent to run against.

The problem is not just as simple as the Democrats pumping unlimited funds into the coffers of their liberal standard bearers. The Republican National Committee, the Republican Party of Arkansas, and even the local county chapters of the Republican Party of Arkansas must bear much of the responsibility for the conservative values of many Arkansans not being represented in political offices. Recent conservative candidates trying to mount political campaigns against Berry and Lincoln have found that they must not only fight their Democrat opponents, but also their own state Republican Party, from which they received little or no help. How can we claim being part of a two-party system when one of those parties disappear when prospective candidates need them?

The time has come for GOP leaders in Arkansan to step up and decide if we are really going to become a two-party state, or if we are only going to give lip service to that idea. If this does not change, then we will have to be content with sending pseudo-Arkansans with Massachusetts values and morals to represent us in Washington.

CHANGE FOR THE SAKE OF CHANGE

I get amused when presidential candidates consistently proclaim how we must *change* the way this country does business, and how the gap between the *haves* and *the have-nots* keeps growing wider and wider with every passing day. The funny part is how most of these candidates can defend either side of any issue, and seem deceptively comfortable in doing so. It is the same old message we hear during each and every election. But if we were totally honest with ourselves, could change simply for the sake of change really be such a good idea? It might serve us well to remember that old adage, "Be careful what you wish for, because you just might get it." Old-fashioned common sense could be allowed to play some role in the decision-making process, but then, why should we allow anything as trivial and insignificant as *common sense* to enter into it?

Like most everything else in this world, nothing is perfect, and the good ol' United States is certainly no exception. But, when compared to all other countries of this world, this nation that we call home is head and shoulders above anything else out there. Although it is admirable to want to better one's situation, perfection is very rarely achieved. One thing that has become abundantly clear, however, is that not everyone is capable of realizing and understanding just how wonderful and unique this nation really is. Shortsightedness of the American people in truly appreciating what we have in this country is perhaps the primary reason for the constant discontent within the citizenry of this nation. Far too many people in this country just cannot seem to grasp the significance of what it means to be a citizen of America. It is indeed a privilege that has been bestowed upon very few human beings born into this world, and it is one that very few within this country seem to appreciate.

Americans have always been very proficient at seeking out and exposing any weaknesses in almost everything we come into contact with, even to the extent that we very often end up killing, cooking, and even eating the goose that lays our golden eggs. As with any government, there are weaknesses and shortcomings in our system of government, but few other governments will allow its citizens the right to contest their leaders, challenge their laws, or even improve their own social standing simply through ambition, initiative, and education.

Regardless of one's political affiliation, all we need to do to see just how far we have come as a nation in the area of race relations is to look at what happened in the 2008 Iowa political caucus. A politically inexperienced black man from Illinois has overwhelmingly captured the Democrats' vote in Iowa, a state whose population is only about 2 percent black. This shows more than one thing concerning race relations in this country. First, in spite of what liberal rabble-rousers continue to portray, this country has come a long way in closing the gap between the races. It also proves that regardless of one's race, anyone with ambition, initiative, and a willingness to accept the reality that we control our own destiny (to some extent) can achieve personal success. In the real world, there will always be those who achieve various degrees of success, regardless of any obstacles placed before them. Unfortunately, there are also those who will accept failure as a way of life and are content with letting their government take care of them. These people seem to be satisfied with far less than what they could have if only they would refuse to accept failure as an unalterable fact of life. Some of our so-called leaders try to justify their own existence by creating dissatisfaction where there is really little or none to be found, and they use the lack of ambition within certain people as the vehicle to propel these *them against us* feelings. The only way they can continue to hold a place of so-called importance is by keeping one group or another in the mind-set of being constantly persecuted and held down. One of the unique aspects of this nation is that regardless of one's inherited situation at birth, that situation can be used as motivation to elevate oneself out of that prison, and achieve success simply through ambition and hard work. Self-pity and satisfaction with being dependent upon everyone else for one's very survival is at the root of failure.

The trend has always been to hire some PhD and pay him thousands upon thousands of dollars to study why people cannot co-exist and get along, when it seems that a much more valid way would be to have everyday people try to work it out among themselves. That word *work* could be used to solve many problems, if it was only put to use more often.

WHO IS BARACK HUSSEIN OBAMA?

What do we really know about Barack Hussein Obama? Remember the old saying that goes, "Birds of a feather flock together?" Who are the *birds* in Obama's flock? What might we expect from an Obama presidency?

Obama receives his spiritual guidance from his minister, Reverend Jeremiah Wright, an ultra-racist, white-hating bigot who encourages his congregation to substitute the words "God bless America" with "God d*** America" (his words, not mine), who refers to this nation as the United States of KKK America, and whom Obama acknowledges as the inspiration for his book *The Audacity of Hope*. Should we be concerned that Reverend Jeremiah Wright gave a *lifetime achievement award* to Louis Farrakhan, the ultra-racist, anti-Semite, white-hating leader of the Nation of Islam? Should we question Barack Obama's relationship with William Ayers, a friend and terrorist bomber with the Weather Underground; or Tony Rezko, Obama's neighbor and convicted felon and Chicago real estate slum lord?

Reverend Jeremiah Wright's brainwashing could possibly be the reason Barack Obama does not wear an American flag lapel pin and doesn't place his hand over his heart during the Pledge of Allegiance. This could also be the reason Obama's attorney wife, Michelle, expresses no pride in this country and thinks America is a "mean place." How could she feel no pride in a country where she received degrees from Princeton University and Harvard Law School; where her husband, Barack, also an attorney, received degrees from Columbia University and Harvard Law School; where her brother, Craig Robinson, received a degree from Princeton University and is head basketball coach at Oregon State University; and where she and Barack Obama claimed a combined annual income of several million dollars in each of the most recent years? Does she not realize that the vast majority of white people as well as black people in this country can only dream of a life of abundance and luxury which she enjoys everyday? If she feels that this country has been so unfair to her, she might consider trading her life in America for a life in Obama's ancestral homeland of Kenya.

Who is Barack Hussein Obama? We still don't have any idea. Despite what he says, can we really be secure in the thought that he says he feels no allegiance to the Muslim teachings of his early childhood years?

What might we expect from an Obama presidency? As the most liberal member of a liberal-controlled Congress, don't be surprised if he leads this nation straight down the road to total socialism, complete with higher taxes and increased entitlements. *Would he respond quickly and decisively if it ever became necessary for him to order military action against Islamic militants or Islamic nations?* We can only hope and pray that he would.

Can this nation survive an Obama presidency? That is something we must ask ourselves when we step into the voting booth.

Barack Hussein Obama, the Candidate of Change

Barack Hussein Obama says he doesn't place his hand over his heart during the Pledge of Allegiance because he doesn't want to take sides. Does this mean that he doesn't want to make decisions that would be viewed as taking sides in favor of the United States? Does he mean that he will not make any decisions as president that would be construed as being in the best interest of America, or *taking sides*? Whose side does he think his decisions as president of the United States of America should favor or protect? Should his priority be to protect America's interests, or to make sure that he doesn't offend our enemies? How long does he plan to continue not taking sides if he becomes president?

Just how stupid does he think the American people really are? Would you feel more comfortable if your president took sides or didn't take sides? How much longer will the blind mice of this country keep listening to the overwhelming amount of condemning evidence about the most liberal Democrat candidate for president we have ever seen, and still feel the conviction to vote for him? When will sanity return to our election process?

If it is change that you want, get ready. The change you get quite likely will not be the change you want.

GOVERNMENT

ORIGINS OF GOVERNMENT

In ancient times, the first forms of government were created to help with flooding and other natural disasters. Later, protection of citizens from bandits and thugs was added to the role of government, but the specific role of government was limited to those things that individual citizens found difficult to do alone, or when they needed the collective assistance of other citizens to survive disasters.

Moving ahead to the twentieth century, we find an era where the role of government had become so greatly expanded that it now feels that it must assume responsibility for almost every aspect of the lives of its citizens. Some now see the role of government as taking care of every need anyone might have from the cradle to the grave. These feelings of obligation were likely fueled by feelings of guilt on the part of some people, which caused them to assume total responsibility to take care of everyone they perceived could not take care of themselves, whether legitimate or not. Not surprisingly, those well-intentioned Samaritans found ample numbers of people willing to allow them the pleasure of assuming this burden of supplying their every possible need, and for as long as government is willing to keep doing it.

This assumed duty of government soon took on another facet; that of convincing these dependent citizens that they were forever indebted to these wonderful Samaritans of government, and in return for their vote, these citizens would continue to receive their entitlements as long as these liberal government providers stayed in office. This practice created an entirely new class of people within this country: the dependent class. To ensure that this class of people remained dependent upon their government, they were encouraged not to pursue such trivial practices as meaningful employment, ambition, trust of business owners, and, least of all, an education that would likely expose the true objectives of these liberal government Samaritans. Thus, the liberal wing of the Democrat Party found its purpose in life, and this once unique country hasn't been the same since.

The Role of Government

When progress is to be made in almost any area, the participants must understand and chose between one of three actions: lead, follow, or get out of the way. Success depends upon choosing the correct one and knowing when to act accordingly. To be successful, business must take the lead in areas such as product research and development. People must apply their individual skills and follow the lead of business. But where government is concerned, it simply needs to just get out of the way so that it will not impede the genius of its people.

In the early days of civilization, people learned to band together to help each other during times when individual efforts in problem solving just were not enough, and this brought about the origin of government. Since that time, government has expanded its role to where we now have the conglomerated mess we see in Washington today, and government now tries to assume responsibility for each and every facet of our daily lives. Government has never learned how to just get out of the way and let the people get the job done.

Old-time political machines saw government as a means to achieve power, and they did so by sending those to Congress who would vote as they were instructed. Voting was manipulated in their territories to ensure their continued success. Many came to Congress with good intentions, only to find that once they learned how the game of politics was played, instead of helping to solve problems, they soon became just another part of those very same problems. If they refused to play the games designed by the political power brokers within their home districts and within Congress, they soon found themselves out of a job. Congress has become a fraternity that protects its own, and its members quickly lose sight of what life is like in the real world. Their primary focus switches from one of working for their constituents to one of self-promotion, in which their own financial security and job security become the priorities.

Congress must be made to understand that the role of government is not like that of an income-producing business, which in many cases government becomes direct competition with the enterprises of its own citizens. It should be limited to providing help in areas that are too great to be handled on an individual basis, such as national defense, natural disasters, the building and maintaining of highways and infrastructure, and passing laws that provide for the safety and protection of its citizens. The assessment of taxes should be limited only to those necessary for carrying out those specified duties and nothing more. Legislating entitlements that provide for the day-to-day existence of its citizens should never be a function of government.

THE UN-AMERICAN FACTOR

We are forced to listen as all of the whiners constantly complain about how terrible this nation is. According to them, anyone and everyone wanting to enter this country, whether documented or not, should be allowed to do so with no questions asked, regardless of their plans to contribute anything positive to this country or not. These bloodsuckers feel that we should provide undocumented immigrants with the same access to entitlements to which tax-paying American citizens are eligible. Many of these immigrants constantly berate the United States on every issue from *A* to *Z,* while at the same time taking advantage of every benefit they can get their hands on. For the most part, this group will not volunteer to help with anything; they find fault in everything while at the same time cursing the brave members of our military who put their own lives on the line every day to offer the opportunity of these individuals to be a drag on our economy.

Congress, on both the Democrat and Republican sides of the aisle, has become home to a group of *career politicians* who feel that they know what is best for the rest of us, even though they refuse to listen to what we are constantly trying to tell them. Congress has become home to a large collection of lawyers who have become quite comfortable with life in their private little kingdom. This group, and many freeloaders just like them, has given us the best reasons for implementing national *term-limit* legislation that we have seen. Their work ethic, or the total lack of one, is the very reason why Congress has the lowest approval rating perhaps in the history of this nation. Can you imagine how Ted Kennedy might react if he ever had to do an honest day's work, like most of us have to do on a regular basis? What are the odds that good ole' Harry Reid or sweet little Ms Nancy Pelosi could survive in the real working world, where an honest day's work for an honest day's pay is what most people have to do everyday? Now, I'm not a gambler, but that just might be as close as one might ever come to a *sure thing*.

WHILE FRANCE LAY SLEEPING

An article entitled *Al-Qaeda and Algerian Group Target France* appeared in the September 15, 2007, issue of my local newspaper in the "Around the

World" section. This article said that even though French leaders decided "not to join the U.S.-led war in Iraq," this would not exclude France from Islamic terrorism. Al-Qaeda has formed a union with a group of Algerian insurgents, and they have decided to also target France as one of their enemies. This proves one very simple but important fact; that a policy of appeasement does not protect anyone in the *war against terrorism*.

France's lack of a backbone, as evidenced by not joining the United States and other democratic nations of the world in putting down this radical Islamic movement, has not gained them any special favors from these crazy Islamic murderers after all. How long will France and the other countries of the so-called *free world* keep acting like the picture of the three monkeys sitting side by side above the caption, "Hear no evil, see no evil, speak no evil"? It makes no difference whatsoever to these radical killers whether a country actually attacks them or not. They see anyone and everyone who does not succumb to the dictates of their narrow-minded, ruthless, and intolerant ideology as their enemy, and they will do everything within their power to destroy their enemies!

Al-Qaeda's best allies in their mission to conquer the world are the "I don't want to get involved" citizens of the free world, those who feel that being "politically correct" is much more important than our own national security, and those who refuse to see and understand the intentions of these Islamic radicals! These people need to ask themselves one question: "Where would the free world be today if the United States of America had listened to those who preached non-involvement in the late 1930s and early 1940s and had turned its back on England and France during World War II?" Believe it or not, the world would have been much better-off if Hitler had been allowed to conquer the world during World War II than we will be if that sentiment prevails today concerning these Islamic radicals, and their plans of conquest are allowed to succeed.

Whether we choose to fight to eliminate these murderers or not, the free world is doomed if their plans are successful! Will France and the rest of Europe continue to sleep through this wake-up call? Will the "silent majority" in the United States become subject to the same fate?

It's time to *wake up, America*!

WHERE IS THE OUTRAGE?

The outrageous behavior we have come to expect from ultra-liberal and un-American cities like San Francisco has snaked its way all the way to the

Bible Belt of America and reared its ugly head in Eureka Springs, a little mountain town in northwest Arkansas.

It is not surprising that the mayor and a majority of the members of the San Francisco city council have shown their appreciation and love for America by banning many military-oriented functions; endorsing the homosexual lifestyle and same-sex marriage; and welcoming illegal immigrants with open arms by proclaiming San Francisco to be a sanctuary city. San Francisco and much of California have been written off as being un-American for some time now, but behavior like this certainly was not expected in a small Arkansas town.

To many people who have visited Eureka Springs, Arkansas, in the past and who plan to do so in the future, this beautifully quaint little village has always been an ideal spot for a family outing; that is, until those in the Eureka Springs city government recently decided that they are more interested in promoting this once-fair city as a desired destination for same-sex couples to stroll its streets hand in hand, instead of promoting it to traditional families, with or without children. What kind of message is this sending? This is just another addition to the growing list of evidence suggesting how this country is headed toward becoming the modern-day *Sodom and Gomorrah*; and if it does, the same results will not be far behind.

Where is the indignation that once would have met this kind of behavior by almost any city or state government—outside of San Francisco, that is—with loud protests and boycotts of local businesses that supported this kind of immoral behavior? Since Eureka Springs depends primarily upon tourism as its main source of income, it would not be a very difficult nor lengthy process to get this point across. This should not be viewed as merely a political issue, but simply as an issue between right and wrong. One does not have to be a goody two-shoes to see what is happening here. Those who choose that lifestyle must not be allowed to shove it in the faces of those who see this kind of behavior as distasteful and immoral. How much longer are we going to allow the ultra-liberal minority of this country to steer our ship right onto the rocks while we just sit back and allow it to happen? Isn't it strange that those who view morality as a positive asset to this or any nation, and who decide to stand up for what is moral and right, are somehow looked upon by the "if it feels good, do it" liberal crowd as being the troublemakers? Phone calls and letters to the Eureka Springs city hall just might work wonders, but I am afraid that San Francisco has been a lost cause for long, long time.

MEXICO-TO-CANADA (NAFTA) HIGHWAY

There is a very interesting development taking place just south of the Arkansas-Texas border that will have a huge impact, not only in Texas, but in Arkansas and the entire nation as well. The *Trans-Texas Corridor* (TTC), also referred to as the "NAFTA Superhighway," is a massive international highway/ rail transportation system that will run unchecked through the heart of this nation from Mexico to Canada. This project is primarily funded by Spanish and other foreign investors, and it appears that our own government will have little or no jurisdiction over it.

Concerned citizens of Texas have been trying unsuccessfully for months to find out more about this project, which will start in their state but will eventually enter Arkansas, Oklahoma, New Mexico, and other states on its designated route into Canada. Concerned citizens asked CNN, the network conducting the recent Texas Democrat presidential debate, to include a question asking Hillary Clinton and Barack Obama their position on this project. After an aggressive letter-writing and e-mail campaign by these citizens, CNN promised to include their question to the candidates if they would stop sending e-mails to the network. Needless to say, CNN reneged on their promise to this citizens' group, and no mention of this project was ever made during this debate.

When news of this project first began to leak out, several state legislators from Oklahoma began their own investigation into some of the more questionable aspects of the project and were shocked at what they found. They discovered that this transportation system could easily become an unimpeded pipeline for the movement of illegal immigrants, drugs, terrorists, and weapons into this country, transported by trains and uncertified and possibly unsafe big-rig truck-and-trailer units originating in Mexico.

If this is such a good and useful project for this nation, why has so much remained hidden from the general public? Why is it being financed almost exclusively by foreign investors and not by financial organizations within this country? My biggest concern, however, is this: "Why would our own government agree to allow construction of this huge project, while being given virtually no control over its operation?" Oklahoma state legislators are very concerned that they will have no input or knowledge of what is being transported through their state over this superhighway system.

Those interested in keeping up with this project can go to the Web site corridorwatch.org, a watchdog group that provides a newsletter. I truly hope I am wrong about this, but if my gut feelings are correct, then all I can say is, "Houston; we have a problem!"

REBUILDING AMERICA

What has happened to that wonderful human spirit that was discovered by our forefathers, and was used to build this unique nation into what the rest of the world has come to know as the United States of America? We have allowed ourselves to be taken in by a group of phony pretenders who just cannot seem to appreciate or enjoy the success which this great nation has achieved, and has tried to share on many occasions with the rest of the world. We have stood by silently and watched as these pale excuses of real Americans have tried to dismantle something so precious, something which our founding fathers and early ancestors toiled so valiantly to bring to life as the Great American Dream. Liberals and their blind robotic followers are now trying to destroy the nation that became known as the most powerful and benevolent nation on Earth, and one which the rest of the world turned to so often for help in their times of need. They desire to turn America into a place that will resemble those weak, socialist, and feudalistic European kingdoms of centuries ago.

How are we going to stop this craziness? We must understand just how and why America was so different from anything that had ever been successfully tried before. This nation is so different from any other that there are many people who call America home that just cannot comprehend what it means to be a real American. Real Americans have burning within them a true entrepreneurial spirit, one where the virtues of ambition, initiative, and drive are the cornerstone, and which is found deep within it's very soul. These virtues, if left unimpeded by a cumbersome and suffocating government, will create and grow an economy that has been found in only one place, and that place is this same America which liberals are now trying to destroy. Just look back at the history of this nation, the real history of this nation, and not that *politically correct* version which liberals would now have us to believe. We must take the reins out of the hands of those who are trying to drive this great nation straight over a cliff, and put them back into the hands of those who possess the strength, courage, and character necessary to put us back on the right course. With the right leadership for this nation once again in place, we will then immerse ourselves in the work of prioritizing the needs of this nation.

Our national security must become the primary issue of this nation! We must make sure that our military is fully staffed and funded, and that the military draft is reinstated. Military pay and benefits must become more competitive with that of the civilian sector. Without our national security intact, we will become just as weak as our once powerful European cousins who have allowed themselves to forget their own true history, and they now seem to have lost the ability or desire to correct their problem. Our European cousins have been infected with some of the same political virus that has been trying to devour America in recent years. In their quest to dilute our once proud heritages, guilt-ridden and success-hating liberals are trying to corrupt our history to the point where our ancestors would no longer recognize us. Some people sadly just cannot bring themselves to appreciate success.

The mission, purpose, and goal of public education in this country must be reevaluated, and the administration of our educational system must be removed from a government bureaucracy, and transferred to proven education professionals. Participation in the public educational system up until a stated age will be mandatory, and continued student involvement will be determined by progress, participation, and skills or interest levels. All dropouts from our public schools age 17 and above should be given the choice of enlisting in one of our military branches, or serving in a version of the Peace Corps or other service organizations. Those under the age of 17 who have either dropped out of school, or who have been expelled due to disciplinary reasons should be given the option of enrolling in and successfully completing a vocational trade school, or into a highly regimented and disciplined boot camp–type military school program, including those who are removed from the vocational trade school. All high school, military school, and vocational school graduates who do not continue their education either as a college or vocational school student, or who do not find gainful employment within six months after graduation, should be immediately drafted into the military or a public service occupation for a period of not less than two years. These measures would help to create a more disciplined, motivated, and more patriotic citizen who will hopefully not become dependent upon entitlement programs.

We must identify American corporations that do business with the enemies of this nation, withdraw all tax incentives and begin imposing penalties on these corporations, and demand that they cease doing business with our enemies immediately. American corporations that move factories or facilities out of this country and relocate in other countries simply to take advantage of the cheap labor costs must be shown clear and positive reasons to reconsider their plans for doing so. By relocating assets to other countries, these corporations have weakened the once strong employment fabric of this nation, and have moved our economy toward decline.

Business and industrial tax incentives must be tied into research and development, especially in the area of developing alternative fuels. This area must be placed on a fast track, and limitations upon oil drilling and refining must be relaxed or removed entirely. Construction of nuclear power plants, solar and wind power development, and any other viable means of energy production must be enthusiastically encouraged. The ultimate goal must be to achieve total energy self-reliance at the earliest date possible. Future tax incentives to the energy industry must be tied directly to progress in the areas of research and development.

The purpose of and need for the IRS should be reevaluated, and if determined to be necessary, restructured into a more fair and just agency. Responsibility for all previously government-funded public assistance programs should be transferred to local private or church sponsored civic organizations, in cooperation with private and public employment agencies. Social Security payments should not be made to those whose private retirement accounts exceed a specified annual income. There should also be no income tax charged on Social Security income.

IS OBAMA CONSTITUTIONALLY QUALIFIED TO BE PRESIDENT?

The presidential election of 2008 has presented us with perhaps the most significant constitutional crisis in our nation's history, and the outcome of which will truly answer several questions about the people of this nation. For one thing, the outcome of this issue will tell us much about the future of race relations in this country, but as we have known all along, the liberal mainstream media has done everything within their power to keep the public in the dark about this matter.

It was long ago determined that we would become a nation of laws, and that these laws were to be established in accordance with that most wonderful document of government ever devised by man, the *U.S. Constitution. Article II, Section I* of this great document clearly describes the qualifications any candidate must meet to be eligible to hold the office of president of the United States, and these are the same qualifications which have been totally ignored and blatantly compromised by the Democrat Party and their apparent winning candidate in this election, Barack Obama.

According to Philadelphia attorney Phillip J. Berg, a very simple and pertinent question about Barack Obama's constitutional eligibility to even hold the office of president has twice been presented to the U.S. Supreme Court for consideration, and twice this illustrious body has declined to hear it. This question could have easily been answered and laid to rest by Obama himself if he would have simply produced his legitimate and verifiable certificate of birth to show that he was indeed qualified to hold this high office. This opens the door for two very urgent and important questions. The first question is, "Why has Obama not taken the simple and proper steps that would put this matter to rest, and produce his legitimate and verifiable certificate of birth?"

The second question would be, "Why does it appear that our Supreme Court is afraid to even respond to this very valid question?" Are they allowing fear of a perceived violent retaliation from the black community to become more important than their duty to make sure that our constitution is followed?

Obama has continually slapped all Americans in the face by ignoring this serious question, and it only gives credibility to the assumption that he indeed has something to hide! It was primarily the responsibility of the Democrat National Committee to make sure that any and all of their party's candidates for this high office meets all three qualifications as outlined in Article II, Section I of the U.S. Constitution. But, as has been the case with any other issue they were afraid to answer, the DNC has ignored this question in the hope that it will just simply go away. The fact that our own U.S. Supreme Court, the highest and most prestigious legal authority in the land, seems afraid to respond to this question is an even greater mystery than why the DNC has ignored this same issue.

What would happen if Obama were to be proven unqualified by citizenship to hold the office of president? Since nothing like this has ever happened before, the timing of any decision on this issue will be of the utmost importance. If Obama is proven to be ineligible to hold this office before he is inaugurated, it is likely that his victory in the election would be declared null and void, and John McCain would then be declared the winner by default. If Obama and Joe Biden have been sworn in as President and Vice President respectively, according to this same constitution which Obama has spat upon and apparently sees as irrelevant, I assume that Joe Biden would ascend to the office of president. Believing the DNC has known for sometime whether Obama was qualified, the timing of any decision would determine which party would occupy the White House for the next four years, and the DNC will do everything they can to delay any decision until after Obama has been inaugurated.

The outcome of any decision on this matter brings up a question about the true intentions of the black community itself. Would that proud race of people actually stoop so low as to approve of a fraud being perpetrated upon themselves and all other American people just to get a black elected to the office of president? Our black brothers and sisters have every right to be excited about having someone of their own race occupying the White House. But, if it is proven that Barack Obama is not constitutionally qualified to hold this high office, pride within the black race should insist that the first black president be one who has every legitimate chance at success, and not someone who reached that office by perpetrating a fraud against all of the American people. Any threats of violence by blacks in retaliation for preventing an unqualified person from assuming this office must be condemned and rejected by black leaders! Such treasonous actions would set back race relations in this country 100 years, and would destroy any and all of the credibility gained by well-intentioned members of the black community since the abolishment of slavery. The black community must ask themselves if it is more important for them to be *black*, or to be an *American*. If it is indeed more important for them to be *black* than to be an *American*, then they will never understand what it means to be an *American*, a real, true *American*!

Have the ethics of this nation become totally abandoned in the interest of liberal socialism? Has the liberal enhanced *white guilt of slavery* actually replaced common sense? Are we actually willing to criminally compromise the most perfect document of government ever devised by man, just to cowardly appease a proud race of people who have shamefully allowed themselves to become duped by a bunch of sleazy liberal hijackers? If these obscene possibilities prove to be correct, then there is not enough pride left in this country to fill a thimble!

Are we now to think that the leaders of the black community, a group of proud people who have been toiling and demanding for centuries that they be allowed to hold their rightful place as a people in equal standing within this nation, would riot and turn the streets of this country into a bloodbath just to keep a suspected unqualified person who is black, but not one of them, in the White House? This would destroy everything the hardworking and patriotic American blacks have been working toward for centuries. There are many well-qualified and legitimate members of the black race who have taken the proper steps to be qualified for this office, and to allow someone who has possibly stolen the White House through deception and deceit, would destroy everything those hardworking and very patriotic American blacks have been working toward for centuries.

CHRISTIANITY

The following is a collection of "letters to the editor" on the subject of Christianity which I submitted to my local newspaper for publication. Those displaying dates were actually printed, while those without dates were not. I have also included responses to some of my letters from liberal contributors, who will remain anonymous.

My Letter
December 24, 2007
Defending our Christian principles

Whether or not you support Mitt Romney or Mike Huckabee in their bid for their party's presidential nomination, one thing that cannot be denied about either of these two men is that they are not afraid to express their own religious convictions and beliefs. It seems that the overwhelming concern about these two men is that certain groups fear that they will govern using Christian principles as their guidelines. This would be in direct contrast to the un-American and un-patriotic principles demonstrated by many liberals placed in positions of leadership today. Since the majority of the population of this nation professes to be of the Christian faith, my only question is, "What the heck is wrong with having someone with Christian principles occupying the White House?" If Hillary Clinton is elected, do we want someone who would force us to accept the gay lifestyle, or who would protect the right to murder unborn babies? If Barrack Obama were elected, would we feel comfortable with a president who just might have a hidden agenda to propose legislation favoring the principles and traditions of his Islamic ancestors?

If we elect a president who is afraid to protect Christian principles and values because he is afraid of offending the *politically correct* crowd, then we had better start folding our tents and look for some other place to call home, because we will have lost this one! When I see certain groups vehemently protesting what they perceive to be a hidden meaning in Mike Huckabee's commercial showing what appears to be a cross in the background, or Mitt

Romney's speech in which he professes his commitment to his personal religious beliefs, my reaction is: "Get over it," or "So what?" or "If you don't like it, tough!" What is wrong with this picture? This nation has become so accepting and tolerant of almost every religion; that is, all but Christianity. Christianity is tolerant of other religions, but that same degree of tolerance is not returned. Do you remember the old saying, "If you don't use it, you'll lose it"? The same advice can be applied to our Christian beliefs and principles, and if we don't stand up for them, use them, and protect them, then we just might wake up one day only to realize that we have lost them forever.

The Liberal Response
December 28, 2007
Careless in Assertions

Mr. Hubbard is careless in his statements on Christianity and the Republican presidential candidates. First, George W. Bush, who campaigned in 2000 and 2004 as a "Christian conservative," has everyone scared to use religion as a qualification for political office. We have seen more bribery, stealing, lying, approval of torture, homosexuality, and dead American soldiers from the Republicans in the past seven years than we care to remember.

It would be nice if our vote assured that a candidate would clearly promote Christianity and all that it stands for. Unfortunately, that isn't true. Even Mr. Hubbard makes statements he cannot validate. While pretending to advocate Christianity, he states that, if elected, Hillary Clinton "would force the acceptance of the gay lifestyle down our throats and protect the right to murder unborn babies." Of course, Mr. Hubbard can't produce any evidence of Mrs. Clinton saying this.

Also, not one Republican candidate has openly stated he will work for a revision of the Constitution to abolish abortion and overturn the Roe vs. Wade ruling. Republicans want the women's votes and won't anger women by stating this publicly. A Republican statement that "I am against abortion, but I believe in a woman's right to choose" is a hypocritical way of not admitting you support abortion.

Also, Mr. Huckabee, on public television, stated he would be happy to accept the support of the "Log Cabin" group of homosexuals. He would not openly reject the support of homosexuals.

Mr. Hubbard uses innuendo to suggest that Barack Obama "might or might not" have a hidden agenda. Mr. Hubbard doesn't know this but is willing to malign someone to get votes for his "politically correct" crowd.

Don't be tricked into believing that morality belongs to one political party. There is nothing wrong with Christianity, but there is something wrong when someone tries to use it to trick you into voting for his politician.

My Letter
Stand Up and Be Counted

It may have become "politically correct" to sit back quietly and allow all mention of God or Christianity to be erased from the American conscience, but at what price are we willing to sell out our Christian heritage to a bunch of left-wing liberals who apparently have neither values nor conscience? In a weak effort to appease these liberals by sitting back and remaining silent as our once-proud Christian principles are continuously and falsely attacked as being unfriendly to other religions, American Christians are assuming a similar stance as did the citizens of Germany during Hitler's rise to power. We see what is happening, but we have become satisfied to blindly and silently sit by as the Christian majority is singled out and accused of religious bigotry, while all other religious and non-religious sects alike are allowed the right to display and celebrate their beliefs unchallenged.

I know these statements will sound judgmental and hypocritical, but I must admit that I am just as guilty of this as anyone else. I must continue to ask myself how can I continue to call myself a Christian, then just sit back and allow my very own faith to be constantly attacked without taking a stand to defend it. Sending a letter to the editor may not sound like much, but it allows me to question myself on these very issues, and I hope that it may elicit a similar response in someone else. Thanks to the continued efforts by several liberal educators who try to discount the importance of teaching this nation's true history in our public schools, we may lose sight of the fact that if we do not stand up and act to protect our faith, we could soon find ourselves in the same situation as those German citizens in the 1930s. And as history has taught us, when that day comes, we may have lost forever our opportunity to take a stand for what we believe in.

My Letter
Remain True to Your Beliefs

This is not intended to be an endorsement of Mitt Romney, but I strongly commend his courage in expressing what role his religious convictions would and would not play in his presidency. I cannot say that Mr. Romney would be my first choice as the Republican presidential nominee, but one thing I can say with no hesitation or reservation is that if we do not place the leadership of this nation into the hands of one who has strong Christian convictions and principles, we will continue our downward spiral into becoming a nation of no consequence.

For those guided by the concept of *political correctness*, ask yourselves whom you would rather your children have as their role models: the Hollywood elite, whose moral guideline is "If it feels good, do it"; college and pro athletes whose press clippings include their athletic performances and their disregard for laws and rules that they feel are meant for everyone but them; or people who value their Christian principles and use them to guide their lives. Our priorities seem to have become somewhat distorted in recent years.

The majority of Americans know the real difference between right and wrong. Most of us understand what we should and should not do as a nation. The destruction of this nation will not come in the form of a massive attack from our enemies. It is the little things that are going to destroy this nation over time, little bits and pieces that we hardly notice but are fatal blows nevertheless—little things such as when we fail to respect teachers, employers, or anyone else in leadership roles. It happens when it becomes acceptable for school kids to wear their pants far below their waists to allow their underwear to show. It happens when we allowed non-patriots to convince us to do away with the military draft, thereby eliminating our obligation to serve in our nation's military. It happens when we begin to view the satanic Hollywood elite or drug-addicted athletes as our moral role models. It happens when minorities are encouraged to believe that they are perpetual victims with no chance to succeed. And it will continue to happen as long as we give any credibility to those who encourage us to think that our government owes us something for nothing.

This nation will not continue to prosper or survive if we allow ourselves to follow the misguided and fatalistic advice of those who worship at the altar of "political correctness," which has become the true Achilles heel of this nation. We have become so afraid of hurting someone's feelings that we avoid realism and common sense in our treatment of others.

The Christian population of this nation has sat by silently far too long in allowing those who want to challenge our right to acknowledge our own Christian beliefs, to do so totally unchallenged. Mitt Romney is not afraid to acknowledge his belief in God and the importance of following his Christian principles. If this is not an important factor in choosing our next president, then we had better reexamine our priorities.

OBAMA'S IDEA OF CHRISTIANITY

Have you noticed that Barack Obama sometimes gives us an early warning of one of the *changes* he has in mind for America? You will find them hidden within the delivery of his flowery speeches. I recently watched a video of Barack Obama making one of his wonderful and insightful speeches in which he so wisely proclaimed that the United States was no longer a

Christian nation. To justify this statement, he pronounced this nation to now be a Jewish nation, a Hindu nation, a Buddhist nation, and—let's not forget, of course—we are now also a *Muslim* nation. As his reasoning for this announcement, Obama proclaims that since there are so many religions other than the Christian religion that are allowed to practice their faith in this country, he no longer considers the United States of America to be a Christian nation. How comforting that is! Thank you, Mr. Obama.

In his proclamation that the United States is no longer a Christian nation, Obama enlightens us as to his understanding of what it is to be a Christian. What else might we expect, considering that he received his exposure to the Christian faith from the Reverend Jeremiah Wright, the leader of the Trinity United Church of Christ in Chicago, arguably the most radical black church in the United States? If Obama's impression of Christianity is the same version he absorbed from Reverend Wright during the twenty years he has attended this church, then there is very good reason to ask questions about the impact of Barack Hussein Obama's Muslim indoctrination in his youth. Wright's version of Christianity doesn't seem very far removed from radical Muslim teachings, and if this is what Obama is referring to when he calls himself a Christian, then we had better look out!

He has overlooked one glaring difference about what it means to be a Christian nation. It is because America was, is, and has indeed always been a Christian nation that these other religions he mentioned are even allowed to practice in this country. If Obama is trying to equate what happens in this country to what happens in countries where any religion other than the chosen religion of that country's government is practiced (like the Middle Eastern countries and their Muslim religion, for example), he has absolutely missed his own point. None of these other religions would be allowed to exist in a Muslim-controlled country, and if discovered, those practicing their outlawed faith would be arrested or executed. If it is Obama's contention that the United States of America is no longer a Christian nation *because* we allow those other religions to exist, he has proven his own lack of understanding of what makes us a Christian nation. As a Christian nation, we are tolerant of other religions, which is something Obama cannot seem to comprehend. If we were no longer a Christian nation, using Obama's reasoning, members of these other religions would not be allowed to openly practice their faiths and would soon find themselves outlawed, punished, or even executed. Under an Obama administration, the United States could soon find itself under the heavy hand of one of those religions that is totally intolerant of other faiths, quite likely a Muslim regime.

This, America, is one of those *changes* Barack Hussein Obama has been impatiently proposing to those who are so blindly following him as their newly discovered messiah. If change is truly what you wish for, be careful! The change you are expecting will not be the change you will get.

Wake up, America!

The Ghosts of Christmas Past

Many of us have very wonderful memories of Christmases long ago—not just those of magical Christmas mornings, but of the entire Christmas season as well. Christmas may not be special to everyone, but to me and many, many others like me, Christmas is the most special day of the year. But these past few Christmases have left many with very empty feelings. Christians have been forced to sit back and watch as the *Grinch Who Stole Christmas* (the ACLU) worked its evil spell in its attempt to kill the true Christmas spirit.

Perhaps it is the shameless way that Christmas has become so commercialized that has hastened the demise of the true meaning of Christmas. Or it could even be the vicious and un-American political climate that we find our nation in today. We have seen this coming for several years, but Christmas 2006 convinced me that this wonderful holiday had truly lost its meaning for many people. There are those whose religious or nonreligious beliefs have denied them the experience of what it means to grow up in a home where Christmas was looked forward to and celebrated as a wonderful and special time.

What did Christmas mean in times past? For young children, the excitement of Christmas was the anticipation of what Santa might leave under the tree for them on Christmas morning. For others, it was the excitement of seeing the joy that filled the hearts of almost every person they came into contact with. Even strangers would smile and speak as they passed you on the street. People wished a sincere "Merry Christmas" to everyone they met. Then there were those wonderful old movies we would watch over and over again, which helped to usher in the spirit of the Christmas season. There are still a few networks that show these wonderful and timeless treasures, but the "politically correct" movement today seems to have brainwashed many people into denying the very spirit of something that requires only the faith of a child to enjoy and celebrate.

Is there really anything wrong with enjoying and celebrating this special time of year, one that allows us to feel a little closer to our lord and savior, Jesus Christ, and to one another? What is wrong with the joy that comes from watching as a child gets caught up in the magic of the season, even though we know that we can no longer experience that same wonderful excitement again ourselves in exactly the same way?

One day, we will come to realize just what we have been missing, and we will decide that it is time to reverse this nonsense and set things on the right track again. After all, it was Christmas that gave us hope and allowed us to dream, once upon a time. Maybe that time will return.

REMEMBERING CHRISTMAS

We have allowed Christmas—the real Christmas, that is—to become something that too many people feel is no longer worth celebrating. We have allowed Christmas to join a list of pleasant but ever-fading memories such as baseball, Mom, and apple pie ... well, maybe not baseball, which has fallen far down on the list in importance. We can blame it upon the commercialization of the holiday if we want to, but everyone knows that when it comes to the almighty dollar, business leaders have placed it above everything else since the beginning of time. The blame for the devaluation of Christmas can be laid at no other place than at the feet of each and every one of us. This is not something that just happened overnight, but with tiny step by tiny step, we have allowed ourselves to leave the importance of Christmas in our dusty past.

Regardless of how sincere we are when it comes to our own Christianity, there were certain aspects of the Christmas season that always seemed to bring out the very best in us and warm even the coldest and hardest of hearts. As children, we started to get excited about Christmas not long after Labor Day—for sure by the time Halloween had come and gone. Although we knew the meaning and importance of the Thanksgiving holiday, one of the ever-present meanings of this holiday was that we knew that Christmas was just around the corner. Santa Claus even appeared at the end of the Macy's Thanksgiving Day Parade, which meant for us to start getting ready for Christmas. Children would now go to sleep each night dreaming about Santa Claus, carolers singing, and the ever-present and magic aroma of popcorn and candy filling the air of every department store in town. Regardless of how young or old we were, Christmas was a very, very, very special time.

People seemed to be nicer to one another and would even go out of their way to speak to strangers. Even though the thought of getting presents was very exciting, giving a present to those dear to us also held its own special excitement for everyone. Parades, Christmas plays at schools, churches, or even at a local community playhouse would bring back pleasant memories of times past. Sitting around the living room with family and friends while enjoying holiday programs on TV or radio—many of which we would enjoy over and over again each year—were special times. Shopping trips with our parents, then later with our own children, created everlasting memories. We looked forward to opening our presents on Christmas morning and going to Grandmother's house for that special Christmas dinner, where we could see some of our aunts, uncles, and cousins that we might see no other time during the year. The fact that many of the people we shared those memories with have passed on and are no longer with us makes those memories even more special to us.

Just as important, though—and to many of us, even more so—was the real and true meaning of Christmas: the birth of our lord and savior, Jesus Christ. Whatever the mention of Jesus held for us during the rest of the year, it seemed to have a very different and even more special meaning during the Christmas season. We seem to have lost sight of this true meaning of Christmas. Many have allowed the shallow and empty concept of "political correctness" cloud our memory of what makes this holiday season special. With the misplaced notion of not offending other religions while we are celebrating our own, we have allowed the hearts and minds of the American people to be hoodwinked into believing that these other religions would allow us the same respect, and in doing so, we have allowed our own faith to become devalued.

THE MOST PROFOUND STATEMENT I HAVE EVER HEARD

Some time ago, I received an e-mail message that makes the most profound statement about life I have ever heard. It is so simple, yet so thought-consuming:

"I would much rather live my life as if there was a God, only to find out at death that there isn't; than to live my life as if there isn't a God, but to find out at death that there is."

A MOTHER ASKED ...

A friend sent me this e-mail message. One can feel the pain in each mother's question to the president.

A mother asked the president, "Why did my son have to die in Iraq?"

A mother asked the president, "Why did my son have to die in Saudi Arabia?"

A mother asked the president, "Why did my son have to die in Kuwait?"

Another mother asked the president, "Why did my son have to die in Vietnam?"

Another mother asked the president, "Why did my son have to die in Korea?"

Another mother asked the president, "Why did my son have to die on Iwo Jima?"

Another mother asked the president, "Why did my son have to die on a battlefield in France?"

Yet another mother asked the president, "Why did my son have to die at Gettysburg?"

And yet another mother asked the president, "Why did my son have to die on a frozen field near Valley Forge?"

Long, long ago, a mother asked, "Heavenly father, why did my son have to die on a cross outside of Jerusalem?"

The answer is always the same: "So that others may live and dwell in peace, happiness, and freedom."

This was e-mailed to me with no author attributed. I thought the magnitude and the simplicity of its message was awesome.

If you are not willing to stand *behind* our troops,
Please, please feel free to stand in front of them.

Note: This was e-mailed to me with no author attributed.

EDUCATION

Education Is the Difference

Once we finally realize and understand that getting a good education is the key to everything, a large portion of our problems could be solved! I am not referring to that educational scam that has been force-fed to several generations of our young people by ultra liberal educators; the very same scam that has attempted to brainwash intelligent Americans, young and old, rich and poor, black and white, into the idea that this world owes us a living, and that all of the wealth of this nation must be shared equally among those who created it, as well as those who never lifted a hand to do anything except to take a handout. I am referring to the type of education that teaches us to be proud of our country, and to answer the call to defend it if necessary; the type of education that inspires people to create and build things, and to discover a cure for cancer and heart disease; the type of education that teaches us how to use our ambition and initiative to design products that improve the lives of millions upon millions of people. I am referring to the same type of education that landed us on the moon and has created thousands of businesses that employ millions of people everyday.

This is what separates the strong from the weak, the rich from the poor, and the haves from the have-nots. Education is the difference between a world power and a third-world country. Education is the one thing that the powerful suppressors of freedom fear most from those being suppressed. Education is what allowed Abraham Lincoln, a poor backwoodsman from Illinois, to become perhaps the greatest president of the United States of America.

No, it is not teaching how to repeat slogans or make banners that build nations; it is not by convincing people that they are victims that helps find cures for diseases; and it is not convincing people to live on government entitlements that allowed an intelligent black educator in Alabama to create hundreds of innovative ways to use the peanut that revolutionized agriculture by bringing new life into previously worn-out farm fields. It is not telling people just how terrible this great nation is that made the difference in 1776. It was teaching people how to build and to do things, and not how to destroy that which is good. It is education that has allowed people to make positive differences in the lives of others everyday. Yes, it is education makes the difference!

A Most Unappreciated Profession

We are often advised or warned to get our priorities straight, and this is one priority that is long overdue in its need to be corrected. The time has come to heed this powerful advice and do whatever is necessary to correct the practice of grossly under-appreciating and properly compensating one of the most necessary and honorable professions in our nation's history; that of the professional educator or schoolteacher. But, when describing the professional educator, the distinction must be made between the truly dedicated teacher, and those within this profession who have become so intertwined within the destructive ideology of liberal teachers' unions, who instead of concentrating their efforts upon becoming more professional teachers, have become a major part of the problem.

Why do we keep losing the better teachers? Believe it or not, it is not always the money that forces them to leave this noble profession, but if they were paid in relation to the importance of their profession to this nation's future, it would be a good place to start. But to the professional teachers themselves, the opportunity to do their job in an atmosphere of safety, and one that is conducive to learning for their students would be the greatest incentive we could give them to continue in their chosen field. These fine people did not take the time to earn their college degrees in education simply to become glorified babysitters. These people are dedicated to the future of this nation, and thanks to the deplorable mess that our public school system now finds itself in, these saints soon lose their excitement to teach and motivate, and in many instances they lose a part of their faith in the Great American Dream itself.

How much importance are we really willing to place upon the future educational development of our children when we allow our dedicated teachers and educators to be viewed as expendable people who probably cannot do anything else? How important is it to properly teach someone the basics that will lead them into developing the cure for cancer? One question to ask would be whether it is more important to pay for new sports facilities, or even some other less-than-urgent physical facilities, than it is to provide a proper income and workplace environment that will support those whose job it is to teach our children, and at a level that is somewhat on par with the projected earnings of those they are teaching. After all, without dedicated and qualified teachers, the need for schools would not exist. Many school patrons erroneously think that it is wrong to pay teachers during the summer months when they are not teaching. But, what most people do not understand is that under the extreme working conditions our teachers are placed in today, if they did not have those summer months to recuperate, many of them simply could not find the strength to return to the classroom in the fall. Although the dedicated teacher loves and enjoys his or her job, it is not an easy job, and under the working conditions found in many of our schools today, it would be appropriate to allow *combat pay* to compensate for the danger some teachers find themselves in. It may be difficult to find the correct working plan, but it can be done.

Ask yourself which role model would most greatly affect the future success of this nation: professional athletes who are paid millions of dollars per year, and many of whom are continually arrested or charged with criminal behavior while being given two, three, or more chances to reform; or dedicated professional educators who are presented with the daunting task of motivating, training, and educating those who will someday aspire to all of the other professions necessary to make this or any nation a world leader. Granted, there are professional athletes who are very honorable and who cast a very good light upon their profession; however, almost everyone will agree that the amount of money paid to even the greatest of these athletes falls dangerously close to being considered obscene, if not insane. If the idea of anyone making this income were to be considered reasonable, who then would honestly deserve it more, the baseball player who hits thirty home runs a year; the basketball player who scores twenty-five points per game; the football player who rushes for a thousand yards in a season; or the classroom teacher who motivates and inspires a gifted but untrained young student to strive to discover the cure for cancer, or to find the alternative fuel that will allow this nation to become totally independent of an expensive and disappearing petroleum fossil fuel?

Imagine a world where children must leave their home at age eight to twelve to find jobs to help feed their families, and where there is no option that would allow them to go to school to study the arts, sciences, mathematics, or even how to interact with others. We would be as backward and undeveloped as any of today's Third World countries who must constantly seek out help to feed, clothe, and defend them from any number of predators. The United States of America would be just another place where people couldn't feed themselves or their families, and where the life expectancy was anywhere from eighteen to forty years of age if not for our dedicated teachers. Now, wouldn't that be something to look forward to?

There would be no factories to design, develop, and produce the products that have become the conveniences or even the necessities of the everyday lifestyles we have come to enjoy today. There would be no hospitals, doctors, or nurses to treat the sick and injured. There would be no one to motivate and train someone to invent, build, or maintain things we now consider to be the necessities of life. For good or bad, we could not be spending our weekends listening to, watching on TV, or attending sporting events as we do today.

The world we live in today is made possible as a result of many factors, but one of the most vital, yet underrated and unappreciated, is the dedicated classroom teacher. These noble people most certainly do not go into this proud profession with any grand illusions of becoming wealthy as a result of the pay this profession provides them. But, after toiling away in the classroom for a few months, or even a few years in a valiant effort to help our young people get the necessary educational foundation, they soon begin to realize that in far too many cases, they are the only ones who are truly excited about the learning experience. And woe be unto them if they ever attempt to discipline the wrong little darling placed into their care. They are expected to maintain strong discipline in the classroom—unless, of course, they attempt to discipline the children of certain members of their community, whether they are the elite or not. When those who really want to learn and achieve an education are hampered in doing so due to the unruly atmosphere found in many of today's classrooms, the teacher is viewed as the one who has failed to do his or her job of maintaining the proper discipline in their classroom.

As with any other profession, there are good teachers and there are bad teachers; but how many times have we seen a truly qualified and gifted teacher forced to leave the teaching field, a profession for which many have a burning passion, for reasons over which they have no control? Far too many! Many of us can recall a time when there were teachers whose careers spanned thirty to forty years and who left their profession only because there was a mandatory retirement age. These were teachers who were very much responsible for the success of the outstanding doctors, lawyers, civic leaders, astronauts, scientists, engineers, and educators of today. It is sad to realize that those same dedicated teachers of yesteryear could not even begin to survive or tolerate the deplorable conditions found in our schools and classrooms today. This is in no way intended to take anything away from today's teachers, many of whom went into their profession with the same dedication of those teachers of years past, but who were fully aware of the conditions in which they would have to teach today. In far too many cases, these teachers of today are also forced to leave their profession because they just can't take it any longer. Both groups of these noble professional educators, past and present, are among a diminishing group of *true American heroes* that we still have around today. They have too long been forced to accept and live with the lack of respect, gratitude, and yes, the financial considerations they have deserved for a long, long time. Let me make it perfectly clear that most of these unsung American heroes have not openly campaigned for the increase in compensation that this noble profession properly deserves, as it would not be within their nature to do so.

One way to provide funding for this is to make our legislative leaders aware of the importance of this issue, and with encouragement from the general public, this can be done. Our government needs to understand just how important it is to the future of our nation that we appreciate and compensate those who dedicate their lives to opening the doors of educational opportunities to our young people, and to allow these education professionals to reintroduce the discipline necessary to allow our schools to conduct the intended business of educating our children, and not being forced to play the perceived role of glorified babysitters or prison guards.

Possibly the most intriguing and compelling reason for correcting these injustices of the past is to convince many of our best and brightest young people of today to seriously consider entering teaching as a most worthy and worthwhile profession. Without the efforts of these dedicated warriors, the educational advantages this nation has previously enjoyed will continue to erode and eventually disappear, just as we have seen happen to our strong family values and other beliefs and principles of the past.

God bless our troops and our teachers, and God bless America!

EDUCATIONAL FAILURES

I recently watched a report on a local TV news channel about how education in this country is in much worse shape today than it was twenty-five years ago. This report revealed that a very high percentage of students in our public schools today could not identify a picture of Adolf Hitler, could not identify the century in which the Civil War was fought, and that many high-school graduates cannot understand even basic eighth-grade mathematics. For many of us who spent at least part of our careers teaching in public schools, we recognize that the real problems go back much further than twenty-five years.

These problems started when groups of liberal malcontents began posing as educators, and began promoting the crazy ideas that competition was unfair, that students must be promoted whether they achieve certain basic standards or not, that most forms of corporal punishment must be eliminated, that the teaching of real American history should be de-emphasized in favor of a more *politically correct* version, and oh yes, to promote this idea of *political correctness* as the acceptable way to live in today's society. These liberal educators also decided that to properly integrate public schools, expectations must be relaxed so that all students would learn at the same pace. These same liberal educators understood that if they could reach students at a very early age, they could brainwash them into believing that everyone and everything must be equal, that competition advanced the strong at the expense of the weak, and that experiencing failure of any kind would only serve to destroy one's self-esteem. This philosophy has produced generations with no ambition, no desire to excel, no pride in their country, and no obligation to defend this country if called upon to do so. Many of them have been convinced that this world owes them a living without them doing anything to earn it, and that the concept of Christianity is inherently evil. We are now being taught that our long-held Christian traditions, values, and beliefs are making certain ethnic and religious groups in this country feel uncomfortable because our beliefs differ from theirs, and that we are expected to abandon our religious principles and traditions, while at the same time allowing these people to celebrate their own.

This, my fellow Americans, is why our educational system finds itself in such an abysmal condition today! How much longer are we going to sit by and allow America to become something that our founding fathers and our own ancestors would not recognize?

THE ONLY HOPE TO SAVE OUR FAILING EDUCATIONAL SYSTEM

It is true that educational programs such as "No Child Left Behind" and others may hold the possibility for great improvements in education, but we can spend all of the money that the so-called *experts* promise will do the trick, and more, but nothing, absolutely nothing will be able to save our educational system until strong discipline is returned to the classroom! Those who see our public schools simply as a place to sell their drugs, bully anyone they choose (including teachers and administrators), disrupt learning, and refuse to take part in the educational process must be given the choice of fully conforming to earning an education, or being placed into mandatory alternative programs. These mandatory alternative programs would consist of enrollment to successfully learn a vocational skill, being drafted into military or community service if they have reached a certain age, or enrollment in a military boot camp/education program if they have not yet reached that certain age. This would be required for everyone age eighteen and under.

Obtaining the best education possible is vital to anyone's career growth. Those who are not willing to take advantage of the many opportunities available in our public education programs—and in such way that does not distract from the overall learning opportunities of other students—should be placed into either a strongly disciplined vocational program or into a military setting. When discipline is finally returned to the classroom, then, and only then, can any programs designed to enhance the educational experience become successful.

RACE RELATIONS

A Recipe for Positive Race Relations

By the chance that there might be readers of this book who call the black community there home, it is my sincere hope that you will not view it as a negative message from the white community to the black community. There has been far too much negativity between the races, and it is time to move in a totally different direction.

Do you believe in *tough love*? Well, this is an honest attempt at a version of *tough love,* coming from one concerned and compassionate American to another. There is no doubt that there are many within the black community who would truly love to see great improvements made in the area of race relations in this country; but, unfortunately, Jesse Jackson, Al Sharpton, Jeremiah Wright, and Louis Farrakhan, are not among them. This group would rather see both races die out than to see them living in complete and total harmony as equal partners in the American dream. Jesse Jackson and Al Sharpton often speak of bringing the races together, but in reality, that is the very last thing they want to see happen. Listening to and following the advice of these so-called civil rights leaders will ensure that the races will never come together in peace and harmony.

This is not intended in any way to be racist, although I am sure that there are those who will view it as such. This is something that has definitely needed to be discussed for a long, long time! I hope we have finally arrived at a point where the white community and the black community can come together and have an honest and open heartfelt dialogue on the subject of race relations. If we are indeed the mature adults we have imagined ourselves to be, this will hopefully open many doors that have previously been closed to one group or the other, and will be very beneficial to all concerned parties.

Everyone recognizes that the black race is one of the oldest, if not the oldest, races upon this Earth. Pride within the black race is the one thing that has sustained them throughout their history, and it is what has allowed them to survive when many other races became extinct during those same time periods. Improvement in the area of race relations in America has long been erroneously determined to be solely the responsibility of the white community. However, events that took place on November 4, 2008 have changed the course of history, and from that date forward, it will be the pride deep within the black community that will determine whether race relations in this country will improve, or if they will continue to divide the American people forever!

On November 4, 2008, the American voter proclaimed that race would no longer be a determining factor when choosing a president. On this date, Barack Hussein Obama, a black Democrat from Illinois, became the forty-fourth president of the United States. The fact that this country would vote a black man into office over his white and more experienced opponents, speaks volumes. Although the result of this election has been clouded by long ignored challenges to Obama's constitutional qualifications of birth, the presidential election of 2008 proved beyond a shadow of a doubt that race relations in this country have indeed improved dramatically since slavery was abolished by the thirteenth amendment to the U.S. Constitution in 1865. Now that this historical event has actually taken place, it is now incumbent upon the black community to realize the true significance of this event, and to do their part to see that continued progress in the area of race relations is no longer blocked by those who see any improvement in this area as detrimental to their own personal financial future.

Blacks have long campaigned to become a truly accepted part of the great American experience, but they must also realize that this acceptance is a two-way street. It will now become necessary for the black community to take very positive steps to see that they allow themselves to become Americans in every possible way. To do this, adult members within the black community must take the necessary steps to assert a strong influence upon younger blacks, and encourage them to become much more responsible American citizens. Young blacks must dedicate themselves to earning a good education; to preparing themselves to become responsible leaders and role models for their own families; and to make sure that their families consist of a home where both a father and a mother are present and supportive. Once these huge steps have been successfully taken, other problems that have prevented blacks from enjoying each and every aspect of the great American dream will begin to disappear, and the American Nation can become a nation of common goals and opportunities for everyone!

One of the most important characteristics that must be instilled into all people of America, regardless of race or color, is that they must think of themselves as Americans first and any other characteristics second! Black parents must understand and instill into their children that they, and not the government, are completely and totally responsible for their own future, and that they must do everything necessary to see that they do not become dependent upon government assistance for their very existence. They must break the bondage of dependence to a liberal Democrat Party who sees the black race as simply a voting bloc that will keep them in power, but at the expense of the loss of productivity and pride of an entire race of people.

Every segment of the black community, along with everyone else in America, must accept some level of responsibility to see that the drug culture is not viewed as an acceptable lifestyle. This may require that those involved in that culture be given the option to get help on their own, or they will be reported so they can receive the help and treatment necessary to break the hold of this fatalistic addiction and destroyer of human self-worth. Improvement in this vital area will also help in other areas, such as the high crime rate.

Becoming a part of the Great American Dream means that there are benefits to be enjoyed, but there are also sacrifices to be made! This is where the two-way street comes into play, and one cannot become a true American unless they are honestly willing to accept both. America cannot survive and prosper if a large segment of its population is only willing to take, while giving back nothing in return! If there is no willingness or desire to make sacrifices for something that we say we love, then we are only fooling ourselves and everyone else when we say we love that something. A return to the greatness America once enjoyed and took pride in is just waiting for its people to say the word. Once that happens, the rest of the world will recognize and understand that the real America is back in its rightful place, and the future of the rest of the world is once again secure.

IMPROVING RACE RELATIONS

Considering the sensitivity of many within the black community toward any comments that might be considered racially insensitive, perhaps Golf Channel announcer Kelly Tilghman should have taken time to edit any remarks she might possibly make, that could be overheard by anyone, before she made her comment about Tiger Woods. On the other hand, this incident simply serves as a perfect example of why race relations in this country will never improve until all concerned parties are willing to use reason and logic when dealing with this issue. Tiger Woods demonstrated his integrity and willingness to recognize Ms. Tilghman's comments exactly for what they really were, and he accepted her apology; case closed. Unfortunately, Al Sharpton, Jesse Jackson, and others like them will invent a problem where none actually exists, because they see any improvement in the area of race relations as a threat to their self-appointed role as a civil rights leader to the black community. For this reason, they will never acknowledge anything that even resembles improvement in the area of race relations.

Soothing any fractured and sensitive relationship should never become the sole responsibility of only one of the involved parties. Conscientious parents of all races will make every effort to see that their quarreling children stop their juvenile bickering and do whatever is necessary to stop fighting and make up. Why, then, should it be any different when dealing with race relations? The time is long overdue for all parties to bite the bullet and do whatever is necessary to come together and make it work. While the white community must try to be more conscious of any actions or remarks that might be viewed by the watchdogs out there as insensitive, the true leaders within the black community must take it upon themselves to lay aside any long-held bitter feelings and stop listening to those whose primary goal is to make sure that the races never come together. One thing is for sure; if we continue to search for ways to keep the races divided, then we will sadly be successful, and we will never come together as one people.

I realize that my comments will likely infuriate those who have no interest in seeing these ancient problems in the area of race relations improve; however, that attitude is exactly why this area will never improve without a positive and determined effort on the part of both sides of this divisive issue. Once both parties are willing to acknowledge that race relations have indeed improved considerably over the years, we can take pride in this fact and move forward with total success as our ultimate goal.

THE FUTURE OF AMERICA

What do we truly want America to look like in the future? Are we honestly satisfied with the direction in which we are currently headed? Are we confident that we will be happy and content with the way this country looks in five, ten, twenty, or fifty years from now? Do we want America to be a land where our cities and communities are safe places, and where we and our families can go downtown, or to shopping malls, or to parks and feel perfectly safe in doing so? Is America now a place where our schools can dedicate their time, energy, and resources to the task of educating our children? Do we want America to be a place where our children can grow up in the traditions and values we hold dear, and where we can worship our God in the way we so choose? Is this what America is like right now? If our founding fathers were to come back to see what has become of the nation for which they had laid the foundation, would they be proud of what they saw?

We all know what both the problem and the answer are, but I am afraid that we have been conveniently avoiding the true and honest answer to these questions for so long that we have lost the true perspective of how to fix it. We need to tell it like it is, and stop worrying about hurting the feelings of this group or that group who always tries to respond to the problem as being the result of something that happened to their ancestors many years ago. There comes a time in everyone's lives when we take responsibility for our own actions, and when this is done, contrary to what liberals try to reinforce, these problems will become greatly improved.

The real question is, "What are we going to do about it?" Our cities and communities are not safe! Our schools cannot dedicate their efforts to education! Our tax revenues are used for building jails and prisons and hiring additional police officers, instead of building parks, schools, and hiring teachers. Americans are being compelled to forget their own traditions and values and to become more open and receptive of the traditions and values of those who came here from other places.

When we speak of race, there must be only one race that concerns us, and that is the *human race!* Black or white, it doesn't matter. If we continue to allow lawless thugs, punks, and gangs to rule the streets of our cities, no one of any color will be safe. Do we want our cities and towns to look like Memphis, Washington DC, Detroit, Philadelphia, or inner-city Los Angeles? Those cities have become war zones, with no one willing to identify and attack the real problems. We have been so concerned over being labeled as racially insensitive that we cannot and will not do what is necessary to fix the problem. We have become so afraid to make any comment that might be seen as negative about one race or another that we are allowing the lack of corrective action to destroy this nation from within. This is exactly what Russian premier Nikita Khrushchev was referring to in the early 1960s when he said that Russia wouldn't need to lift a finger to defeat America, because we would destroy ourselves from within.

Political correctness is quickly becoming the weapon of our own self-destruction.

Wake up, America!

It Is What It Is

Thanks to Reverend Jeremiah Wright, we can see exactly why race relations within this country have gone absolutely nowhere. Although many within the black community have taken advantage of opportunities designed to help bring them into the social and economic mainstream, there are also those who have never known anything but hating white people, simply because they are white people. A perfect example of this is the case of Reverend Wright, who clearly demonstrated his hate for white America with his racist and hate-filled sermons to his congregation. People such as Jeremiah Wright will not allow that portion of the black community he sees as in his charge to gain any confidence in a relationship with the white community. Since the church is the strongest social segment of the black community, it is this group to which he constantly reinforces the "them against us" mentality that prevents his followers from ever separating themselves from the comfortable *victim* label.

The glaring finger of racial prejudice has long been pointed, and with some justification, solely at the white race as being the cause of the racial divide in this nation. However, certain facts cannot be disputed. Although it was white Europeans who brought black men, women, and children from the African continent to North America and some of the surrounding islands, one very important fact has long been overlooked and even ignored. It was their own African countrymen who captured their black brothers and sisters, sold them to European slave traders for profit, and then returned to hunt and capture many, many more.

Is it possible that Reverend Jeremiah Wright has provided—unintentionally, of course—the most revealing piece of the puzzle to date suggesting that the banner of racism can no longer be laid exclusively at the feet of the white community? This matter of racism has long been the most divisive issue in the history of this nation, but thanks to Reverend Wright's undeniable proof, it is clear that the black community has also played a major role in the continuation of racial intolerance. Once the true leaders of the black community admit that they are also responsible for racism in this country, we can then move forward into a new era of understanding, and only then can real progress be made. Jeremiah Wright's accidental back-door revelation just may have achieved the unlikely results that will remove the wedge that has divided the races for centuries. The black community must move past those bleak years of slavery and realize that this wonderful opportunity may come only once in our lifetime. If we don't take advantage of this opportunity to do something positive in the area of race relations, it will never happen. The first and perhaps most important step in this process is for the black community to once and for all deny this *victim* charade that has been wickedly implanted into the minds of many blacks, both young and old, for generations.

Blacks in America today, unlike many of their ancestors, have never toiled under the bondage of slavery, except of course for that self-imposed version laid upon them by the likes of Jessie Jackson, Al Sharpton, Louis Farrakhan, and, as we have now learned, Reverend Jeremiah Wright. This group of whiners enjoys a much more affluent lifestyle than does the vast majority of the same black community to which they constantly preach their message of doom and gloom. If their followers ever stopped listening to their bleak message, they would quickly lose their gravy train. Jeremiah Wright has finally proven what many have known all along: that there are white racists, but there are also black racists!

Neither race has totally escaped the shackles of slavery. Blacks and whites have both suffered greatly from slavery—not equally, of course, but in varying degrees. For Black Americans, it was the unspeakable bondage of the institution of slavery itself. For White Americans today, it is the guilt of the injustice of slavery and the fact of actually knowing that what happened was wrong. All of our hearts bleed deeply from the knowledge of this injustice!

Since that dreadful period of slavery legally ended many years ago, both races have been guilty of doing things to keep the idea of racism alive. The white community was very reluctant to acknowledge either social or economic equality for the black community. The black community has been reluctant to understand that government entitlement programs were only intended to help move them out of poverty and toward self-reliance, and not to become their livelihood. Many within the black community have been led to believe that they cannot survive without the benefit of these suffocating entitlement programs. The real effect of these programs is that they robbed many blacks of the ambition and drive that would have lifted them out of poverty. Liberals saw this as a way to buy the black vote and keep them in a state of permanent dependence upon government. It is definitely not the responsibility of government to block the opportunities blacks need in order to achieve the independence and equality they so rightly deserve. But, once self-reliance is achieved, the proud black man must take steps to ensure that this ideal of success and self-reliance is passed along to all current and future generations, with the understanding that all Americans of all races are responsible for their own future and success.

THE DREADED WHITE MALE

Have you ever listened closely to the Democrat presidential candidates' speeches and tried to pinpoint who their specific target might be? For Barack Hussein Obama and his supporters, they talk about rising above four hundred years of racism. For Hillary Clinton, she is the poor little female trying to make it in a man's world. For each of them, the enemy of the American people is *the dreaded white male*. It would appear that according to them, all of the world's problems would simply go away if only *the dreaded white male* were to be eliminated from the face of the Earth.

When will blacks, gays, feminist, and Hispanics in America finally come to realize that their chances for success will be much better when they stop viewing themselves as perpetual *victims*? They hope everyone will feel sorry for them because they want us to believe that they are always being picked upon by white males. It is very doubtful that this world could last very long if any category of people were to become extinct. Although it usually comes about by accident, we have often learned that things turn out much better when we all work together for the common good.

VICTIMS

It appears that the Democrat presidential debates are becoming a version of *last one standing*. On alternating days, each one takes his turn at playing *good cop, bad cop*. So far, no single candidate has assumed the position of pack leader.

Remember when we were told by leaders within the Democrat Party that Barack Obama might have finally hit upon an approach as the New Age leader of the black community that could take giant steps toward improving race relations within this country? The only thing Barack and Michelle Obama have in common with the black community is the color of their skin, and their involvement with their racist minister and his church, which they apparently used to get votes from the black community. They consider themselves to be no more a part of the black community than do most other political and business leaders in their income category. Their connection to the black community is totally and selfishly for whatever political advantage it will give to them.

Democrats have tried to convince us that Obama does not appear to be consumed by same old worn-out approach of the Jessie Jackson's and Al Sharpton's of this world, who keep portraying blacks as being *perpetual victims*. They have failed to realize that the only way a successful black leader is ever going to help bring the races together is to stop preaching to the black community that they are now and have always been *victims,* and that they have no control over their own destinies. We are told that Barack Obama is one of the few black leaders who truly understand the difference between success and failure, but whether he is willing to pass his secrets along to the black community is yet to be seen.

Well, to no one's great surprise, it didn't take long for Obama to jump on that tired old racism horse and ride it into the ground. For someone billed as one who was supposed to unite all races and classes, it turns out that it is Obama who has used the *race card.* It is Obama who has initiated class warfare. And it is Obama who has made an issue of John McCain's age. Racism is the one thing the black community just will not allow to die. They have used this issue to their confused advantage for decades, and they are so comfortable with being perpetual *victims* that they have dismissed any attempts that might bring the races together, and they are now the ones who are keeping racism alive.

If those in the black community continue to think of themselves only as *victims,* they will never realize their true potential as a people, and they will always be dependent upon the liberal political philosophy that proclaims that it is the role of government to take care of them. If I were a member of the black race, I would be very upset with and untrusting of any political or government entity that constantly reminded me that I must always remain dependent upon it and its policies for my very existence. Liberals will quickly become a nonfactor as a political movement once those in the black community find their own self-worth and finally break the bondage of slavery that has long been the primary weapon of the liberal Democrat Party. If Obama really had the best interest of the black race in mind, he could expose the obvious and transparent truth that it has long been the Democrat Party that has kept blacks down as a race, and convinced them that they can only exist through the entitlement programs sponsored by the Democrat Party. But, that isn't likely to happen either.

The black community has much to offer this nation and the entire world. The only way they will ever realize their own value to the world community is for them to break the ties of bondage that have kept them chained to the liberal Democrat Party for centuries, and to begin to make decisions for themselves. When they finally begin to think of themselves as *Americans,* and not as *victims* of America, the black community can then assume their rightful place, not only within the American community, but the world community as well.

SAME SONG, ONE-MILLIONTH VERSE

Columnist Leonard Pitts seems to have earned membership in a very exclusive club that also includes none other than Jessie Jackson and Al Sharpton. This illustrious group has apparently made a pact with the devil himself, and in return for his blessings, they have agreed to make sure that harmony between the races will never be achieved. They will do everything within their power to keep the theory alive that the black race is now, has always been, and always will be the victim of racial prejudice. Their greatest fear is that members of the black community will come to realize that they are just as capable as anyone else, and that by breaking the bonds that have convinced them that they are not capable of taking care of themselves, and understanding that by taking advantage of the opportunities of education, they can achieve success that up until now has been only dreamed of.

The *victim* tag has always been a very useful tool by this group and others like them, primarily liberal Democrats. The current presidential campaign has exposed this long-used practice of the Democrat Party toward minorities. They have always attempted to buy the votes of the black community by offering entitlement programs that will provide just enough subsistence that they will feel forever indebted to the Democrat Party, but not enough to allow many of them to escape this orchestrated level of poverty. Democrats have always assisted a select few members within the black community in achieving certain positions of political success, but they are always careful to ensure that this success is confined within certain limited, designed parameters. This time, however, the chosen minority candidate whom they selected to run and finish second to their presumed queen, Hillary Clinton, actually turned out to be a much more formidable opponent than they had ever imagined. So, to not appear to be the party of *racism,* which they truly are, they began to read between the lines, and even threw their Queen Hillary under the bus in the interest of perpetuating their charade as the party of minorities.

The advancement of a victim class, although somewhat weakening as more and more people realize that we all are capable of controlling our own destinies, is alive and well, thanks to the likes of Al Sharpton, Jessie Jackson, and columnist Leonard Pitts. These purveyors of doom and gloom are still trying to sell buggy whips in the modern automobile age. This group has once again demonstrated that they just can't get past something that happened almost 150 years ago, and in order to justify their self-appointed role as watchdog for the black community, they must make sure that the *victim mentality* continues to thrive.

This group will soon lose their gravy train if the black community continues to realize that the only way to improve one's station in life is to improve one's ability to function within society. Success cannot be achieved by depending upon the government to supply one's every need to sustain life. The "them against us" brainwash theory is a motto for losers. Education, ambition, and a burning desire to succeed is the only way to bury the past and move successfully into the future.

A local reader responded to Mr. Pitts's column in our local paper on March 4, in which his never-ending obsession to keep this victim mentality alive, or at least on life support, is doing nothing but reinforcing the racial division within this country. He just can't understand the value of not spending his life reliving the past. He keeps pointing fingers at this group or that group as being the problem, but in reality, all he needs to do is to just look in the mirror to see who suffers by this constant complaining. People must realize that this is not the 1860s, and the problems of that time will never be fixed until people of today decide to take it upon themselves to improve their own station in life instead of depending upon government to fix everything.

Although it is fact that the great majority of Southerners did not own slaves, Mr. Pitts implies that they are not truthful when they said that they fought for reasons of *states rights* instead of slavery. Mr. Pitts also refuses to apply the same logic to the Civil War as he does to the war in Iraq. Pitts uses statements made by the president of the Confederacy that indicate that all Southerners were following the orders of their political leaders in fighting to keep the institution of slavery, as his proof to show that all Southerners were fighting exclusively to preserve slavery, and that reason alone. This simply is not true!

He uses this same false analogy in his attempt to discredit President George W. Bush's contention that the war in Iraq was about democracy for the Iraqi people. We all understand that Iraqi democracy was one of the reasons, but oil and its availability was also a major reason, one that Bush has acknowledged many times. Why is it so hard for Pitts to accept either of these facts; that the majority of Southerners never owned slaves and that they were fighting to preserve their way of life, and that the war in Iraq was about democracy *and* to protect our vital oil supplies of that region?

After almost 150 years, it is sad that some people want to keep reliving the Civil War instead of getting past it and moving into the future. Wake up and smell the coffee, Mr. Pitts!

FACTS OF LIFE

Everyone living today was born long after the institution of slavery was abolished. As far as I am aware, none of my relatives owned slaves; therefore,

I am not responsible for the institution of slavery, and I am not responsible for the poverty and unemployment rate of blacks in America today.

Modern-day white Americans do not and did not own slaves; therefore, they are not responsible for something their ancestors or even their race did 150 years ago. Today's white race is no more responsible for bringing the ancestors of today's black race into slavery than the innocent members of today's black race are in the high crime rate of their race. Although liberals will plead differently, no one can be held responsible for something that took place even before they were born, or that they had no involvement with or control over.

Life for most blacks in America today is considerably better than it likely would have been if they were living in Africa. Instead of finding comfort in the tag of the perpetual victim, if blacks in America are ever going to rise above the levels of poverty and unemployment that have consumed much of their race for decades, they must take responsibility for their own fate and do whatever is necessary to secure their own future. The black race cannot depend upon liberal Democrats, the white race, or anyone but themselves to improve their lot in life. No one can ever help anyone to succeed who does not possess a burning desire for success.

Many brave American heroes put their lives on the line every day to protect the rights all Americans enjoy, including the rights of those who apparently see themselves as being so inadequate that they are compelled to constantly disrespect everything that makes this nation great.

THE BLACK BLESSING IN DISGUISE

For those of us who claim to be Christians, we have come to learn that when God bestows a blessing upon us, he often will also present us with a challenge to go along with that blessing, and sometimes that challenge is an almost insurmountable one. For Moses and the children of Israel, it was forty years of wandering in the wilderness. For those castoffs and indentured servants from other lands who were to make up the core of what would become the United States of America, it was to follow a dream that had never before been successfully accomplished. And for our brothers and sisters of the black race, as hard as it may be to understand and appreciate, slavery just might have been a blessing in disguise, as well as their most difficult challenge ever. Maybe, just maybe, God had a plan for what he allowed to happen.

In the formative years of this great country, there were many immigrants who made their way to this wonderful land, and many of them would soon realize their dreams, and many of their sorrows here. But the prevailing feelings of that time allowed very few members of the black race from Africa or anywhere else to immigrate here, or to assimilate themselves into that American society. The institution of slavery that the black race has long believed to be an abomination upon its people may actually have been a blessing in disguise. The blacks who could endure those conditions and circumstances would someday be rewarded with citizenship in the greatest nation ever established upon the face of this Earth. Often we just don't understand God's grand scheme of things, but if we believe that God does indeed test us at times, we just might begin to understand why he did things as he did them.

It just might be that he knew that the black race was indeed a strong and courageous people who could endure an existence in the strange land into which they were about to be placed, and that they would one day reap the reward handed down to them by their brave ancestors: that of being an American. The existence and lifestyle of the people of Africa has been almost unchanged since the beginning of time, and if our black brothers and sisters can allow themselves to see it this way, maybe they can in time develop a better understanding of how and why they were placed here. Would it have been better for black Americans of today if their ancestors had never been brought to these shores? Would their lives honestly have been better as African tribesmen? If things had been reversed, it is very doubtful that the white race would have been able to cope and endure such challenges if enslaved in Africa, as the black race did in America. The question now is, with the black race several generations into this process, will they allow themselves to take advantage of the gift that was given to them, and redeem those trials and tribulations of their ancestors?

Blacks today must ask themselves, "Is their life better spent as U.S. citizens living in America, or as African tribesmen living in grass huts and constantly searching for their food?" Is life better for black Americans to be living in an America that is still evolving in its understanding of what it means to be a multicultural nation, or would they be more content living under the same conditions as those endured by most living in Africa today? Wouldn't life for blacks in American today be more enjoyable and successful if they would only learn to appreciate the value of a good education? Also, wouldn't life for blacks in America today be more successful if they would only see government entitlement programs as a last resort, or as for those who simply cannot provide for themselves due to physical or mental handicaps?

Will black pride ever convince their race to take full advantage of those things that would encourage their fellow Americans to see them as equal and contributing members of the American experience? Is black pride enhanced or diminished by the continued acceptance of the *victim* label, as encouraged by liberal whites and far too many impressionable leaders within the black community?

Blacks today have been taken in by a liberal ideology that sees their vote as their only asset. Many blacks have become great contributors to the American way of life, and although there have been numerous success stories about blacks in America, too many blacks today have bought into the *them against us* mentality and have fallen into the pit of racial or class warfare as being their only option. Especially for those in the younger generations, a life of crime is seen as having a more acceptable future than the completion of a good education, followed by the accomplishments gained only from a productive occupation.

Regardless of what members of the black community have been tricked into believing in the past, their success or future cannot be placed in the hands of anyone but themselves. We are all responsible for our own actions, and just as with the white community, success or failure is the result of many individual choices, and how we react as a result of those choices.

THE NEW SLAVERY

As most of us are aware, slavery was abolished by the thirteenth amendment to the U.S. Constitution in 1865. One huge fact that liberal Democrats and their liberal media cohorts try to keep quiet is that it was a *Republican* president (Abraham Lincoln), and not a *Democrat*, who ended slavery. Since that time, blacks have enjoyed various degrees of freedom, and by the mid-twentieth century, the black race had become somewhat assimilated into American society.

Slavery of the black race in America is still very much alive today, but contrary to what Michelle Obama would have us believe, it is not white America that holds her people in bondage. The liberal Democrat Party, along with civil rights activists such as Jesse Jackson and Al Sharpton, constantly reinforces the assumption that blacks are not capable of taking care of themselves, thereby encouraging them to remain addicted to government entitlement programs for their very survival. This logic is responsible for keeping blacks from reaching their full potential and achieving what they are obviously capable of achieving. Once the black race awakens to the fallacy of this charade, these predictors of doom and gloom will soon find themselves out of a job.

For many years, and with but a few exceptions, athletics seemed to be one of the few ways blacks could rise above their preconceived plight of poverty. Unfortunately, many young blacks have also turned to a life of crime to find their way out of poverty, a path that has proven to be like a cosmic black hole, where things fall in but never come out. The black race, if not the oldest race on Earth, is certainly one of the oldest races, and they did not survive thousands upon thousands of years as a race of people without having the intelligence and resourcefulness to take care of themselves. Those who constantly keep reinforcing the idea within the black community that the white race is responsible for holding the black race back, and that blacks are not capable of taking care of themselves without government help, have certainly done no favors for the black community. Ambition, desire, initiative, and pride are what make people survive and prosper, not entitlement programs that keep them dependent upon others. The ability to recognize and take advantage of situations is what moves us to the top of the ladder, not waiting for someone else to carry us up the ladder.

We are all very fortunate that many within the black community did not listen to this group that was intent upon making sure that blacks would never rise above their appointed status of being *perpetual victims*. During the most recent twenty to thirty years, many within the black community saw education as their way out of poverty. For those who did make their way out of poverty through education, often the world became their oyster. Some relied upon affirmative action programs to open doors for them, but in the long run, the primary reason for their success was their own ambition and the desire to take every advantage of a good education, which was much stronger than the pull of those failures within the black community who accused them of being an Uncle Tom, or trying to become part of the *white man's world*. When enough people within the black community acknowledge that education is the path out of poverty, this will be the point at which we see a dramatic change of direction in the fortunes and future of the black community.

THE OTHER SIDE OF RACISM

Thanks to the ranting and raving of a delusional Jeremiah Wright, we are now exposed to a side of racism that we have always been told couldn't possibly exist. Is there any doubt about the real agendas of Jesse Jackson, Al Sharpton, Louis Farrakhan, and now Jeremiah Wright, those self-appointed leaders of the black community who constantly preach white racism? They blame white America exclusively for the institution of slavery, while at the same time completely ignoring the prominent role played by African tribesmen who captured and sold their black brothers and sisters to European slave traders, who then transported them in chains to these shores.

These charlatans have duped the black community into believing that their true objective is to improve the economic and social status of blacks while seeking equality among the races. They keep telling blacks that by supporting their efforts to achieve equality, this will eventually promote better race relations. The reality is, however, that improving race relations is the very last thing these con men want. They realize that if race relations in this country really were to improve, their own little gravy train to riches and power would become permanently derailed.

If race relations in this country were to improve to the point where the black community no longer sought direction from this group, what do you think would happen to the posh lifestyles these crafty opportunists have long enjoyed at the expense of their black brothers and sisters? They do not try to convince their people that the best way to defeat poverty is through education, or that a complete family unit containing both the mother and the father helps to stabilize their entire community, or that living within the drug culture leads to certain death and destruction, or that having children out of wedlock condemns both the mother and the child to a life of poverty. Instead of encouraging the black community to strive for success or to become contributing members of society, this group continues to beat the same old, dead horse, suggesting that almost 150 years after slavery was legally ended, blacks are still *victims* and have no control over their own destiny. If the black community ever stopped listening to these forecasters of doom and gloom, a majority of the feelings described as *racism* in this country just might evaporate!

Only Blacks Can Save the Black Race

This statement will, at first, seem bigoted to many people, but, in reality it is simply stating the unvarnished truth! Will it ever become possible for black people in the United States of America to firmly establish themselves as inclusive and contributing members of society within this country? The sad truth is that this should be very easy to fix, but only if all parties involved would simply step back and apply common sense in discovering the obvious answer. To do so, the black race must first be willing to brush away the *victim chip* that has long occupied a very comfortable position upon their shoulders.

History has shown that whites in America have exclusively assumed the entire mantle of guilt for the institution of slavery in North America, and with a great degree of success. At one point in time, there was some justification for those who owned slaves to make amends to those they had once considered to be their personal property. They should have allowed those newly freed former slaves the option of returning to the homeland of their ancestors, or if they chose to remain in America, deeded to them plots of land that could support them and their families, along with enough financial assistance to get them started, and made available every opportunity for them and their families to receive a proper and unobstructed education. Since education is the foundation for almost anyone in this country to achieve success, this would have been the best thing the former slave owners could have possibly done for those newly freed Americans.

The institution of slavery was legally abolished by *Republican* president Abraham Lincoln in the 1860s, which was approximately 150 years ago. Assuming that a generation is a period of about thirty years, there have been four, five, or more generations of black families that have lived in America as U.S. citizens. This is not to say that these generations have enjoyed all of the immunities available to whites in America during that time, but neither did the American Indians or the Irish, Polish, or Italian immigrants who came to this country and suffered the indignities of being outsiders. It can be argued that these Irish, Polish, and Italian immigrants came here of their own accord, and it can be further argued that these immigrants came from countries where their lives were likely somewhat better than most of the ancestors of the early slaves who were brought to North America in bondage. The one aspect that is always overlooked is that their bondage was often the result of being captured by their fellow African countrymen, who then sold them into bondage to European slave traders. It can also be argued that, except for the unspeakable and unfortunate loss of their freedom, and for those who spent a lifetime in an existence in some of the more brutal situations, life in slavery was in some ways better than the lives they would have led in the jungles of Africa. Certainly today, most of those in this country that are of African descent would not trade their lives in America, regardless of how bad they perceive them to be, for a lifetime spent in sub-Saharan Africa.

Now we get to the real issue. After four, five, and more generations of exposure to the opportunities found in the United States of America, where does the blame really lie for the poverty, the high unemployment, the high crime rate, the high out-of-wedlock birthrate, the failure to take advantage of a proper education, and the lack of ambition, initiative, or self-esteem found in the black race today? A portion of the blame can, without question, indeed be placed at the feet of the white race; however, a large portion of this blame is due to the reluctance of the black race to assimilate themselves into the whole American community and to become valuable contributors to the American spirit, as did those indentured servants and other people who were considered members of the poverty classes of the European countries they left behind when they immigrated to America. You can use the *chip on the shoulder* or the *victim* tag just so long, but then that old excuse quickly loses its validity and relevance. At some point, regardless of the barriers placed before us, everyone must eventually take responsibility for his own future and progress. Either we accept those obstacles placed before us as being insurmountable, or we do everything within our power to improve ourselves to rise above those obstacles (and I am not referring to just reaching out one's hand to accept those entitlements that a liberal socialist government uses to buy votes). We must take it upon ourselves to gain the necessary skills and knowledge to become successful and productive members of society.

Many American citizens of all races were less than successful in realizing their dreams, but the only reason anyone should be ashamed of the lack of success would be if they had not done everything within their power to achieve it. Although there were surely many obstacles thrown into the paths of those of the black race who could have enjoyed success, far too many blacks have chosen to give up, take the easy way out by expecting a liberal, socialist government to provide for their subsistence throughout their entire lives, and continue to accuse the white race for them not being successful. Not only did they allow themselves to become sour toward the white race, they also passed their feelings of hatred and mistrust of whites along to the members of the black race who followed after them.

What can blacks do to save their own race? First, they must learn to love themselves and to love their own race. Next, they must allow themselves to fall in love with the United States of America and learn everything they can about the sacrifices that were made by many people of all races, and how and why our founding fathers pursued their vision to give birth to the closest thing to a perfect nation this world has ever seen. They must also understand that even while in the throes of slavery, their lives as Americans are likely much better than they ever would have enjoyed living in sub-Saharan Africa. A lifetime spent in poverty in America is still easier than life within most African villages.

These steps will take a lot of work to accomplish, but realization of the opportunities available only through education is a giant step toward achieving those goals. Once they learn to love themselves and their own race of people, they will discover a newfound feeling of self-worth and value that they have never known before. Self-respect is vital to success in any field, and once this ingredient becomes an ingrained element of one's makeup, the world can indeed become one's oyster. When we learn to love ourselves, doors will begin to open that would have been impossible to enter before.

This is not unlike the struggles experienced by the likes of Andrew Carnegie and many others who entered this country as paupers and with enormous obstacles placed in front of them, but whose burning desire to succeed made it impossible for them to fail. The real success stories of this country are rarely achieved without sacrifice, and in many cases it requires blood, sweat, and tears. The rewards of success, however, are truly indescribable.

The absence of true family values by many within the black community is an obvious reason for low self-esteem within their community, especially where black youths are concerned. This leads to a blatant denial of the importance of a family unit that includes both a mother *and* a father! Subsequent generations within the black race look at their own family situations and do not understand why they should be any different. Once strong family values are established, the family unit becomes the center point of a strong neighborhood, a strong community, and a strong race of people. They will then want to see their children strive for and achieve success in all areas of their lives.

A major ingredient for success by the black community in assimilating into the total American community is to realize the need to obtain a valuable and useful education. Members of the black community generally do not feel that the early history of the United States of America is their history. It has long been the goal of liberals to see that races within this country remain separated, and one of their favorite tools in doing so is to paint early American history as not being inclusive of all ethnic and racial groups within this country. The fallacy of this theory is that many of those groups were not present during the early days of the United States, just as American citizens had little or no involvement in the early history of the homelands of those same races and ethnic groups. To really feel that they are truly a part of America, blacks must take part in the continual building of America, and if they do not allow themselves to become involved, they will never feel that they are real Americans. This is very sad, because this can be achieved simply by learning to truly love this country and see themselves as true Americans.

The United States of America is a country of many people, but it can only be one country once all of those people feel themselves truly to be *Americans*. We cannot be African-Americans, German-Americans, Irish-Americans, Mexican-Americans, or Arab-Americans. We are all *Americans*, pure and simple.

IMMIGRATION

Teddy Roosevelt's Ideas on Immigration.

In the first place we should insist that if the immigrant who comes here in good faith becomes an American and assimilates himself to us, he shall be treated on an exact equality with everyone else, for it is an outrage to discriminate against any such man because of creed, or birthplace, or origin. But this is predicated upon the man's becoming in every fact an American, and nothing but an American ... There can be no divided allegiance here. Any man who says he is an American, but something else also, isn't an American at all. We have room for but one flag, the American flag, and this excludes the red flag, which symbolizes all wars against liberty and civilization, just as much as it excludes any foreign flag of a nation to which we are hostile ... We have room for but one language here, and that is the *English* language ... and we have room for but one sole loyalty, and that is a loyalty to the American people.

—Theodore Roosevelt, 1907

SEVEN STEPS TO SOLVING THE IMMIGRATION PROBLEM

How do we stop the suffocating flow of immigrants into this country, both illegal and legal? It appears that this is a question for which no one has been able to come up with an answer, at least one that works, while at the same time fitting into the acceptable guidelines of what is "politically correct." Believe it or not, I think I have come upon the perfect seven-step plan that will, in time, solve this problem, once and for all.

The **first step** would be to stop any and all attempts at hindering the influx of our neighbors south of the border. The **second step** would be to reverse the roles in this process and start encouraging all able-bodied U.S. citizens to immediately migrate to Mexico, which surely would welcome us with open arms, since the Mexican government obviously sees nothing wrong with unopposed border crossings. **Step three** would be when enough of the movers and shakers within the American capitalist brotherhood have relocated to Mexico and begun calling it their new home, the Mexican immigrants to America would then see that they can no longer continue receiving the American prosperity they had hoped to receive when they began crossing our border several years earlier.

Eventually, **step four** would be when these former residents of Mexico started becoming disenchanted again with living in a country that could no longer support its masses of unskilled and uneducated laborers (after all, you can only use just so many sod-layers and crop-pickers), and they would again start making their way back toward the Mexican-American border, only this time heading south instead of north. **Step five** would be when the time finally came for the growing economic culture that had migrated from the United States into Mexico, to start relocating back north of the border, and when the former Mexican citizens had decided it was now time to migrate back to their original homeland, where they again would reap the fruits of those gringo American entrepreneurs. Give these former citizens of Mexico a little time, and before you know it, **step six** will occur, when they will have returned en masse to their homeland.

The prosperity of this newly created Mexico that our robber barons are now ready and willing to leave behind should support these former original Mexican citizens just long enough for us to initiate the glorious **step seven**. We go home, clean up all of the old junked cars and all of the other mess they left behind, rebuild our dilapidated infrastructure, and immediately begin construction of a foolproof border security system that will keep out anyone we do not want as our neighbors. Who knows, maybe with a little luck, we will have become the recipient of enough good fortune that a large portion of those bleeding-heart liberals that caused so many of our problems in the beginning will have become so confused about where they belonged and will have become trapped south of our totally secured border.

Then, and only then, can the good ole' United States return to its rightful place as the arsenal of democracy. Only this time, we will have learned a valuable lesson about who our true enemies really are, and we will immediately institute a national legal program of *ideological profiling*.

God bless the good ole' USA!

RECIPROCAL IMMIGRATION

We no longer appreciate or hold dear the reasons for protecting the very borders of this nation. To some Americans, the unlawful invasion by suffocating numbers of illegal immigrants is simply looked upon as a potential increase in votes. As long as they haven't taken our jobs or moved in next door to us, then we see it as being irrelevant.

Have you ever wondered what would be the reaction of the Mexican government if we were to take busload after busload of Americans into Mexico, drop them off on some street corner in downtown Mexico City, and give each one of them a map showing how to find the local office of the Mexican government agency responsible for distributing entitlements? They would be instructed to blend into the masses, use some unsuspecting Mexican citizens' personal identification info for their own benefit, and to send most of what they earn back to friends and family living in the United States. We could only hope that the Mexican government would have its share of liberal legislators who, like our own liberal Democrats, would not see these transplanted Americans as just absorbing huge amounts of Mexican resources, but instead would welcome them with open arms as simply potential voters who would support anyone that would promise them entitlements.

MORE ENTITLEMENTS

The following is a collection of excerpts taken from stereotypical political philosophies that might possibly show up on the floor of Congress as proposed law in the near future. Although this is not taken from direct quotes by any specific liberal legislators, it does conform directly to liberal ideas on how to reward the suffocating number of illegal immigrants crossing our borders, who in the eyes of liberals represent more votes that can be bought simply by offering more and more entitlement programs. See if this sounds familiar to you.

LIBERAL'S PLAN TO FINANCE ILLEGAL IMMIGRATION

Madam Speaker Nancy Pelosi hopes to propose a windfall tax on all stock market profits, including retirement funds, 401(k)s and mutual funds! Alas, it is true. All this will be done under the pretense of helping to fund health care to the twelve million illegal immigrants and other unemployed minorities!

This woman and her gang of liberal, socialist Democrats is frightening. Should their liberal, socialist movement be enhanced by voting into the

White House one Barack Obama, the most liberal socialist of them all, this nation, as we have known it, may never recover. Can true Americans really stand for this?

Nancy Pelosi has condemned the new record highs of the stock market as "just another example of Bush policies helping the rich get richer. First Bush cut taxes for the rich, and the economy has rebounded with new record low unemployment rates, which only means wealthy employers are getting even wealthier at the expense of the underpaid working class."

She would then say, "Despite the billions of dollars being spent in Iraq, our economy is still strong, and government tax revenues are at all-time highs. What this really means is that business is exploiting the war effort and working Americans, just to put money in their own pockets."

Her response to previous stock market highs would be, "Only the rich benefit from these record highs. Working Americans, welfare recipients, the unemployed, and minorities are not sharing in these obscene record highs. There is no question that these windfall profits and the income created by the Bush administration need to be taxed at a 100 percent rate and those dollars redistributed to the poor and working class. Profits from the stock market do not reward the hard work of our working class, who, by their hard work, are responsible for generating these corporate profits that create stock market profits for the rich. We in Congress will need to address this issue, either by taxing these profits or by controlling the stock market to prevent this unearned income to flow to the rich."

When asked about the fact that over 80 percent of all Americans have investments in mutual funds, retirement funds, 401(k)s, and the stock market, she might offer, "That may be true, but probably only 5 percent account for 90 percent of all of these investment dollars. That's just more *trickle down* economics, claiming that if a corporation is successful, everyone from the CEO to the floor sweeper benefits from higher wages and job security, which is ridiculous. How much of this 'trickle down' ever gets to the unemployed and minorities in our county? None, and that's the tragedy of these stock market highs."

She might go on to add, "We Democrats are going to address this issue after the election when we take control of Congress. We will return to the 60 percent to 80 percent tax rates on the rich, and we will be able to take at least 30 percent of all current lower federal income taxpayers off the rolls and increase government income substantially. We need to work toward the goal of equalizing income in our country and at the same time limiting the amount the rich can invest."

When asked how these new tax dollars would be spent, she would suggest, "We need to raise the standard of living of the poor, the unemployed, and minorities. For example, we have an estimated twelve million illegal immigrants in our country who need our help, along with millions of unemployed minorities. Stock market windfall profit taxes could go a long way to guarantee these people the standard of living they would like to have as Americans."

Buying the future vote of an illegal immigrant will be very expensive for working Americans! Are we really ready for this?

WHY IMMIGRATE TO AMERICA?

Are you coming here because of the freedom enjoyed by Americans? Are you coming here because of the employment opportunities available to Americans? Are you coming here because of the educational opportunities available to Americans?

If you are coming here to accept the many opportunities available to Americans, do you also feel that you owe anything to this country in return? Do you owe it to this country to obey our laws? Do you owe it to this country to learn our history, make our language your language, and adopt our customs and traditions? Do you owe it to this country to defend this country if called upon to do so?

If this country provides you a better opportunity than that provided by that country from which you came, why would you not want to do everything necessary to become an American in every way? If this country provides you the opportunity to improve your life beyond your wildest dreams, why would you not want to do everything necessary to become an American in every way?

If you are willing and eager to do all of those things necessary to become an American, welcome!

If you are only willing to take but give back nothing in return, we don't want you!

EPILOGUE

To fully understand the meaning behind this book, we must first understand and accept the fact that of all the nations on this Earth, America is truly unique. For something to be truly unique, it means that it is one of a kind, single, unduplicated, and without comparison or equal.

To further understand that America is truly unique, we must be willing to accept two undeniable facts: (1) it takes a very special person to be able to live in and to appreciate living in a unique land; and (2) not everyone is capable of living in, and appreciating living in, a unique land. After finally putting together these pieces of the puzzle, it begins to make sense why most, if not all, of the people living in this unique land who constantly complain about being victims—and are rarely willing to make any sacrifices for this country—are simply just not capable of being true Americans.

America, oddly enough, is a land that is hated for its virtues, not its vices. At the same time we are being appreciated and even idolized by our enemies, but for our weaknesses instead of our strengths. Our opponents, both at home and abroad, long ago abandoned all rules for playing in the game of life.

For many people in America today who treasure a conservative philosophy of life, it has become more and more apparent over the past several decades that liberalism is the most destructive threat to the survival of this nation that we have ever seen. When the world and our nation were threatened by the Hitler's and Tojo's of World War II, and the Kaisers of World War I, we were fighting an enemy we could see, an enemy we could put a face with. When our enemy was Russia and the USSR during the Cold War, we knew we had a fight on our hands, but we had a very good working knowledge of what we were fighting for and against. We had some idea of the troop strength we would be going up against, and we had wise and capable military leaders who knew what they were doing. We were confident that the resolve of the American people would somehow prevail.

Today, we are fighting a much different enemy. Today we are fighting an enemy who resides within our midst. Fighting the liberal menace is much different than fighting the Kaisers, the Hitler's, and the Tojo's of wars past. This enemy identifies itself as just another American, as someone we work with, or go to church with, or live next door to. During his speech to the United Nations during the Cold War, Russian premier Nikita Khrushchev boldly predicted that we would destroy ourselves from within, and that there would be no need for his military to even fire a single shot. How prophetic and insightful Nikita Khrushchev was. Although he felt that our self-destruction would take place during his lifetime, he saw that the seeds of this self-destruction had indeed already been planted, and that this nation was ripe for the taking.

In their quest for turning America into a socialist state, liberals have employed a systematic program to gradually chip away at the very fabric and core values and traditions our founding fathers understood to be vital to the establishment of this unique nation. While America indeed has been the strongest nation on the face of the Earth, we were also a very compassionate people. When liberals learned that they could bond this compassion with the strong *guilt of slavery* they had been encouraging within this nation for years, this combination would become the perfect formula for the successful transition of this nation into a socialist state, one that would be very little different from those obsolete and failed systems found today in Europe.

Their first plan of attack would be to infiltrate the best educational system on Earth with ultra-liberal teachers, professors, and administrators. In time, these liberal soldiers would plant within the young minds of several impressionable generations the ideology that *good* is *bad*, that achievement and ambition are simply a means used by big business to overrun the common man, and that to ensure equality, no one must ever experience failure. Those who excelled would be viewed as *eggheads*, and the notion that this world owed each and every one of us a living would become the prevailing theory.

Next and likely the most vital element of the liberal plan would be to gradually erode the value and importance of the Christian faith, because this was the unseen factor that gave meaning to the rich traditions and values upon which this nation was founded. The very idea of people placing any value on something that could not be seen was viewed as an easy target, especially when liberal educators began to incorporate their brainwashing techniques into the educational curriculum. After all, how could anyone with any common sense place any value on something they couldn't see, feel, or touch (which just happens to be the basic meaning of the word *faith*)? Churches were for goody two-shoes or people who were weak and couldn't face life under their own power.

As soon as these two elements were in place, all liberals had to do was to sit back and just let their festering socialist indoctrination do its work. Now they would turn their attention to the black and other minority communities and begin to reinforce the idea that they were being targeted by ancestors of those who had created the institution of slavery centuries before. The biggest fear in the ongoing development of this idea was that the black race might learn the importance and power of gaining an education, because if that ever happened, the transparent plans for a socialist world would come crumbling to the ground. Blacks first had to be convinced that they were not capable of taking care of themselves in this white man's world, and that the only way they could survive was to place themselves totally into the hands of the liberal Democrats, who would then take care of their every need through entitlement programs. Enlisting the cooperation of spokesmen within the black community as civil rights leaders would further guarantee the success of this liberal charade.

Now that the liberal infrastructure was set into place, the next step would be to create civil unrest and make sure that divisions would arise among the various races and ethnic groups, thereby destroying all prospects of unity that had been established over the past two hundred or so years. Have these generations of liberal socialists been successful? Well, during the past several decades, their plan appears to have been dangerously successful.

But whether this socialist revolution is to be successful in the future is totally up to you and me. The outcome of the 2008 general election will indeed affect the very future of this nation, but even if liberals should prevail, right-thinking Americans must express their concerns, and very loudly!

Are we honestly so weak as to turn over the future of this unique nation to a group of liberal socialists? Are we truly the legitimate citizens of this unique land we call America? Do we really understand what it means to be a true American?

Our actions will indeed provide the answers to these questions!